THE FACE ON YOUR PLATE

Altruistic Armadillos, Zenlike Zebras:
A Menagerie of 100 Favorite Animals

Raising the Peaceable Kingdom: What Animals Can Teach
Us About the Social Origins of Tolerance and Friendship

The Cat Who Came in from the Cold: A Fable

Slipping into Paradise:
Why I Live in New Zealand

The Pig Who Sang to the Moon:
The Emotional World of Farm Animals

The Nine Emotional Lives of Cats:
A Journey into the Feline Heart

The Evolution of Fatherhood:
A Celebration of Animal and Human Families

Dogs Never Lie About Love:
Reflections on the Emotional World of Dogs

The Wild Child:
The Unsolved Mystery of Kaspar Hauser

When Elephants Weep: The Emotional Lives of Animals
(with Susan McCarthy)

My Father's Guru:
A Journey Through Spirituality and Disillusion

Final Analysis:
The Making and Unmaking of a Psychoanalyst

THE
FACE
ON
YOUR
PLATE

The Truth About Food

J EFFREY M OUSSAIEFF M ASSON

W. W. NORTON & COMPANY

NEW YORK   LONDON

Copyright © 2009 by Jeffrey Moussaieff Masson

For information about permission to reproduce selections from this book,
write to Permissions, W. W. Norton & Company, Inc.,
500 Fifth Avenue, New York, NY 10110

For information about special discounts for bulk purchases,
please contact W. W. Norton Special Sales at
specialsales@wwnorton.com or 800-233-4830

Manufacturing by Courier Westford
Book design by Lovedog Studio
Production manager: Anna Oler

Library of Congress Cataloging-in-Publication Data

Masson, J. Moussaieff (Jeffrey Moussaieff), 1941–
The face on your place : the truth about food /
Jeffrey Moussaieff Masson. — 1st ed.
p. cm.
Includes bibliographical references and index.
ISBN 978-0-393-06595-4 (hardcover)
1. Food of animal origin. I. Title.
TX371.M37 2009
641.3'06—dc22   2008052733

W. W. Norton & Company, Inc.
500 Fifth Avenue, New York, N.Y. 10110
www.wwnorton.com

W. W. Norton & Company Ltd.
Castle House, 75/76 Wells Street, London W1T 3QT

1 2 3 4 5 6 7 8 9 0

To Leila, whose love and knowledge
has brought me closer to all the creatures in
our world and to greater health and happiness;
and to my beloved children, Simone, Ilan, and Manu,
shining examples of compassion for all living beings.

CONTENTS

ACKNOWLEDGMENTS

A NUMBER OF PEOPLE PROVIDED ME WITH INFORMA-
tion on the research in the field, which has proved invaluable.
I want to thank them for their help. They are: Neal Barnard,
Culum Brown, T. Colin Campbell, Matthew Cole, Antonia
Demas, Gidon Eshel, Gary Fraser, Bruce Friedrich, Phil Gee,
Kristen Hawkes, Padmanabh Jaini, Tim Key, Hans Kriek,
Philip Lymbery, Karen Morgan, Jeff Nelson, Ingrid Newkirk,
Christine Nicol, Jeff Novick, Wayne Pacelle, David Pimentel,
Vaclav Smil, and Kim Sturla. For graciously agreeing to inter-
views I am grateful to John Coetzee, Caldwell B. Esselstyn,
Temple Grandin, Francis Moore Lappé, John Mackey, John
McDougall, Milton Mills, Michael Pollan, Stan Sesser, and
Alice Waters. Special thanks go to my friends Jenny Miller and
Marti Kheel, who read every line and made many transforma-
tive suggestions that improved the book immeasurably, as well
as the wise Michael Greger, who did the same. I also wish to

thank my agent Miriam Altshuler, who believed in this project from the start and worked hard to make this book a success, and her assistant, Jake Nabel, for much help. At Norton I want to thank Amy Cherry, the perfect editor (who added wonderful phrases and discreetly took out those that were not so wonderful), and her assistant, Erica Stern, on whom I could always rely. In addition I want to thank all the team at Norton who worked on my book, Deborah Morton-Hoyt, Chin-Yee Lai, Anna Oler, and Nancy Palmquist. A very special thanks to Ann Adelman, who has a special touch and made little magical changes that delighted. Finally, this book would not have been possible without the love and intelligence of my soul mate, Leila Masson.

Introduction

THE GOLD STANDARD
IS GREEN

WHEN I WAS TEACHING SANSKRIT AT THE UNIVERSITY of Toronto in the 1970s, I came across a phrase that stopped me dead: *ashrayaparavrtti*—a sudden moment of life-changing insight. *Paravrtti* is like a somersault, and *ashraya* is one's home base, so it means letting go of everything you have always believed or understood for a leap into the unknown. The Christian equivalent is known as the Road to Damascus experience in which Saul (later St. Paul) underwent a conversion on his way to Damascus to slaughter Christians and instead became one.

Many people become vegan in just that way: a sudden moment, a blinding insight, a turning one's back on conventional wisdom, in this case, conventional diet. How did it happen for me? Well, I had the good fortune to grow up in a vegetarian family: my parents were "disciples" of a vegetarian guru, Paul Brunton. Even when I gave up the belief in the Hinduism and Buddhism that he taught, I still maintained my belief in the value of *ahimsa*, not doing harm, which included not doing harm through one's diet. Later, at Toronto, I had a negative epiphany: what was I doing teaching this language that had lost its magic for me? I entered psychoanalytic training. Alas, giving up Sanskrit somehow entailed giving up my vegetarian ways. One day, after becoming a Freudian psychoanalyst, I had another transformative moment: I was sitting at Freud's desk at Maresfield Gardens in London. I opened one of the drawers, and found a stash of letters, all of which dealt with the "hidden" reality of the sexual abuse of children. That was to become my concern (some would call it an obsession) over the next ten years. Only when I decided that I could no longer be a psychoanalyst in good conscience did I reconnect with my former vegetarian self: I started investigating the emotional lives of animals, and what I learned turned me back into a lifelong vegetarian.

During that time, I can remember hearing César Chávez say that if you want to lessen animal suffering, you would do better to eat meat and give up dairy and eggs. Again, one of those defining moments for me. Everything I thought I knew was suddenly challenged, but I also knew that I was not yet ready for such a challenge. I turned my back on that moment. Yet I understood even then that sooner or later I would have to face up to what I could no longer ignore.

That moment came for me when I began to visit dairy farms and hen-laying facilities and saw the misery and suffering that the animals endured just so that we could enjoy their milk and eggs. My denial was no longer possible, and I took the leap. I have asked some other vegans how it happened for them, and got some interesting answers. John Mackey, the CEO of Whole

Foods, told me: "I remember one day in August of 2003 I made the decision to become (near) vegan and that once the decision was made I felt great emotional alignment within my heart. I knew this was the right thing for me to do and I also knew that I was making a decision that I would be committed to for the rest of my life. At last my beliefs and my ethics had come into alignment." Stanley Godlovitch, one of the people who began the back-to-vegetarianism movement in the 1970s (he and a friend first confronted Peter Singer, then a graduate student in philosophy at Oxford and now the best known animal rights author, about eating meat), told me recently that every vegetarian who drinks milk or eats eggs knows from scratch that there's "something not quite right." But for him and his wife, "the push came from our teenage son Daniel, who brought out the ancient Consistency Cannon over dinner and fired at will. I guess I must have been poised, ready, and that was it."

There is a general feeling among the public at large that to be concerned with the way animals live, or to become vegetarian or even vegan, is now not nearly as odd as it once seemed. Consider that the mainstream group Conservation International (CI) has partnered with McDonald's to promote *The Bee Movie*! When I saw that movie, I heard kids walk out vowing never to eat honey unless it was "bee-approved." On their Web site, CI asks that children take the following pledge: "I recognize that I play an important role in the future of our planet. I pledge to get outside and do my part to learn about nature and to protect all living things. I will be a force for good in my neighborhood." *Protect all living things*—even bees. Sounds good. But how, exactly, does eating at McDonald's accomplish this? The old cliché still applies: We want the steak but don't want to hear about the slaughterhouse. That is why I devote a full chapter to denial.

Sometimes denial, though, is just ignorance. I was having dinner in Thailand in 2007 with my friend Stan Sesser, a writer for the *Wall Street Journal* (he has also been a staff writer at *The New Yorker* and food critic for the *San Francisco Examiner*). He asked me why I don't eat eggs or dairy. I told him it was because of the cruelty involved. He was taken aback, never having heard of this problem before. It had been the same for me, and I am convinced that most people just are not aware of how these animals suffer so that we can eat their eggs and drink their milk.

We don't hear the assertion very often today that animals were born to be slaves, destined to be eaten, that they evolved for our benefit. It would take a certain kind of religious fundamentalist to assert this. However, there is an assertion that is not all that far removed. This time it is not about the animals, it is about us. That we are the ones born to eat meat, the ones destined to do the eating (as opposed to being eaten), and the ones who evolved to hunt and kill our food. I have rarely seen this more baldly expressed than by John Buffalo Mailer, in a dialogue with his father, Norman Mailer: "You know, one of the outcomes of living in such an organized society where everything is taken care of—men don't go out, kill their food, and bring it back, etc.— is there's a complicity, almost a sense of deliberately forgetting that when you get right down to it, ultimately we're animals. We will fight each other down to our last bite when our own is attacked. And I don't know if this is true of everybody, but 95 percent of the time when I meet another man, under it all is that sense of 'Could I take you or could you take me?' "[1]

Perhaps if you are the son of Norman Mailer, this is understandable. I doubt that the rest of us constantly wonder about the outcome of a fight with every male we encounter. But the greater cliché is the earlier one, that in the past a man went "out," killed a formidable adversary, and returned with food for his famished family. You can't blame John Mailer for believing this myth—after all, it has been fed to us for many years now by the leading lights of anthropology departments in American universities: Man the hunter. The myth goes back a long way, and has an impeccable scientific pedigree. No less a scientist than Charles Darwin believed it, along with the view that women depended on men for survival—"Man is more powerful in body and mind than woman, and in the savage state he keeps her in a far more abject state of bondage than does the male of any other animal."[2]

Hunting has been described as "the master behavior pattern of the human species," something that men have been practicing for 99 percent of human history. The main message of the influential book *African Genesis* (1961), by Robert Ardrey, the anthropologist and Hollywood screen writer, was that we are killer apes, who wiped out our peaceful vegetarian brothers. His last book, published in 1976, was simply called *The Hunting Hypothesis*. These books had a notable influence on Arthur C. Clarke and Stanley Kubrick's film *2001: A Space Odyssey*. But in the 1980s this view was challenged, successfully it seems to me, by female anthropologists with a broader vision, which culminated in an excellent collection of essays called *Woman the Gatherer*.[3] This showed that all the evidence suggests that the early human diet was omnivorous, so that meat was far less important than previously thought. Plant foods provided the

staple diet of most hunter-gatherer societies (with the exception of those in the Far North) and these foods were provided
by women. Gathering plants required less energy than going
after mobile animals, the food provided a more stable diet, and
it was less dangerous to acquire. The women who gathered
these plant foods were social, food-sharing, and nurturing people, and they were able to exert enormous pressure on men by
choosing those same qualities in men as mates.

This hypothesis has received very strong support recently
from Milton Mills, a researcher who graduated from Stanford
University School of Medicine in 1991 and now practices medicine at the Fairfax Hospital in Fairfax, Virginia. He is writing
a book which takes the position that people are slowly backing
into the truth: That humans are anatomically and physiologically adapted for a diet comprised primarily or entirely of plant
foods. I spent some time with Stephen Jay Gould at Harvard
in 1999, and he too told me that his study of human dentition
had convinced him that we were, evolutionarily speaking, primarily herbivores.

Dr. Mills has taken this hypothesis further than anyone else
I know, and had already started to do so while he was a medical
student at Stanford. He uses as evidence comparative anatomy.
The simple proof is the shape of the human head—carnivores
have wide mouths, suitable for swallowing large chunks of
meat; we have small mouths, suitable for softer plant foods—
and the human jaw—when the jaws of a carnivore close, there
is a slicing motion that we lack; our jaw joint would be easily
dislocated if we tried to subdue struggling prey or crush bones.
Carnivorous animals do not chew their food but gorge rapidly,
whereas we humans need to eat slowly; the capacious single-

chambered stomach of carnivores contrasts with the stomach of herbivores, which is a simple structure, with a long small intestine; and the human colon has the pouched structure typical of herbivores. Finally, human teeth are similar to those found in other herbivores: our canines are neither serrated nor conical, but flattened, blunt, and small; our incisors are flat and spadelike, useful for peeling and biting relatively soft materials. Human saliva contains the carbohydrate-digesting enzyme, salivary amylase: if we attempted to swallow a large amount of food poorly chewed, we would choke—just watch how your dog swallows meat. In short, concludes Dr. Mills, human beings have the mouth and gastrointestinal tract structure of a committed herbivore.

Think, too, how difficult it would be for an early human, not armed in any way, to use his own body to kill a large animal. After all, humans at the time were less than five feet tall, and weighed less than 110 pounds.[4] They were hardly a formidable adversary against the much more powerful hunting and scavenging animals. Our nails are not claws. Notice the damage that even a small animal like your cat can inflict on unprotected human skin. Cats are obligate carnivores: killing machines. Imagine meeting and trying to subdue an animal ten times that size. Indeed, in a recent book, the anthropologists Donna Hart and Robert Sussman argue that for much of our evolutionary history, humans have been hunted by other, more powerful animals.[5] In effect, we were the prey of any number of predators, including the big cats, as well as dogs, hyenas, snakes, crocodiles, and even birds. As a species, we would have been wiped out long ago had we not depended on easily accessible plants and fruits.[6] Moreover, when researchers feed animal fats and animal protein in large amounts to captive primates, it produces atherogenic effects (that is, they give you heart attacks, hardly a good survival strategy).[7]

The archeologist Lewis Binford has published a series of influential books arguing that there is no evidence for the human transport and consumption of large quantities of meat. Instead, he suggests that members of the early hominids were marginal scavengers, at the bottom of the hierarchy of meat eaters on the African savannah, sneaking in after the lions, the hyenas, and the vultures had had their fill.[8]

Consider how gross just about everyone finds the idea of eating carrion or rotting flesh. Dogs don't mind at all. In fact, as we all know, they revel in it—rolling in it and eagerly seeking it out. Carnivores prefer raw meat to cooked meat. Except in unusual cases, we like our meat disguised. The more natural it looks, the more likely it is to cause disgust and physical aversion. Part of this, I recognize, is custom. Nobody, surely, takes pleasure in the thought of killing a rabbit with their bare hands and then dismembering it and gulping down the raw flesh. Just reading these lines, I imagine, will make many a reader queasy.

We really know very little about what is "natural" when it comes to human behavior, and all attempts to proclaim some preferred behavior as entirely "natural" is almost always doomed to failure. This is especially true when it comes to human diets in the past. For a while we were treated in the mass media to the Paleolithic diet. Much can be learned from traditional diets and just about any traditional diet would be preferable to the junk food and heavily processed food we eat today. Yet I agree with the authoritative recent opinion of *The*

Cambridge History of World Food that we are not going to return to a hunting-and-gathering lifestyle, and that, in fact, history sheds no light on an ideal diet.

Nor, really, can we rely on the argument that we are "animals," since animals eat entirely distinct foods. Primates? Yes, chimpanzees do engage in hunting behavior, from time to time,[9] but gorillas do not. The kind of generalizations that were common among popular historians at the beginning of the twentieth century have fallen out of favor, and when one reads the German amateur historian Oswald Spengler, famous for his *The Decline of the West,* one can see why. He said, "The human race ranks highly because it belongs to the class of beasts of prey . . . [Man] lives engaged in aggression, killing, annihilation. . . . Man is a beast of prey. I shall say it again and again. The traders in virtue, the champions of social ethics, are but beasts of prey with their teeth broken."[10]

What some people mean when they talk about eating meat is that since other animals hunt, kill, and eat one another, and we are just another animal, why should we not do the same? But if you observe what your cat and dog like to eat, you will immediately recognize that we are somewhat different in our tastes. Even more important, which animal are we meant to resemble most? After all, of the approximately 4,200 mammals, only a small number are carnivores. There are surely as many herbivores as there are carnivores, and many animals never kill other animals. It is true that animals seem to have no choice in the matter. No member of a carnivore species has ever been known to choose only roots and fruits. We seem to be the only animal that can "decide" to become a vegetarian.[11] But vegetarians cannot always take the high ground when it comes to other behaviors, such as believing that if they eat no flesh, they are automatically a better person. A vegetarian can be as dangerous to his or her neighbor as someone who eats meat. Similarly, animals who do not eat meat are not necessarily more gentle. There is a common myth that carnivores are more dangerous to humans than herbivores. Carnivorous wolves, however, avoid humans whenever possible, and herbivorous elephants sometimes "decide" to kill people (as I learned when I attempted to get too close to a matriarch with a small baby next to her). No animals are more dangerous to humans than the completely non-carnivorous Cape buffalo, rhinoceros, and hippo. They would not eat us; but they often kill us. You can be as bad-tempered eating only grass as you can be eating only other animals. So I would not argue that human vegetarians are more peaceable than other humans—except to other animals.

What about the claim that the human brain owes its size to eating meat? It is true that the human brain is twice as encephalized as is the brain of an adult chimpanzee and three to five times as large as would be expected for average body mass. Reviews of hunter-gatherer diets indicate that meat varies from 12 to 86 percent of the total daily caloric intake per capita. In contrast, animal products represent only about 5 percent of the average daily calories consumed by chimpanzees, most of them eaten by adult males. Thus, many researchers have claimed that meat is what accounts for our large brains. But brain growth in humans is generally restricted to a critical window of opportunity following birth, for brain weight accounts for 12 percent of body weight at birth in *all* primate neonates, including humans.

The greater rate of growth occurs in humans during the first year and any dietary advantage therefore must be transferred through breast milk. But milk quantity and quality is surprisingly consistent cross-culturally and it is not dependent on diet. The macronutrients are supplied by nature and have little to do with any other variable. Comparisons of breast milk from vegan, vegetarian, and omnivorous mothers have shown no difference in DHA (docosahexanoic acid) content. There is absolutely no evidence that the breast-fed children of vegan mothers suffer smaller brain sizes. Regardless of the ecological circumstances, it would seem that all infants obtain or produce enough of the specific lipids they need to create the large brains distinctive of our species.[12]

Some people, when they speak of eating meat as "natural," are not necessarily referring to our evolutionary past. They simply mean that they have always eaten meat, and that most other people on earth have always eaten meat. It is the human tradition. Yet, as Gary Francione, distinguished professor of law and philosophy at Rutgers University, points out: "Were we slaves to tradition, Rosa Parks would still be riding in the back of the bus."[13] It should also be pointed out that many traditional societies either did not eat meat for ethical or religious reasons (as in India and many Buddhist countries) or ate very little because it was simply not feasible on an economic basis (rural China and other countries in Southeast Asia). I recently visited the island of Efate in the New Hebrides, and learned that except in Port Vila, the capital, most people rarely eat meat simply because they cannot afford it. The men, who go just about everywhere by running barefoot, look remarkably fit and athletic. The fact that your parents ate meat is not an argument unless you feel that you must maintain all the values of your parents or the community in which you were raised.

But even could we maintain that it is, in fact, natural to eat meat, this would not weigh very heavily in the ethical scale. Aristotle argued that it was natural to keep slaves. We believe he was wrong. But even if he were right, would we not argue that what is natural may not be what is moral or what we choose to do? "Fighting," or even weighing ourselves against other men, may indeed be "natural," but few men wish to be enslaved to their nature in this way. Indeed, are we not human precisely because, unlike just about any other animal, we can choose our diet? The big cats have no choice, which is why they are called obligate carnivores. But we can choose what we eat for reasons that have nothing whatever to do with our species, our traditions, our parents, or even our genes. We can choose to stop eating meat because we feel it is wrong to do so. I don't believe any other animal has this astonishing ability.

"Don't you care about humans?" I have been asked more times than I like to think. ("You're on a lifeboat: it's your life or the life of the dog. Which do you choose?" We are rarely on lifeboats.) Of course I do. I am one. My wife is one. My three children are. I care enough to want to save their health and our planet. Why, I wonder, does caring for anything other than our own species mean to some people that we don't care about ourselves? Perhaps, if we are suffering, if the world looks to be in a bad way, we do feel sometimes that we have only a limited amount of empathy and need to save it for ourselves. In extreme conditions, conventional wisdom maintains, we are not concerned with "lesser" beings. But as is often the case, the conventional wisdom is only conventional—not wise, and not even true. Think of those people who survived the Holocaust only to discover that this sharpened and deepened their compassion for animals. Isaac Bashevis Singer's famous comment springs to mind: "When it comes to animals, every man is a Nazi."

We humans have a divided attitude. On the one hand, we want to claim that we are just like animals (which, when you consider that mice and men share about 97.5 percent of their working DNA, only 1 percent less than chimps and humans, is obviously true at some fundamental level). On the other hand, we see ourselves as entirely separate, not just a different species but an altogether different category of species. We are, above all, *not* animals. I have recently noticed how often the phrase "like an animal" is used in outrage. In David Lynch's film *The Elephant Man*, John Merrick is chased by a crowd until he has no escape. Finally, turning unmasked to his tormentors, he bellows: "I am not an animal!" This seems to imply that had he been an animal, the torment would be legitimate. In *The Road to Wigan Pier*, George Orwell sees an exhausted woman, with a desolate and hopeless expression, for a fleeting instant:

> It struck me then that we are mistaken when we say that "It isn't the same for them as it would be for us," and that people bred in the slums can imagine nothing but the slums. For what I saw in her face was not the ignorant suffering of an animal. She knew well enough what was happening to her—understood as well as I did how dreadful a destiny it was to be kneeling there in the bitter cold, on the slimy stones of a slum backyard, poking a stick up a foul drain-pipe.[14]

No doubt there are people who truly believe that if animals are unaware how appalling the suffering they must bear is, then we should have no compunction in perpetrating it or feel no obligation to end it. Yet if animals do not "know" they are being tortured but merely suffer at an elemental level, surely this means we have an even greater responsibility to stop the suffering? Jeremy Bentham's famous remark belongs here: "The question is not, 'Can they reason?' Nor, 'Can they talk?' But, rather, 'Can they suffer?' "

Another argument put forward to "prove" that humans are not by nature vegans is that there has never been a single society in the history of humanity that was vegan or nearly vegan. While this is strictly true, a claim could be made that Jainism comes as close as any society has to encouraging a near-vegan lifestyle.[15] Perhaps this is why George Bernard Shaw once said, "I would like to be reborn in a Jain community."

A few months ago, I went to visit my old friend Professor Padmanabh S. Jaini, Professor Emeritus of Buddhism, Jainism, and Hinduism at the University of California at Berkeley, and arguably the preeminent Jain scholar in the world. Professor Jaini is a bit like me. We both enjoy unusual gems from ancient literature. When I told him the purpose of my visit (to learn more about Jain attitudes toward vegetarianism), he immediately provided me with one such gem. He told me that Jains speak of the three *makaras* (or words that begin with the letter "m") that must be avoided. They are *madhya, mamsa,* and *madhu*—liquor, meat, and, to my surprise, honey!

Jains are not, strictly speaking, vegan. They eat no eggs, but they do eat butter and cheese. So I was surprised by the remark about honey. Vegans do not eat honey because it is an animal product. The argument (with which I agree) is that bees make honey for themselves, not for us. So, when we take their honey, we are engaging in theft. *Robbing the Bees* is incidentally the name of an excellent book about bee keeping! How could I learn more about this prohibition? From my host, of course. Professor Jaini immediately chanted a verse for me from a twelfth-century text, the *Yogasastra,* by the Jain author Hemacandra, which translates as:

> *One who eats honey, which is manufactured by the destruction of tens of thousands of tiny beings, is worse than a butcher, who only kills a single animal at a time.*[16]

I remember visiting Jain temples in India. Often over the main entrance I would see inscribed: *Ahimsa paramo dharmah*—*Ahimsa* (non-violence) is the highest religion. Jainism as a religion predates Buddhism, probably by about 250 years. It is the only religion in the world founded on this principle of *ahimsa. Ahimsa* refers to the attempt to live without causing any harm to other sentient beings. It is a noble ideal. The Buddha believed in it, as did Mahatma Gandhi. The Jain scriptures explain that all living beings want to live and do not want to die. This idea has occurred to many people, religious and irreligious, over the centuries. It is the kind of insight that even small children suddenly develop. I have heard a seven-year-old child say that she will not eat meat because the animal from which the meat derived "did not want to die."

I do not find it surprising that the Jains, the Buddhists, and the Hindus have all taken seriously the lives of others. The ability to imagine ourselves into the minds and bodies of "others"—whether humans we term different from us

(Down syndrome children; Alzheimer sufferers; the so-called mentally ill) or the animals we use for our food—is of central importance because the failure to do so is precisely what led to the horrors of Auschwitz. So, when people ask, Have you nothing more important to think about? the answer is: There *is* nothing more important to think about than the heart of empathy, which in the final analysis is nothing other than the ability to love. Becoming a vegan is simply one manifestation of that love.

THE FACE ON YOUR PLATE

Chapter One

THE ONLY WORLD WE HAVE

The human appetite for animal flesh is a driving force behind virtually every major category of environmental damage now threatening the human future—deforestation, erosion, fresh water scarcity, air and water pollution, climate change, biodiversity loss, social injustice, the destabilization of communities and the spread of disease.

—*World Watch* magazine[1]

USUALLY, PEOPLE GIVE THREE REASONS WHY THEY ARE vegetarian: for their health; for the health of the animals; and for the health of the planet. Until very recently, the third reason got short shrift. That is finally beginning to change. A consensus seems to be building that the Standard American Diet (SAD) is not sustainable: it is damaging our environment in many ways, including as a major player in global warming. I say "seems" because there is resistance from various sources.

There are scientists who believe the case has been overstated; there is a bewildered public of ordinary people who are reluctant to believe that "the way we have always eaten" could prove to be a disaster for the planet; and there are industry representatives who cry "alarmist."

Recently, I have become sensitive to words that are not meant to further debate but rather to stifle it. So, when I read that an article about the environment is called "alarmist," I wonder whether this is not merely a rhetorical feint to avoid dealing in depth with a topic that makes the writer uncomfortable. Though it's almost impossible to shed the label of being alarmist, I want to address the frightening connection of our diet to the planet's health.

Strange as it seems, we appear to be the only species who do not have an instinctive ability to know what food we should eat to stay healthy. All other animals do. We consider ourselves a superior species, yet we are destroying the only planet we have, endangering our very existence. I have been deeply influenced by the early work about IQ that one finds in a groundbreaking book by Richard Lewontin, Steven Rose, and Leon J. Kamin entitled *Not in Our Genes*. This book argued that the classic intelligence tests were ideologically driven by racism, class considerations, and outright fraud. It concludes: "Nothing demonstrates more clearly how scientific methodology and conclusions are shaped to fit ideological ends than the sorry story of the heritability of IQ."[2]

I was never a great fan of intelligence tests for humans. When I turned my attention to animals, it is not surprising that I carried over these views, and could never quite understand the human obsession with "how intelligent is that animal?"—

whether asked about dog breeds, cats, chimps, bonobos, or any other animal. I always felt the correct answer was: "As intelligent as the animal needs to be in his or her environment." I did wonder, though, what was driving this question. Why were people so interested? Could it have to do with a seemingly built-in species bias: that we simply want reassurance that we are the most intelligent of all animal species? Our sense of uniqueness is not confined to intelligence: we have for years insisted we are the only animal to use tools (false, as Jane Goodall was able to show for chimpanzees; many animals, including birds, use tools on a regular basis); the only animal with culture (false; every wolf has to be taught wolf culture); the only animal to use language (false, if language is defined more broadly as communication, which of course it ought to be); the only animal who has self-consciousness (false, as the Harvard biologist Donald Griffin showed in *The Question of Animal Awareness*); the only animal who has a theory of mind (still being ferociously debated); the only animal who has complex emotions (false, as I have attempted to show in a series of books over the last fifteen years, and as Darwin demonstrated as early as 1872); the only animal who reasons (false, as a whole series of books about animal thinking in the last ten years demonstrates); the only animal who has a sense of death (false; elephants mourn their dead perhaps as deeply as we do); and finally, the only animal who can see himself or herself existing in the future (false; see the face of your dog when you use the word "walk," which brings an ecstasy of anticipation).

The very need for such reassurance with respect to intelligence hints that there are probably a lot of people who are not quite so sure how we should define intelligence. Count me among them. It is not that I doubt we are the only species to write books, compose symphonies, use cell phones, drive cars, and wonder what the twenty-first century will bring. But surely whatever type of intelligence it takes to do these things is not the only kind of intelligence out there. I have many friends who do none of these things and I think no less highly of their intelligence. We use words like "street-smart" to refer to people who are intelligent in ways that are often impossible to measure. Even moral intelligence can be selective.

Despite our seemingly greater intelligence, we are the only animal to have deliberately conceived the extermination of a particular group from among our own species: the killing by the Nazis of Jews, Gypsies, the "mentally ill," and "malformed children"; the Armenian holocaust; Pol Pot; Stalin's Terror—the list is long and depressing. We humans have also reached a point where we have put in jeopardy our own future and that of most other animal species on our planet, even if this has not been deliberate. This fact does not inspire much confidence in human intelligence. The mega-animal farms, known as "factory farming," and the concentrated animal feedlots—those vast, barren pens containing hundreds of thousands of animals trapped as they are fattened up for slaughter—are polluting our air, our water, and our land. Humans as well as all other species of animals and plants are all affected.

Today, everybody who looks at the scientific research accepts and fears global warming. The very words "human-caused greenhouse gas emissions" terrify us because they contain the implicit criticism that we are the cause of our own impending destruction. But when people hear these and other phrases associated with climate change, they still tend to think of planes, cars, industrial smokestacks, and large oil corporations. They rarely think about farms, animals, and agriculture. In fact, it is the global food system in all its many manifestations—from how we grow our fruits and vegetables to the way we raise animals for food and what we do with their waste—that accounts for at least 33 percent of human-caused greenhouse gas emissions, according to the Pew Center on Global Climate Change.[3] (I am not fond of the term "greenhouse gas," because the words make me think of a greenhouse for plants, which sounds innocuous and benign.)

What scientists are worried about is the amount of methane and nitrous oxide emitted by industrial farming. Methane has 23 times the global warming effect of carbon dioxide, and nitrous oxide 296 times. A full three quarters of the nitrous oxide emissions in the United States come from agriculture (mostly from the use of nitrogen fertilizer). Nearly two thirds of all methane emissions around the world are from agriculture. A lot of this comes from the massive waste lakes created by giant animal farms. EarthSave International points out that the world's 1.3 billion cows are a serious concern when it comes to methane. Figures from the U.S. Environmental Protection Agency (EPA) indicate that this source accounts for almost 20 percent of human-related methane emissions.[4]

ANIMAL WASTE

TO GIVE SOME IDEA of the scale of the pollution we are creating by eating the way we do, think of the fact that the planet's population of more than 2.5 billion pigs and cattle excrete more than 80 million metric tons (1 metric ton is 2,204 pounds) of waste nitrogen annually. By comparison, the entire human population produces just over 30 million metric tons. In the United States, the amount of animal waste is 130 times greater than that of human waste.[5] The EPA, hardly considered a radical environmental group, takes the view that factory farm runoff (we are talking about 3 trillion pounds of waste) is a greater source of pollution of our rivers and lakes than all other industrial sources combined.[6] The figures defy our imagination.

Animals on factory farms in the United States produce 87,000 pounds of waste every second, or, put a different way, 130 times more than the entire population of the United States. This is equivalent to about 5 tons of animal waste for each person in the United States every year. Most people react with disbelief when they hear about the vast lakes of raw waste, consisting of excrement and urine, often larger than small cities (a typical pig factory farm generates as much waste as a city of 50,000 people).[7] How can the nitrates from these lakes not contaminate nearby water sources, given the invariable leaks and spills? And contaminate them they do: the Centers for Disease Control and Prevention (CDC) has warned that high nitrate levels in the drinking water of people who live close to these excrement lakes suffer high levels of spontaneous abortions, or, worse, "blue baby" syndrome, which can be fatal.[8]

There is the constant scourge of E. coli, Salmonella, and of Cryptosporidium, a diarrheal disease involved in the contamination of Milwaukee's drinking water in 1993, which killed more than 100 people and made 400,000 sick.[9] Hydrogen sulfide gas wafting from these lakes, an acidic gas known to burn the eyes and respiratory tract, can lead to brain damage. In 1998, the National Institutes of Health (NIH) reported that nineteen people died in the United States from these sulfide emissions.[10] The number of fish found dead in our streams is increasing. Millions of them die from what could only be spills from these lakes. Imagine the destruction that occurs when these open-air manure lagoons the size of several baseball fields simply burst their banks due to hurricanes and tornados.[11] The "dead zones" in the Gulf of Mexico caused by algal blooms (themselves a product of nutrients in animal waste and of ammonia, the toxic form of nitrogen released in gas) increase every year, extending over thousands of square miles, roughly half the size of Maryland. They are called dead zones because just about everything they touch dies.[12]

The hazards to humans involve many objects we do not see, or rarely even think about. Consider, for example, the dust raised by the millions of animals in feedlots throughout the United States: in Texas alone, one study found more than 7,000 tons of particulate dust in a single year raised by animals.[13] That dust contains bacteria, molds, and fungi from the animals' feces and the food they eat (almost never the grass they are evolved to eat). Children, asthmatics, and people who are sensitive to particulate matter (pm; the sum of all solid and liquid particles suspended in air) can all be adversely affected—in fact, no threshold has been identified below which a person's health is not affected.[14] (We should also be concerned with the health of the workers on these large farms: as many as 30 percent of Concentrated Animal Feed Operations (CAFO) workers suffer from occupation respiratory diseases such as acute and chronic asthma.)[15]

Animal waste here does not refer to the old-fashioned cow

manure, pig feces, or chickenshit that on family farms was simply plowed into fields and vegetable gardens and made for rich fertilizer. The reason is simple: on these traditional farms, the animals ate what they were evolved to eat and what they would want to eat, given the choice. They were never fed antibiotics and hormones, and certainly not ground-up members of their own species. Today, all of these are routinely fed to all animals in agribusiness.[16] We know that as much as 75 percent of these antimicrobials can be excreted unmetabolized in animal waste.[17] Obviously, this is bound to contaminate both the soil and the groundwater, with disastrous effects on human health. Researchers at Tufts University in Boston found that these substances are endocrine disrupters, which can lead to increased risk of breast and ovarian cancer in women, and testicular cancer and a lower sperm quality and sperm count in men.[18] High nitrate levels in wells near animal feedlot operations can be dangerous to women and young children. High nitrates carry a greater risk of miscarriage in pregnant women. In extreme cases, nitrate contamination can cause "blue baby" syndrome where the blood's ability to transport oxygen is greatly reduced, sometimes to the point of death.[19]

Generally speaking, people don't have much choice when it comes to where they live. Would anyone choose to live near an industrial animal farm? Not likely, when they learn that those who do have higher rates of respiratory problems, nausea, fatigue, plugged ears, and irritated eyes, noses, and throats, according to a study published in the *Journal of Agricultural Safety and Health*. These are only the physical symptoms. Research conducted at Duke University has found that residents living near pig farms report more tension, depression, anger, fatigue, and confusion, and less energy.[20] And these people don't even visit the place! Imagine, then, what the pigs themselves experience.

A number of environmentalists do not seem as alarmed by the McChicken farms as they are by the cattle farms on the grounds that they are less detrimental to the environment. But we must take into consideration the fact that there is good evidence that bird flu could become a human pandemic because of the way chickens are raised on these mega-farms. According to the World Health Organization's coordinator for zoonoses control, "The chief risk factor for emerging zoonotic diseases [such as avian flu] is environmental degradation by humans." This includes degradation caused by global climate change, deforestation, and, as WHO recognizes, intense animal production.[21]

The effect of an outbreak of bird flu on the human population and on the environment is almost unimaginable. Michael Osterholm, the director of the Center for Infectious Disease Research and Policy at the University of Minnesota, believes that "An influenza pandemic of even moderate impact will result in the biggest single human disaster ever—far greater than AIDS, 9/11, all wars in the twentieth century and the recent Tsunami combined. It has the potential to redirect world history as the Black Death redirected European history in the fourteenth century."[22] And the executive director of the Consortium of Conservation Medicine, A. J. McMichael, has said, "Show me almost any new infectious disease, and I'll show you an environmental change brought about by humans that either caused or exacerbated it."[23]

Disease is not the only problem. Limits of land use is another. As we will see, the vast majority of dairy cows in the United

States and in Europe rarely get outdoors. But even those cows who are allowed to graze (in New Zealand and many parts of Australia, and for beef cattle elsewhere) put an enormous strain on our environment. Each head of cattle needs about 30 acres of pasture for grazing and will "yield" (awful word) about 500 pounds of beef. If we planted a single acre with looseleaf lettuce, we could get from 530 to 900 boxes of lettuce (each weighing about 35 pounds) twice a year, for a minimal cost (water and energy together priced at approximately $171).[24] We are talking about 63,000 pounds of lettuce versus 500 pounds of beef. And if we take into account that other crops and herbs could be interplanted with the lettuce, we are looking at a remarkably irresponsible use of land. Remember, a single cow produces twenty times as much body waste as a human does. The lettuce, of course, produces no body waste.

WATER

WATER IS BECOMING A MORE and more precious commodity and the raising of animals can consume a lot of water. Agriculture is the largest single user of water in the nation, consuming approximately 80 percent of total pumped fresh water. Professor David Pimentel of Cornell University's Ecology Department has calculated that it takes 13,000 gallons of water to produce a single pound of beef.[26] Granted, this sounds extreme. But even when we use more conservative figures, we find that most people simply have no idea how much water is involved.

When reporters at *National Geographic* asked people about water use, they were surprised at how far off the mark the average person was. For example, researchers calculated that it takes 2,600 gallons of water to produce a single serving of steak, but the average person guessed 99 gallons (for comparison, it takes 6 gallons of water to produce a head of lettuce, or for grain anywhere from 25 to 250 times as much, depending on your source). Put a different way, producing 2 pounds of animal protein requires about ten times more water than producing 2 pounds of grain protein.[27]

Beyond the amount of water used, consider what these huge animal farms do to the *quality* of the water. According to the EPA, chemical and animal waste runoff from factory farms is responsible for more than 173,000 miles of polluted rivers and streams. As a single example, consider the area bordering the Chesapeake Bay along the eastern shore of Maryland. This area raises 62 million chickens annually, which produce nearly 3.3 billion pounds of raw waste;[28] and this waste contains approximately 13 million pounds of phosphorous and 48 million pounds of nitrogen.[29] Since farmers use the phosphorous- and nitrogen-rich chicken waste on croplands, scientists and environmentalists believe that it is precisely the waste from these farms that is a primary cause of *pfiesteria,* a single-celled microorganism referred to as a dinoflagellate. The symptoms of exposure in humans are reddened eyes, severe headaches, open sores, sleepiness, blurred vision, nausea, vomiting, difficulty breathing, kidney and liver dysfunction, memory loss, and severe cognitive impairment. Over time, these symptoms improve. But does anybody want their children and other loved ones exposed to *pfiesteria* by breathing in the airborne toxins, or by open wounds or contact with intact skin?[30]

E. coli, a common pathogen present in the feces of farmed

animals, is found in our surface water. How much? Extraordinary amounts. In Michigan in 2001, samples of water downstream from a cattle feedlot contained 1,900 times the state's maximum standard for *E. coli* in surface waters.[31] In Walkerton, Ontario, more than 1,300 residents were affected by *E. coli* poisoning, after the town's drinking water was polluted by nearby cattle operations.[32]

In congressional testimony, the Environmental Protection Agency said that agriculture is the main source of pollution in U.S. rivers: "Based on . . . reports from all 50 States, we estimate that agriculture generates pollutants that degrade aquatic life or interfere with public use of 173,629 river miles (i.e., 25% of all river miles surveyed) and contributes to 70% of all water quality problems identified in rivers and streams."[33]

It is not just the poisoning of water that is of concern, but the disappearance of water altogether. Globally, farmers are "abstracting" water in such enormous quantities, mostly for the animals on these giant farms, that all over the world aquifers are beginning to run dry.[34] The amount of irrigation water used annually to produce feed for U.S. livestock is a staggering 17 trillion gallons.[35]

All of this is going to get a lot worse. As living standards rise in the developing world, so does the appetite for meat and dairy. Annual per capita meat consumption in developing countries doubled, from 31 pounds in 1980 to 62 pounds in 2002, according to the Food and Agriculture Organization (FAO) of the United Nations, and global meat production will more than double by 2050. In a recent editorial, *The New York Times* concluded: "As the world's appetite for meat increases, countries across the globe are bulldozing huge swaths of land to make more room for animals and the crops to feed them. From tropical rain forests in Brazil to ancient pine forests in China, entire ecosystems are being destroyed to fuel our addiction to meat. According to scientists at the Smithsonian Institute, the equivalent of seven football fields of land is bulldozed every minute to create more room for farmed animals."[36] Nearly 40 percent of world grain is being fed to livestock rather than being consumed directly by humans.[37]

Yes, the rain forests are being destroyed to grow soy, but be assured that only a minuscule portion of that ends up in the tofu of vegetarian diets. The vast majority of it is used to feed animals. To be precise, according to Lester Brown, guru of the environmental movement and president of the prestigious Washington, D.C., Earth Policy Institute, in 2007 farmers produced 222 million tons of soybeans. Of this, some 15 million tons were consumed directly as tofu or other products based on soy used by humans.[38] If instead of investing water, energy, and time in fields of monocultures meant to be fed to animals, we concentrated on growing fruits and vegetables, what could we expect to see?[39] What, for example, would be involved in producing one acre of organic fruits and vegetables?

As a child of twelve I lived in the hills of Hollywood, near Fern Dell Park. Once, some other children and I decided to turn a vacant lot next door to our house into a garden. The garden could not have been much bigger than the size of a small house, maybe 1,000 square feet. We read gardening books and talked to some knowledgeable adults, and in no time we had planted corn, melons, cucumbers, tomatoes, lettuce, and onions. It was extraordinary to see the first plants press themselves out of the soil. In a few months, we had so many vegetables that we opened a roadside stall in front of the lot and sold the vegetables to people driving by. I was amazed at how much food came from such a small place.

I regret to say that this exciting experiment did not transform my life. I did not go on to study agriculture and figure out ways to grow more and more on less and less land. But other people have. At the time, we grew all our vegetables organically. Today, if I were doing the same thing, I would go a step further and grow them using the methods and principles of permaculture, or eco-agriculture, which involves a more natural, sustainable, and harmonious balance between the needs of a place (an ecosystem) and the people in that place. As Bill Mollison, one of the two Australian founders of permaculture (the other is David Holmgren) puts it, it's the philosophy of working with rather than against nature.[40]

Using permaculture, what could I expect on, say, one acre of land? John Jeavons, an organic gardening expert, explains that whereas conventional farming practices deplete the soil of nutrients and lead to wind and water erosion, permaculture is a sustainable, soil-friendly way to feed the world. He claims that with his methods, "you can actually build up to 20 pounds of farmable soil for every pound of food eaten."[41] In the 1970s, he went to the San Joaquin Valley, where approximately 30 percent of the food in the United States was being grown at the time, and he asked farmers this question: "What is the smallest area you can grow all your food and income on?" They were not sure, but the answer was usually close to 1,000 acres, and they were referring to wheat. Whereas, he calculated, it takes about 15,000 to 30,000 square feet of land to feed one person the average U.S. diet, he figured out how to get this down to 4,000 square feet by focusing on growing soil, not crops.

One acre (43,560 square feet) is nothing when you think about raising a cow to the age where she will be slaughtered. But if instead you think about doing something else with that acre, the possibilities are endless. And this is hardly a trivial issue. Consider that worldwide more than 3 billion people in the world are currently malnourished, the largest number and percentage of malnourished humans ever recorded in history.[42]

Using the philosophy of permaculture, on far less than a single acre, you can easily feed your family. In fact, if you really hew to the principles closely, it has been calculated that you could actually feed twenty to thirty families on half an acre of land.[43] You could plant vegetables such as broccoli, cauliflower, kale, mushrooms, chard, many varieties of lettuce, spring onions, tomatoes, potatoes, corn, and fruits such as figs, pawpaw, kiwi fruit, plums, cherries, watermelon, cantaloupe, and nuts of many kinds, not to mention medicinal herbs. You do this by "companion planting." Green beans thrive next to strawberries, corn provides shade to cucumbers, and fast-maturing radishes grow well in between slower-growing carrots, just to give a few examples.

Permaculture imitates the forest, and the result is a forest garden, with plants assigned to one of seven specific layers. The canopy layer is made up of large fruit or nut trees. Then comes the low-tree layer, perhaps made up of dwarf fruit trees. Underneath these trees would be the shrub layer, with fruit bushes. Next the herbaceous level, with plants that die back in winter. Comfrey (a favorite plant for permaculturalists) would live here, as would leafy vegetables and herbs. The rhizosphere is the zone where root vegetables live. Then there are the ground-hugging plants. For example, strawberries make an effective ground cover when they are allowed to spread naturally. Climbers and vines form the final layer.

Using the principles of permaculture, the state of California could produce enough fruits and vegetables to feed the world. We already have the know-how, we have the space; all we lack is the will and the necessary political structure. Moreover, the price would be insignificant in comparison to raising meat. Permaculture requires almost no care once the initial work is done. The cost of planting, caring for, and harvesting one acre of land devoted to fruits and vegetables sufficient to feed a family of four for one year would be minimal; the cost of feeding that same family with beef would be significantly more.

Permaculture and eco-agriculture are increasingly used all over the world. In a hillside farm near a pine forest on the edge of the remote village of Pacayas in central Honduras, Elias Zelaya used the principles that he learned from the non-profit organization, World Neighbours, to turn what had been an abandoned lot, deemed useless for cultivation, into a farm where there are now twenty-eight types of crops and trees. In the fields he grows legumes as green manure and uses composts so that the soil is thick, dark, and spongy to the step, often reaching two feet deep. A bit further to the west lies another transformed farm in the village of Guacamayas, also in the hills. Here Irma de Guittierez Mendez has transformed her land, working with rather than against nature: "Her farm is covered with *terracita*, small terraces to conserve soil and water. She grows maize; cassava; and four beans; seven vegetables; bananas; guava and avocado; and coffee under apple trees at the top of the slope. These crops are rotated in order to control diseases, and Irma brings wasp nests from the forest to hang on the farm trees, which control pests."[44]

Jules Pretty—one of the leaders of eco-agriculture and head of the Department of Biological Sciences at the University of Essex—and his students have looked at more than two hundred projects in fifty-two countries, including forty-five in Latin America, sixty-three in Asia, and one hundred in Africa. They calculated that almost 9 million farmers were using sustainable agriculture practices, more than 98 percent of which emerged in the past decade. Ninety percent of these farmers are in areas with less than five acres. Using these agro-ecological approaches, they are getting extraordinarily high yields, often increases of 150 percent over conventional methods. And they do this with minimum or zero pesticide use, zero tillage, and innovative water methods, without losing nitrogen, phosphate, and potassium nutrients from the soil. Because the organic matter contains carbon, the soils can act as sites for carbon sequestration—something that has only become obvious in about the last ten years. So, these sustainable agriculture farmers provide a benefit to everyone by sequestering large amounts of carbon from the atmosphere, and in this way mitigating the effects of climate change.

The households with these small farms with their double-dug beds are eating a far more diversified diet (kale, onion, tomato, cabbage, passion fruit, pigeon pea, spinach, pepper, green bean, and soya are all planted by the women). The land, formerly useless, is fertile; wildlife has increased; there is water in the soil, and the people are much healthier and happier because they feel in control of their destiny. Pretty and his team reviewed twenty-six communities; they found that three quarters of participating households are now free from hunger during the year, and the proportion having to buy vegetables has fallen from 85 to 11 percent.[45] We always thought that "organic" meant elitist, expensive, of small import, without benefit to the larger population. All that received wisdom turns out to be wrong.

In a sense, it is counterintuitive. These people grew a larger crop with no or very little pesticide, yet we have come to believe that to be able to "cultivate" plants, we need to use pesticides. Not surprisingly, pesticide companies have been busy for decades invoking this basic bedrock assumption. But, in fact, it was upside down. The paradigm-shifting moment occurred in the early 1980s, when Peter Kenmore and his colleagues in Southeast Asia discovered that the more pesticides they used on rice, the more the pests attacked.[46] The reason was actually quite simple: pesticides were killing the natural enemies of insect pests, such as spiders and beetles. The key was biological diversity. Pests and diseases thrive on monocultures and monoscapes. They then have no natural enemies. Similarly in Bangladesh, when fish were put into the paddy fields and vegetables in the rice field dykes, suddenly everything was different: "Our fields are singing again, after thirty years of silence," said one farmer joyfully. He was referring to the frogs who had returned to the richly diverse fields full of fish, rice, and vegetables.[47]

I don't know if anyone in the conventional sectors of California agriculture is paying attention to these innovative methods, but I would suggest they should give it more than a cursory glance. After all, California produces more than 350 crops. The average family, however, probably subsists on less than a dozen. Moreover, only in California are almonds, artichokes, figs, olives, persimmons, pomegranates, prunes, and walnuts commercially grown. So, yes, California does grow more than half of the nation's fruits, vegetables, and nuts from less than 4 percent of the nation's farmland. But just imagine how these figures could climb if natural methods of farming were employed, and think, too, of the health benefits for all. After all, farms cover one third of the entire land area of California. That is about 50,000 square miles (about 32 million acres), *precisely the amount of tropical forest that is cleared every year in the world.*

Imagine if those 32 million acres were planted with fruits and vegetables using the principles we have seen here. We could help fight against climate change. When Jane Goodall, the leading field researcher in the world, signed the "Forests Now Declaration" in New York in late 2007, she noted, "If we lose forests, we lose the fight against climate change." Deforestation leads to desertification. It is that simple. (Forests absorb carbon dioxide during photosynthesis, storing it above and below ground, and producing oxygen as a byproduct of photosynthesis. Forests are vital in that they remove CO_2 from the atmosphere to mitigate the effects of climate change on the environment.) There is little doubt that we are losing forests at rates unprecedented in the history of the earth. Eighty percent of Thailand's forests are gone; 85 percent of the Philippines' are history; the massive forests of Indonesian Borneo will collapse by 2010. The rain forests ("the lungs of the earth," as they are so often and correctly called) of South America are under constant assault from logging companies and ranchers, often working in tandem.

Another way of looking at the figure of 50,000 acres is that, according to scientists at the Smithsonian Institution, every minute land the size of seven football fields is currently being bulldozed to create room for farmed animals and the crops needed to feed them (not us).[48] As we have seen, nearly 70 percent of former forests in the Amazon have been turned into grazing land for animals, and Amazonian Indians are not profiting, nor are the animals, nor is our planet.[49]

We should not believe, however, that nobody is paying attention. More people than ever before are aware of these problems. More and more people know that if we continue to destroy the forests at the present rate, in just the next four years we will have pumped more CO_2 into the atmosphere than all the flights in the entire history of aviation.[50] There *is* concern.[51] The oldest public health institution in America, the American Public Health Association, recently issued a statement which resolved that the APHA should urge "federal, state and local governments and public health agencies to impose a moratorium on new Concentrated Animal Feed Operations (CAFOs) until additional scientific data on the attendant risks to public health have been collected and uncertainties resolved."[52]

●　●　●

THESE ARE NOT JUST theoretical problems, or problems with no bearing on our species. If humans believe they can live without the aesthetic pleasure of looking at forests, nobody believes they can live without food. More people are hungry today than ever before in history—854 million, to be exact, nearly a sixth of the entire population of earth (the figure is much larger if we include undernourishment as well).[53] At the same time, scientists note that the world produces more food than ever before: enough to feed twice the global population. The problem is that the food that exists is being consumed by the richer half of the world, with the effect that that half becomes obese.

What lies behind these terrifying statistics? Greed, for one thing; a small number of people want to profit at the expense of the vast majority of other people. Al Gore in his film *An Inconvenient Truth* quotes the great Upton Sinclair: "It is difficult to get a man to understand something when his salary depends upon his not understanding." Many other factors, too, play a role, and we will examine them in detail later. The odd thing is that most of the factors that are promoting this state of affairs, which puts our very existence into jeopardy, are recognized by just about everyone. We are often urged to take immediate steps, which many of us do, to stave off the worst: we put in CFL light bulbs; we use less gas, ride more bicycles, buy smaller hybrid cars, and recycle. But this is not the case for large business agriculture, which also seems to be grounded in greed (one of those attributes oddly missing in the animal world outside of humans).

I am not the first to point out that one inconvenient truth Al Gore omitted to mention in his marvelous film is the price we pay for industrial agriculture. The most inconvenient truth of them all is the effect that eating meat and other animal products is having on our planet. Agribusiness not only harms animals in ways that most of us cannot even imagine; it also financially destroys small farmers (chasing them off desired land, or forcing them into bankruptcy). Large firms want mono-crops, not staple foods, because that is where the big profits lie. Their Web sites announce that they are in the business of feeding the world, but they are really just in business, period. Farmers using the wisdom of the land never grew rich in the past, true, nor did they harm their own environment. It takes a corporation to think of genetically modified seeds, chemical fertilizers, and synthetic pesticides, seemingly indifferent to the risks involved (pesticide use on farms is a growing concern, with nearly 1 billion pounds of active ingredients now being applied to our soil every year).[54] Global agriculture uses 3 millions tons of pesticides each year. According to Polly Walker at the Center for a Livable Future at the Johns Hopkins Bloomberg School of Public Health, these pesticides and herbicides contain over 1,600 chemicals, and "most have not been tested for toxic effects on humans."[55]

Sometimes we simply do not take into account dangers we do not conceive of. For example, the Union of Concerned Scientists pointed out in 2001: "Many consumers will be surprised to find that tens of millions of pounds of antimicrobials are used in livestock systems. We estimate that every year livestock producers in the United States use 24.6 million pounds of antimicrobials in the absence of disease for nontherapeutic purposes." This is more than is used for humans by a factor of 8![56] Eventually, this may lead to the creation of superbugs that kill people and are immune to our superdrugs.

Few people have stopped to consider, too, what intensive agriculture does to wild animals who depend on habitat that has not been so degraded. In an article with the ominous title

"The Second Silent Spring?," John R. Krebs, from the Edward Grey Institute of Field Ornithology at the University of Oxford, and his colleagues, "estimate that, in the past 20 years, ten million breeding individuals of ten species of farmland birds have disappeared from the British countryside." In all, 116 species of farmland birds—one fifth of European avifauna—are now of concern to conservationists.[57] Nature is suffering.

Nothing I have written above is in any sense controversial, even if it is not always explicitly recognized. Most scientists who study these questions admit these facts. Where it does become controversial is when we assign blame. When it comes to recognizing the role of animal agriculture, and so ultimately the eating of meat and other animal products, the major environmental organizations, much like the winner of 2007's Nobel Peace Prize, shy away from stating the obvious. Gore, in his new book and on his Web site, has a single sentence: "Eat less meat." Nothing wrong with that, but a single sentence can hardly be considered a clarion call to the conscience of the West. We can do better.

On October 17, 2007, the UK organization called Compassion in World Farming distributed a report entitled *Global Warning: Climate Change and Farm Animal Welfare*. Their conclusion is that

> *if the projected doubling in global meat production takes place (mostly in poor and developing countries), methane, with 21 times the warming (more like scorching) potential of CO_2 (carbon dioxide), and nitrous oxide emission from the digestion and manure of animals will continue to rise steeply, the demand for feed-crops will*

lead to further deforestation, overuse of scarce water resources, competition for arable land, damage to soil fertility and desertification of grazing land. These trends can only exacerbate the unavoidable effects of climate change, such as floods, drought and harvest failure. Resource conflicts, human conflicts and human and animal suffering are almost certain to be increased by current livestock production trends.[58]

Consider *Livestock's Long Shadow: Environmental Issues and Options,* by H. Steinfeld, et al., the 390-page United Nations Food and Agriculture Organization report on the impact of the livestock industry on the environment for 2006, which states that "livestock production accounts for 70 percent of all agricultural land and 30 percent of the land surface of the planet" and concludes that "livestock's contribution to environmental problems is on a massive scale and its potential contribution to their solution is equally large. The impact is so significant that it needs to be addressed with urgency."[59] This report found that livestock accounts for 18 percent of human-induced greenhouse gas emissions in carbon dioxide equivalent terms—in other words, global warming. That percentage is more than the entire transportation sector of the whole world, including cars, ships, airplanes, and trains. Livestock, the UN report warns, accounts for 37 percent of all human-induced methane, which has 23 times the global warming potential (GWP) of CO_2, and 65 percent of human-related nitrous oxide, which has 296 times the GWP of CO_2. Livestock also accounts for 64 percent of ammonia emissions, which contribute significantly to acid rain and the subsequent

loss of biodiversity. Plants die, animals die, people die; everything we have loved about our planet is reduced. What are we
thinking?[60]

•   •   •

CLEARLY, THE ETHICAL CLIMATE must change almost as
rapidly as our atmospheric one. At the same time, I concede
that it is hard to be a responsible, well-informed citizen today.
There are so many demands made on our conscience. We are
pulled in many different directions and cannot go in all of them.
Yet we want to do the right thing. Each day, a new issue comes
to our attention. I recently looked at the Web site of the Polaris
Institute and, convinced by what I read, took what is called the
"Think Outside the Bottle Pledge." I would not buy any more
bottled water. Why? As they put it in a nutshell on their Web site:
"Though many bottled water brands come from the same source
as public tap water, they are marketed as somehow more pure.
What's more—bottled water corporations sell water back to the
public at thousands of times the cost. Plastic bottles also require
massive amounts of fossil fuels to manufacture and transport.
Billions of these bottles wind up in landfills every year."

So many issues require our urgent action. Like you, I get
asked for donations constantly. Sometimes, just as I am about
to give to Bioneers and *Earth Island Journal,* I am bombarded
by dozens of other, equally worthwhile organizations short of
cash. I hesitate; I feel overwhelmed. I feel poor. I feel like reading Richard Russo's new novel instead. Yet those of us privileged to live in the developed world who have the means are
obliged to inform ourselves and take action.

Speaking of reading, where do we get our news and how do we make the decision as to what sources we trust? I know how long it takes to be able to make an informed choice. My wife is a pediatrician, and we have two young children (my eldest is grown-up). We have both read a good deal about child rearing, and yet we are both often stumped. What is true? What is right? How long should a mother breast-feed? Two years, more? How long should our children share our bed? Until they no longer want to, or until we no longer want them to? Are there any objective criteria, or are we adrift on a sea of conflicting evidence and studies? How is it that in spite of our access to the world's best universities, we still don't know the answer to simple and urgent questions and don't know for sure when we can trust our own instincts?

Even when there is general agreement—as there now seems to be for global warming—we sometimes throw up our hands in frustration, wondering what a single individual can do. What possible difference could I make? But if we took this attitude all the time, we would never make any change in our life, not even bothering to recycle or, as bad, vote. Going vegan saves on average 2,000 animals over a person's lifetime. This is hardly trivial. By the time a dozen or so friends are influenced by your change, you are saving a large number of lives.

Two geophysicists from the University of Chicago, Gidon Eshel and Pamela Martin, have concluded that changing one's eating habits from the Standard American Diet to a vegetarian diet does more to fight global warming than switching from a gas-guzzling SUV to a fuel-efficient hybrid car.[61] Eating meat is like driving a huge SUV. A vegetarian diet is like driving a midsized car or a reasonable sedan; and eating a vegan diet (no dairy, no eggs) is like riding a bicycle or walking. If we want to fight the warming trend, we need to walk away from SUVs and an SUV-style diet. And Eshel lives by his study. I called him with a single question: "Are you vegetarian?" "Better," he answered. "I am vegan."[62]

If we don't have children, perhaps we don't need to know everything about child rearing. But here is the thing: we eat every day. We put our forks into something or someone three times a day. We cannot disengage ourselves, even if we wanted to. We are all involved in agriculture on a daily basis. We vote with every meal. We make a difference with every bite. We cannot choose to ignore this issue, thinking it has nothing to do with us. It has everything to do with us.

We are programmed not to question too intensively what society deems essential to its own survival. Marshall McLuhan may have put it best when he said, "I don't know who discovered water but it wasn't a fish." We can no longer see the problem in a practice as pervasive as eating meat. To see the impact on our environment means to step out of the box and our daily habits. We must be prepared to perceive something we have been encouraged and accustomed to ignore.

The editors of *World Watch* magazine concluded in the July–August 2004 edition that "the human appetite for animal flesh is a driving force behind virtually every major category of environmental damage now threatening the human future— deforestation, erosion, fresh water scarcity, air and water pollution, climate change, biodiversity loss, social injustice, the destabilization of communities and the spread of disease." As Lee Hall, the legal director for Friends of Animals, put it: "Behind virtually every great environmental complaint there's milk and meat." Even the British government maintains that "Production of meat and dairy products has a much bigger effect on climate change and other environmental impacts than that of most grains, pulses, fruit and vegetables."[63] When the British government asks its citizens to eat less meat, we know the world is changing. For the better.[64]

Chapter Two

THE LIVES THEY LEAD

"And even the miserable lives we lead are not allowed to reach their natural span. For myself I do not grumble, for I am one of the lucky ones. I am twelve years old and have had over four hundred children. Such is the natural life of a pig. But no animal escapes the cruel knife in the end. You young porkers who are sitting in front of me, every one of you will scream your lives out at the block within a year. To that horror we all must come—cows, pigs, hens, sheep, everyone."

—George Orwell, *Animal Farm* (1944)

MANY ANIMAL BEHAVIORISTS AND OTHER BIOLOGISTS consider the question of animal happiness to be pointless. We can never know, they say, what it takes to make an animal happy. I think they are wrong, and that in fact we can know quite easily.[1] Animals are happy if they can live in conformity with their own nature, using to the utmost those traits in a natural setting. To live according to nature will differ for each species, but the answers are not unfathomable mysteries.

Cows are herd animals. When transported in dark trains to the slaughterhouse, they cannot help but feel panic.[2] You cannot speak of happiness inside that boxcar. Cows did not evolve to take such terminal voyages. Nor did cows ever have to face a situation where their newborn calves were removed from them at birth. The calling sound they make is a mourning call; it cannot be mistaken for a happy sound. A chicken likes to take a sunbath. She will roll onto her side, extend one wing, exposing it to the sun, then roll onto her other side and do the same. A chicken who never sees the sun cannot be said to be happy. Ducks need water. To keep them in vast indoor pens without access to a pond or river is to deprive them of expressing their innermost nature. Anyone who has observed ducks in the wild playing in the water knows that this, not confinement, constitutes happiness.

Geese are more monogamous than humans and as faithful as dogs. If a goose's mate or gosling becomes sick, she will refuse to leave, putting her own survival in jeopardy. Even with winter approaching, she will watch her flock head south rather than abandon her loved one. Separation, as happens on geese farms, means unhappiness. A flock of sheep needs a leader; this is how they are saved from mountain lions and wolves in the wild. If they are separated from the flock, they immediately become prey. Is it surprising then that they "appear" so miserable when they are deliberately removed from the flock for shearing, slaughter, or any other reason? The security of the herd is part and parcel of what it means to be a happy sheep.

The question of animal happiness is hardly a trivial matter from a philosophical point of view, a scientific one, or a moral one. Almost gone are the days when we could quote Bertrand Russell, who began *The Conquest of Happiness* in 1930 with the patronizing comment that "Animals are happy so long as they have health and enough to eat." Recent comments, alas, by the philosopher Roger Scruton that farm animals who are housed together in the winter and allowed to roam in the summer "are as happy as their nature allows" are not so different.[3] How can Scruton or anyone else arbitrate what limits there are to the nature of any other creature?

By observing animals in the wild, we begin to get a sense of what kinds of lives they lead, and hence what makes them genuinely happy. This is why the early studies by women scientists such as Jane Goodall, Dian Fossey, and Biruté Galdikas, who went into the field and simply observed wild animals, was such a breakthrough and proved so valuable. What we still require is their equivalent on the farm: patient scientists who are willing to devote years to simply observing farm animals under conditions that simulate as far as possible their wild homes. Only then can we get a sense of the complexity of the requirements of these animals for true happiness.

Most people, in theory, want animals to be happy. When asked if they care about the lives that animals lead before they eat them for dinner, an astonishing 80 percent of Americans polled said that they did. I suppose that is not all that surprising. What kind of person with any moral compass is going to answer: "I really couldn't care less"?

Far from being separate realms, it could even be argued that total indifference to the lives of other animals is a sure sign of something seriously wrong. A whole field of research has arisen in which cruelty toward animals in childhood is seen as the first stirring of hatred toward humans. I am not impressed with the new movement where people, chefs included, no longer deny the suffering involved, but claim that somehow viewing and recognizing it makes the cruelty less cruel. From the animals' perspective, whether we acknowledge their suffering or not is irrelevant. The point is, we perpetrate it.

What do scientists think? Though they may wish to hedge their answers and request more specific details, in fact, the majority of animal scientists subscribe to what has become known as the Five Freedoms for farm animals. Ruth Harrison, an Englishwoman who died in 2000, was the primary mover behind these freedoms. She wrote a book in 1964, *Animal Machines,* which did for animals what Rachel Carson's *Silent Spring* did for the environment. Harrison explained how she came to write her book:

> In 1960 I received a letter containing a leaflet that dramatically changed the course of my life. On the front of the leaflet was a picture of a veal calf standing in a crate and emblazoned over it was the question "Cheap food yes, but is it good food?" This started me on a course of investigation which culminated in my writing Animal Machines. *The book looked at the ways in which farm animals were kept, fed and slaughtered; at the many drugs and additives used; and at the resulting quality of the food produced. It also looked at the effects on the environment and the problem of world hunger. The conclusion was that it was not good food, and that change was urgently needed.*[4]

Harrison's book was widely read at the time, and led the British government to appoint nine experts, known as the Brambell Committee—after the zoologist F. W. Roger Brambell—to examine the basics of animal welfare. Their 1965 report defined welfare to take into account "the feelings of animals,"[5] an important early recognition of the significance of emotional well-being to all living creatures.

One recommendation of the committee was to establish a group devoted to the study of farm animal welfare, which would advise ministers, and make recommendations for legislation and research. In 1967, the UK government set up the Farm Animal Welfare Advisory Committee (it became the Farm Animal Welfare Council in 1979). The committee's first guidelines recommended that animals require the freedoms to "turn around, to groom themselves, to get up, to lie down and to stretch their limbs." These have, since 1993, been elaborated to become the Five Freedoms of animal welfare:

1. Freedom from hunger and thirst by ready access to fresh water and a diet to maintain full health and vigor.
2. Freedom from discomfort by providing an appropriate environment including shelter and a comfortable resting area.
3. Freedom from pain, injury or disease by prevention or rapid diagnosis and treatment.
4. Freedom to express normal behaviour by providing sufficient space, proper facilities and company of the animal's own kind.

5. Freedom from fear and distress by ensuring conditions and treatment which avoid mental suffering.

Because the Brambell Report specifically recognizes that farm animals have feelings, its authors were far ahead of most scientists, veterinarians, and indeed the general public. They clearly had these feelings in mind when they devised freedoms 4 and 5. If we think about these last two freedoms, we realize that they have far-reaching implications.

So, when I talk to farmers about how they treat the animals on their farms, I come up against a strange fact: while the general public and most research scientists all acknowledge that farm animals suffer, the farmers responsible for them have a tendency to deny it. Let me give an example. Almost all hens kept for laying eggs have their beaks trimmed when they are small chicks. It is generally done with an electric machine that uses a hot blade to cut off half the upper beak and one third of the lower beak of the young chick (how many of them actually die from shock during the operation is not currently known). The rationale behind the procedure is that otherwise, given the crowded conditions the hens are forced to live in, they will inflict injuries on one another by pecking.

I have asked farmers who debeak about the procedure and have been told it is like humans cutting their fingernails. But this is manifestly untrue. There are no nerve endings in my fingernails, while there are many in the beaks of hens. A more accurate comparison would be to liken the procedure to cutting off the tip of my finger. Brambell said so in no uncertain terms, and as far as I know no scientist has ever contradicted his observation: "Between the horn and bone [of the beak] is a thin layer of highly sensitive soft tissue, resembling the quick of the human nail. The hot knife blade used in debeaking cuts through this complex horn, bone and sensitive tissue causing severe pain."[6] The nerve endings do grow back, but because of the trauma inflicted on them, they grow into what is known as a neuroma—a tangled mass of nerve fibers and surrounding scar tissue that often weeps discharge. Since the tip of the beak is richly innervated and has pain receptors in the same way that our hands do, both acute and chronic pain is the inevitable result of debeaking.[7]

If we were to take seriously the Brambell Report's recommendations, we would have to insist that "normal behavior" for a bird such as a chicken is actually quite complex. We may have modified the appearance of modern chickens, in much the same way that we have modified the appearance of dogs, but a chicken is still very much a Red (wild) Burmese jungle fowl. They are the same species, and if we want to understand what chickens need, we need to understand what their wild cousins need. These birds, found throughout South and Southeast Asia, are notoriously wary. Of course, they have to be. Many other animals would like to eat them for dinner. So they roost in trees to minimize the risk of being attacked at night. This means any chicken kept in captivity needs a perch. The Burmese bird lays an egg in a carefully constructed nest, which must be in a quiet, secluded spot. The more hidden, the safer the bird feels.[8]

So, we need to provide similar nests. The purpose of the nest, of course, is to receive one egg, and then another, and then another, until there is a clutch; the hen then decides it is worth sitting on her eggs (almost all of which are fertilized) until they hatch some twenty-one days later. In a year, a normal wild hen will lay only 20 eggs, instead of the 260 or more she is now bred to lay in captivity. A "brooding" hen is one sensitive bird: it is her job, her very raison d'être, to hatch these eggs into her genetic inheritance, the chicks. So she must see to it that no harm comes to these eggs (for example, a snake that wants to eat them). Then she must make certain the chicks learn to be chickens. They must know how to dust their feathers in clean dirt to regulate their temperature and keep the feathers free of debris and parasites. They must be shown how to spread their wings out in the sunshine. The hen will teach them to drink. She will call them to her to show them where they can find the best food (bamboo seeds and insects, hidden under the leaves; hence the deep-wired urge to scratch beneath covering). All the while the hen makes the elaborate sounds that alert her young to danger from predators. She uses different sounds for predators on the ground or in the air, and may even make a special sound to indicate that an alpha predator—us—is coming. Her maternal affection and training will last many weeks and the bonds that form can last a lifetime.[9]

Does it need to be said that "battery hens" never approximate this life? The chickens are kept four to ten in a cage (usually 20 by 20 inches large, around the size of a filing cabinet drawer), with each bird allowed *two thirds* the space of an 8 × 11 sheet of typing paper; the cages are stacked sometimes as high as six tiers, with up to 100,000 birds in a single shed. They cannot stretch their wings (each has a wingspan of about 32 inches, much larger than the width of her cage). Battery hens don't have perches. They don't have nests. They have nothing to scratch except a wire cage (hence many have crippled feet). A very high percentage develop caged layer osteoporosis. Their legs are so brittle they often snap like twigs when handled.

You can imagine all the other health hazards from a complete lack of exercise. These hens don't see sunlight at all, for they have no access to the outdoors, and some of the sheds are kept permanently semidark. They don't get to keep their young, and the overcrowded conditions destroy any bonding between the animals. Dust-bathe? Of course not. Is that a problem? Well, consider what Dr. Marian Stamp Dawkins, research lecturer in the Department of Zoology at the University of Oxford (no animal rights fanatic), writes: "If such dust-deprived birds are eventually given access to something in which they can have a real dust bath, like wood shavings or peat, they go in for a complete orgy of dust bathing. They do it over and over again, apparently making up for lost time."[10] These barren cages are as far removed from the natural world of the Red Burmese jungle fowl as it is possible to imagine. It is hard to avoid thinking of them as concentration camps for chickens.

As for the instinct to hide their nests, it is completely frustrated. Konrad Lorenz, who won the Nobel Prize for his work on animals, understood the plight of farmed chickens. He wrote that "the worst torture to which a battery hen is exposed is the inability to retire somewhere for the laying act. For the person who knows something about animals it is truly heart-rending to watch how a chicken tries again and again to crawl beneath her fellow cage mates to search there in vain for cover."[11]

Desmond Morris, the former head of the Royal London Zoo and a prominent animal behaviorist, said, "Anyone who has studied the social life of birds carefully will know that theirs is a subtle and complex world, where food and water are only a small part of their behavioural needs. The brain of each bird is programmed with a complicated set of drives and responses that set it on the path to a life full of special territorial, nesting, roosting, grooming, parental, aggressive and sexual activities in addition to the simple feeding behaviour. All these are denied the battery hens."[12] Lesley Rogers, a professor of neuroscience and animal behavior at the University of New England in New South Wales, Australia, who has written perhaps the most complete book about the brain of the chicken, is of the same opinion. She concludes, "it is now clear that birds have cognitive capacities equivalent to those of mammals, even primates."[13]

In the European Union (which has more or less the same number of hens as the United States, roughly 300 million), these cages will be phased out in the year 2012. And the Dutch have announced that they will no longer permit battery cages as of January 2009, an unprecedented step. This shows that veterinarians, the public, and governments now recognize the harms that cages do to chickens. About 98 percent of the eggs produced in the United States, however, come from hens in these cages. That is a lot of misery, and the hens know it. They make a sound that has been mistakenly identified as pure noise. In fact, it is communication: some bird experts believe that the specific sound the hens are making is a call of help to the rooster. I know that sounds like anthropomorphism. But why, then, is the sound identical to the one a hen makes to a rooster when under attack, but never at any other time?

Chickens are birds, and long-lived ones at that. In the wild, they could live anywhere from seven to ten years, perhaps even longer (nobody has conducted studies, partly because the Red

Burmese jungle fowl is so shy that few humans have encountered one, let alone studied a wild flock). But caged hens' productivity declines by 25 percent in the first year. Now called "spent" hens, before their second birthday most are sent for slaughter to be used as pet food. Increasingly, they are simply buried alive because slaughterhouses will not accept them any longer (they are fragile and have little meat left on their small overworked bodies, so it is not worth the effort to kill them—they are no longer "valuable resources"). It is hard to tell if male chicks have it worse. They are "macerated" at one day old—crushed to death by a high-speed grinder while they are still alive. Or else they are "bagged" and left to suffocate or die of dehydration.[14]

"But I like eggs," I can hear you say. "What can I do?" True, you can buy eggs that are labeled "organic." Organic means no antibiotics and better feed. That's good for your health, but it generally does not mean much for the bird. And "free-range" or "cage-free" are subjective terms that mean whatever we choose them to mean. "Free-range" conjures up idyllic images of chickens in sunshine with the freedom to roam. But this is a false image, as you will frequently find if you actually visit a farm that advertises free-range eggs. Often the birds have a few feet of grass but are otherwise kept in sheds.[15] In the United States, no organization regulates the use of these terms.

Moreover, even if the reality did correspond to the image, we could still legitimately ask what happens to the male birds hatched in these facilities. Like the male birds in battery operations, they are killed immediately at birth, often left to suffocate in large plastic bags. Since they are thin little things, they are not bred for their meat. There is no "profit" in them for the farmer. And the hens from free-range farms, even the good ones? Well, they too are considered "spent" hens within two years, and are slaughtered. The farms are not there for the hens. The hens are there for the farms. So what matters is profit, not the life of the hen. When she is not worth her keep, she is killed. It is as simple and implacable as that. Labels like "happy hens" or "compassionate chickens" are mere marketing devices. The food writer Michael Pollan has a terrific expression for this: "empty pastoral conceits."

The exception is the old-fashioned family farm, of which I need not remind you there are fewer and fewer every week. In principle, could these places provide healthy and tasty eggs from truly happy hens? Each farm would have to be seen on its own, but the descriptions I have read in the literature are not reassuring. The novelist Barbara Kingsolver (*The Bean Trees* and *The Poisonwood Bible*) has published *Animal, Vegetable, Miracle: A Year of Food Life,* which chronicles her own and her family's time spent on a farm growing their own food.[16] Alas, included in the term "growing" are animals slaughtered in their own backyard. She tells the unedifying story in the chapter called "You Can't Run Away on Harvest Day." Kingsolver says on the first page that she has kept half a dozen roosters and as many tom turkeys in a room of the barn she calls "death row." And that, in two words, is the problem: the animals on this farm, like any other, live in the antechamber of death.

Kingsolver's daughter Lily may find it sweet and harmless that the hens she raised from chicks are giving her eggs. But sooner or later, she must face the issue of what you do with hens that are now too tired or too old to continue producing eggs. They may not be spent at two years, but they will certainly be an economic liability long before their natural life span is over. Do we reward them for service given or must they too face the ax her mother wields?

Barbara Kingsolver was describing her own family farm, which was not intended as a commercial venture. Some might consider Joel Salatin's Polyface Farm in Virginia's Shenandoah Valley the ideal family farm that is still meant to turn a profit. It is artfully described by Michael Pollan in his beautifully written *The Omnivore's Dilemma*. Although the chickens have more freedom to roam than most (within the confines of the Eggmobile, which Salatin invented), and get to follow the cows in their organic pastures, the work of killing them is not pretty. Pollan was not just an observer, he participated as well. He did not succeed, however, in convincing me that there was anything noble in the enterprise. He may have salved his own conscience by claiming that the chicken whose throat he was about to cut betrayed no flicker of fear in his black eye. I found this neither comforting nor illuminating. He tells us that his companion in the slaughter, Daniel, "has been killing chickens since he was ten years old, and doesn't seem to mind it."[17] We are all able to bring to mind other situations in which people accustom themselves to killing. This fact in itself does not reveal the moral dilemma such killing may pose.

Of course, I am not claiming that everyone who eats chicken or enjoys eggs is a sadist. But the account of Dick Cheney seen at the Clove Valley Rod & Gun Club blasting away at birds is pertinent here. These are birds, raised in packed pens for canned hunts, that can barely walk, let alone fly. They needed to be kicked so they could "fly" enough to be shot at by the vice president.[18] Were he to be called to account (if only!), Cheney could argue that the pleasure he derives from killing birds is hardly different from the pleasure others derive from eating them or their eggs, and he would have a point. The moral dilemma lies in the lives these animals lead—and there seems no way in which we can leave the moral low ground.

Let me bring in a personal element to this account, by describing a visit I made recently to the largest egg farm in New Zealand. I was invited to visit one of the Midlands bird farms near Auckland that has approximately half a million hens. Also present were a visiting British scientist who works for the company's head office in Christchurch, Larna Craig; the executive director of the Poultry Industry Association of New Zealand, Michael Brooks; and the livestock manager, Kevin Jensen. All three took several hours out of their day to show me around and answer my questions, even the ones they might have found offensive. The farm is in a rural area, about half an hour's drive from downtown Auckland. There is nothing on the road to indicate the vast structure within, just a number on a mailbox. I was grateful that I was permitted to visit the farm, for I made no secret of the reason for my visit. It speaks well for New Zealand in general that secrecy is not a prized attribute of the Kiwi character. It is sometimes referred to as "fair go." That is, your critic should be allowed his say, and should be listened to, if not followed. We disagreed, but at least we knew what we were disagreeing about.

Before going in to see the hens, we had to take a shower and dress in special clothes, with boots that we dipped into a sterile solution. We entered a long, narrow room, with many hundreds of cages in tiers of six running along each side. Each cage contained six hens. I believe there were probably 50,000 birds in the room we were in. In front of the cage was an automatic feeding system, and a watering trough. Underneath was a conveyor belt taking away the feces. I did not smell what I feared: ammonia gases coming from this large number of hens. Also, I was expecting a loud sound to greet our entry, something in the nature of panic, but was surprised to hear just a kind of murmur. The foreman was proud of this; he said it meant the birds were not stressed, and I believe him. The sound grew as we stood talking, and the explanation was that the hens were becoming increasingly curious about us. That is true: when I looked down the line, I could see almost every hen's head in the room turned and looking intently in our direction. It was spooky: 50,000 pairs of eyes looking at you. Why were they so curious? What were they wondering? There is no way that their minds were empty while they searched our faces as we walked by. Perhaps they were thinking about what we were up to, and what our intentions were.

I wondered if the hens couldn't use more space. Six birds in a single cage meant they could not stretch their wings and there was no room for perches for them to sit on. The floor was of wire mesh and could not be comfortable for claws meant for wrapping themselves around narrow wooden branches. My hosts said they were looking at something better: "This system will be phased out in the near future, and we are looking at furnished colony cages." "You mean, 'enriched' cages?" I asked. "Exactly. Each cage will contain a nest for each hen, litter, and wooden perching systems to allow them to get off the wire floor of the cage."

But for me, as for many researchers who have more than only a scientific interest in the matter, a cage is still a cage. And these minimum improvements, while definitely improvements, were still a long way from the definition of enrichment. This is why they are being phased out everywhere in the developed world. But cages are not the only concern for people who care about chickens as sentient beings.

The farm had other decent treatments. "We don't trim the beaks of our hens, and we do not engage in forced molting," my hosts explained. Still, something was nagging at me. If you wanted high-quality eggs from healthy chickens, this was a successful operation. But if you were concerned with the *life* of the chicken, with the *happiness* of the hens, then something important was missing.

All three assured me that the birds are well looked after. That was true. Were they, though, I wondered, happy? One might believe that if they have all the food and water they want, are not sick, and have no predators to threaten them on a daily basis, they have all they could possibly want.

Yet these hens were destined to be sent to slaughter at seventy-eight weeks. A complicated mathematical formula determined that was the optimum time to make way for new hens. By then, the current hens' capacity to lay just about an average of one egg a day was beginning to fade. My hosts did not seem particularly comfortable with this phase of egg production. Understandably. They were not eager to give me any details of precisely how the hens met their end.

How do hens generally get from here, a relatively comfortable place, to there, the hell that is a slaughterhouse, no matter how well run? They have to be caught, one by one, by somebody whose sole job this is. It does not require an advanced degree and is not well paid (in some U.S. slaughterhouses, the job turnover rate is 100 percent per year).[19] Gentleness, compassion, and empathy are not part of the job description. At the time of catching and crating, levels of the stress hormone corticosterone in battery hens rise ten times higher than normal. Once caught, the hens are held by their legs, carried upside down out of the shed, and packed into crates for transport, often breaking their bones in the process.[20] On average, nearly a third of hens in the United Kingdom arrive at the slaughterhouse with at least one freshly broken bone; removing them and hanging them upside down on the shackle to await slaughter simply increases the proportion of hens with broken bones.[21]

In the Brambell Report, there was still one freedom that these hens did not have. It is undeniably the most important freedom of all, the one that makes the others worthwhile: *Freedom to express normal behavior*. These hens, cooped up their entire lives in small cages, could not do what hens normally do. If they did, they would no longer be economically viable *commodities*. They would then be living, breathing, sentient beings. They would be chickens just as nature designed them.

It is interesting that chickens who have escaped captivity and become feral, often existing on the side of the road in many countries, revert back to natural behavior. Even though they were bred to behave in a zombielike way, they become, with every generation, more like the Red or Burmese jungle fowl from which they originated.[22] Each chicken wants to fly to a low-lying branch of a thick tree or bush at dusk, where she can perch out of harm's way, invisible to predators, listening to tropical rainstorms in safety and warmth. Each chicken wants to scratch in the dirt, to keep her wings in perfect condition by dust-bathing them frequently, to find tasty morsels to eat. Each chicken wants to warm herself in the sun, feel the evening breeze, wake up to the dawning light as the rooster informs the flock that sunrise is close, and form close friendships with other hens. She also wants to lay her one or two clutches of ten to fifteen eggs every year, build a secure nest, and in that nest brood her eggs, raising the chicks that emerge twenty-one days later. She will do this for her entire life span. This is how they have lived for hundreds of thousands of years. Until we came along.

For centuries, human cultures—with the exception of the Chinese—rarely ate eggs (Cervantes, in the seventeenth century, was the first to warn us not to put all of them in a single basket). Partly this had to do with the fact that the birds were used for divination, or there were food taboos involved (especially for pregnant women); but it was also considered wasteful to eat the egg rather than to wait for the chicken. And some cultures in ancient times thought it disgusting to eat the product of the semen of a cock.[23]

Most people don't stop to think what an egg is when they see an omelet. The egg is the protective casing for the chicken embryo. In nature, there is no such thing as a non-fertile egg, except by accident. In its complexity, the egg is still a bit of a mystery to scientists, but of no small importance. In 1949, A. I. Romanoff and A. J. Romanoff published a book in which they attempted to compile all the facts known at the time, about the eggs of birds. It contained over 2,400 reference citations.[24]

What is inside a chicken egg? It is a mixture of proteins, fats, vitamins, minerals, and water. The egg yolk, produced by ovulation in the hen's ovary, contains the nutrients that the embryo needs during its incubation period—an elaborate rich brew of fats, cholesterol, protein, six B vitamins, as well as vitamins A, D, and E. The yolk also contains the antioxidants lutein and zeaxanthin, and trace amounts of β-carotene, phosphorus, iron, magnesium, and other metals. The reason the yolk is either yellow or orange is because of the plant pigments, xanthophylls, that the hen eats. The egg white, or albumen, is the cytoplasm (the jellylike material that fills cells), containing seven major proteins. It serves the function of protecting the egg yolk (and the embryo at its center) by absorbing shocks. In the last portion of the oviduct, the vagina, a thin protein coating called "bloom" is applied to the shell to keep harmful bacteria or dust from entering the eggshell pores.

Eggs are immensely complex. If you stop to think about it, there is something a bit odd about eating the egg of a bird—frying the yolk and scrambling the albumen. If we don't think about it, however, or simply refuse to do so, it can feel entirely natural.

In the last ten years or so, it has become more common for people to choose as their companion animal a hen, or a flock of hens. I puzzled over this, even after reading outstanding accounts, such as the one by William Grimes, the former food critic for *The New York Times*,[25] or the books by Karen Davis and many others, until I acquired two chickens of my own.

Chickens are funny, curious, affectionate, stubborn, ingenious companions. My two followed me everywhere, even for walks on the beach, and even though a dog and three cats also accompanied us. They got on with everyone—except our three pet rats, for reasons I do not entirely understand (perhaps because rats in the wild eat chicken eggs). It was interesting to see people visit the house. Usually, they made some disparaging comment about the chickens, invariably involving some version of the silly and inaccurate word "birdbrain." But by the time they left, most had a much more positive view of chickens. People watched them watch me at the computer (alas, nobody has yet invented the necessary chicken diaper), saw them perch in my bookshelves to be near me while I worked, and saw how bonded they were to one another: one could not move anywhere without the other following.

It turned out they were rooster and hen, although we did not know this at first (chickens are not easy to sex when first born). Eventually our hen, with great pride, produced a single egg. Although she brooded it for a long time, nothing came out. I think it affected her more than we might have thought. She really wanted to be a mother. Their relationship with me came to a premature end after a year. They had learned to trust other species too much: they assumed that other dogs and cats on our beach would be as tolerant of them as their house companions. It became too dangerous to keep them in freedom, and I did not have the heart to lock them into a cage, even for their own safety. They now live on a large farm as free birds and are producing chicks as they were meant to by nature. I miss them and their very distinct personalities, as does everyone who got to know them. What I believe I learned from living with them is that there were giant characters inhabiting their small bodies, and given the chance, they were happy for us to see them, get to know them, and become friends with them.

•   •   •

Is the picture any different for cows?[26] Why do animal activists call milk "liquid meat"? Isn't that extreme? Not if it can be shown that you cannot get milk without involving the death of an animal, hence meat. The claim, when I first heard it (from César Chávez back in the 1970s), made me very uncomfortable. But when I did my research, I had to admit that it was entirely justified. Of course, literally speaking, milk is not meat. And it is theoretically possible to get milk without harming a cow. Theoretically. In fact, however, that is not how milk is obtained today. At one time it might have been true. But at one time we would never have been able to get even remotely close to a cow with a calf: a bull would have made short work of us. And had we somehow managed to avoid him, the cow herself would never have permitted us to take milk destined for her calf. From her point of view, that's pure theft. (I can't see any way to counter her view, either.)

The way we dealt with this problem was to "domesticate" the cow, that is, to breed her over the centuries until we had a more docile animal on our hands. We still had a problem, though: no cow gives milk unless she gets pregnant and gives birth to a calf. (I remember one dairy farmer I visited insisting that the cow would be in pain unless she was milked; true, but only because she had just given birth to a calf who was no longer present.) The milk is meant for the calf. She produces, like every mammal, just enough for her calf. That is, roughly speaking, 10 pints of milk per day.[27] But our greed is greater than any reasonable person could expect: we do not allow the calf even the small amount he or she would normally take in a day. We want it all. So the calf is separated from the cow immediately upon birth. The industry says this must happen instantaneously, for otherwise there is a risk—no, it is a certainty—that the two will bond. In fact, they have already bonded, just as much as would a human mother with her baby. The strong bond is inborn in all mammals.

The terrible sound one hears on any dairy farm after a cow has given birth is the call of a lost calf, calling her mother, and the mother answering in desperation.[28] If that is not suffering, I don't know the meaning of the word. John Webster, Emeritus professor of animal husbandry at Bristol University's Clinical Veterinary Science Department, who is widely considered the world's leading authority on dairy cows, acknowledges that the removal of her calf is the single worst incident in the life of a dairy cow. Temple Grandin, professor of animal science at Colorado State University and the world's leading expert on animal slaughter, put it even more strongly. Oliver Sacks tells of how he and Grandin visited a dairy farm and of the great tumult of bellowing that they heard when they arrived: "'They must have separated the calves from the cows this morning,' Temple said, and, indeed, this was what had happened. We saw one cow outside the stockade, roaming, looking for her calf, and bellowing. 'That's not a happy cow,' Temple said. 'That's one sad, unhappy, upset cow. She wants her baby. Bellowing for it, hunting for it. She'll forget for a while, and then start again. It's like grieving, mourning—not much written about it. People don't like to allow them thoughts or feelings.' "[29]

Surely it is a source for rejoicing that moral progress is possible: farm animals used to be considered simply "goods." But now in a 1997 protocol to the Treaty of Rome, the founding document of the European Union, thanks to the efforts of the UK organization Compassion in World Farming, they have been recognized as sentient beings, that is, beings capable of a full range of emotions.

Now that the calves are separated from their mothers, sometimes before they've had their first meal of colostrum, what happens to them? The answer depends on whether the calf is male
or female. If female, then most will go to replenish the dairy
herd. If male, however, well—I will come to that in a moment.
What do they get to replace the milk she would feed them on
demand (four to ten meals per day)? Almost entirely, commercial milk replacer, made with whey, soy, wheat, red blood cell
protein and plasma proteins, vegetable fat, vitamins, minerals,
and amino acids.[30] It is cheaper than milk from the cow, but
hardly what a calf is designed to eat. They are also fed digest-
ible dry feed, which promotes rumen (the first stomach in a
ruminant animal) development, and helps wean the calf off any
form of milk as early as four to five weeks. Under natural conditions, a calf could nurse for up to a year, and possibly beyond.
They begin to forage early on, usually around eight weeks. At
eighteen weeks they will be consuming nearly as much as an
adult.[31] It is an entirely unnatural arrangement. We are the only
species who drink, as adults, the milk of another species. Perhaps that is why lactose intolerance is high among humans. The
calves get neither the nourishment nor the suckling they need.
This is not merely a matter of indifference to the needs of a different species. It is rather that our main concern is for economic
profit. Eventually, these female calves will start on the cycle of
pregnancy and milking just as did their mothers.

The male calf born in a dairy herd, however, can have no
future there—except for the very occasional one kept for breeding purposes. Dairy cattle are not meant for meat, so to raise
a male until adulthood is not economically feasible. There are
many descriptions of male calves being carted off on a trailer,

often before they can even walk, to slaughterhouses. Temple Grandin, the leading authority on slaughterhouse methods (and the woman responsible for most of the reform that has taken place in them), has witnessed this often enough to say, "The worst thing you can do is put a bawling baby on a trailer. It's just an awful thing to do."[32]

The ones who are not killed are often turned into veal (even the industry itself claims veal as a product of the dairy industry). The word "veal" was chosen because it has no resonance in English. In fact, it is simply the translation of the French *veau* (calf) because it would offend some people's sensibilities to be asked if they would like to be served calf for dinner. It's not dissimilar from "pork," which comes from the French *porc*, meaning pig. Americans don't like to ask for a pig for breakfast. "Bacon" means nothing to us beyond its use for breakfast; we have no other associations. "Hamburger" or "burger" do not resonate with us or conjure up images of cows peacefully grazing, minding their own business and getting on with their own lives. (We do, however, speak of chicken, lamb, and calves' liver without blushing—so, go figure).

When we see veal on our plate, it does not generally occur to people to wonder how the animal got such pale flesh. The calves have borderline anemia, which is achieved by feeding the small animal an all-liquid diet. That is the meaning of "milk-fed veal" on the menu; but it is also hypocrisy to give the impression the calf was nursed. The calves do not receive the nutrients they require—no iron or fiber. In addition, they are fed a large amount of antibiotics and hormones, for this unnatural diet would make them deathly ill without them.

The calves to be used for veal (about 1 million of them

every year in the United States) live from sixteen to eighteen weeks. As soon as they are removed from their mothers, they are put into a small crate about two feet wide, with no straw or bedding, sometimes chained by the neck, making it almost impossible for them to turn around, stretch, or even lie down comfortably.[33] Mortality rates are typically about 20 percent, probably because of the stress and separation from any family member.[34] They are fed an iron-deficient diet, and receive no colostrum from their mothers. Unable to move, they cannot exercise, and will have no muscles, keeping the flesh "tender." If you see "bob" veal on the menu, you can be sure that the animal you are eating lived only a few days or even just a few hours, but certainly less than one month. Today, many restaurants in the United States have taken the "no veal" pledge that was urged upon them by the Farm Sanctuary and the Humane Farming Association. Many people, not necessarily vegetarian, were sickened when they learned how veal was created, and refused to eat it or even eat in restaurants that served it. Still, the United States produces 14 million pounds of it every year.

As for the cows who are used for producing milk, what kind of life do they lead? Pictures on milk cartons and industry advertisements would have us believe they lead quiet lives, resting in the shade of a tree on a green hill in the country. The vast majority of the 225 million milk-producing cows in the world today actually live in confined sheds, tethered in standing cubicles while being fed and milked by automated systems. Those who live on dry lots with no grass in them at all have it even worse: they are not protected from the weather, and the lots are cleaned once or at most twice a year, leaving the cows to stand in their own urine and feces.[35] A vacuum machine milks each cow two to three times a day for six to eight minutes, to yield from 60 to 120 pints a day, roughly ten times what that cow's calf would have taken, thanks to genetic manipulation and the artificial food she is fed. Many are injected with growth hormones to increase the milk yield. Most milk farms use rBGH (recombinant bovine growth hormone, also known as rBST— recombinant bovine somatotropin). The average Holstein cow will now produce ten to fifteen times the normal amount of milk. The physical cost of this overproduction is enormous. According to John Webster, "The dairy cow is exposed to more abnormal physiological demands than any other farm animal. She is the supreme example of an overworked mother."

This high milk production quickly depletes the cow of minerals and nutrients, causing metabolic imbalance and susceptibility to bacterial and viral infections—notably chronic mastitis, a painful infection of the udders that occurs in half of all cows.[36] Because of how they are housed, the cows suffer from a variety of leg problems. They must stand on cement floors while being milked, with their hind legs spread to allow for the enlarged udders, causing lameness.[37] Often their stalls (cells) do not allow them to even lie down. The constant wet conditions and manure-covered floors contribute to fungus, laminitis, and foot rot. It is expensive to have vets on hand, so there is minimal medical care, which is why huge amounts of antibiotics are given on a preventive basis. This lasts for ten months. Because, like humans and all other mammals, cows only lactate when they have given birth, the cows are artificially impregnated, and the cycle begins again. In the United States, as opposed to much of Europe, cows are raised according to the "zero grazing system," meaning they basically never walk and hardly move, spending their entire life indoors.[38]

Evolved to eat grass, it is the rare cow today who does so. The vast majority are fed a pellet mixture, called a TMR (total mixed ration), which contains cheap filler from "rendered" animals, including bonemeal and processed manure.[39] In the United Kingdom, the indoor cows are fed a diet of silage (wet fermented grass) and high-protein concentrate (a mixture of cereals, rape meal, sunflower meal, maize, and soya, most of which are genetically modified). The wet silage causes wet manure and the cows often develop mastitis and lameness. The high-protein concentrates cause a buildup of toxins which creates laminitis (inflammation of the tissue that lies below the outer horny wall of the foot), a severely painful condition.

How strenuous is a dairy cow's life? John Webster writes, "The amount of work done by the cow in peak lactation is immense. To achieve a comparable high work rate a human would have to jog for about 6 hours a day, every day."[40] The cows are soon exhausted, and by the time they have reached the age of four, they are called "spent" cows and are sent to slaughter. Under natural conditions, cows can live sixteen years or longer. One of the major scandals of 2008 was revealed by the report of the Humane Society of the United States' (HSUS) investigation into the mistreatment of cows, most of which were spent dairy cows. Video footage showed cows who were too sick or too injured to walk on their own ("downers") subjected to terrible abuses, including being stunned with electric prods and jabbed in the eyes to force them to walk when they were deathly ill and unable even to stand up.[41] Moreover, these ill cows were being used for meat, which is illegal. The factory was shut down and meat recalled from 150 school districts.

I have not been able to bring myself to visit a slaughterhouse, so I cannot give a firsthand report here. I can only urge you to read the harrowing account by Gail Eisnitz, chief investigator for the Humane Farming Association; to look at the haunting paintings of the celebrated American artist Sue Coe, who visited forty abattoirs to produce her book *Dead Meat*; and to buy *Fast Food Nation* by Eric Schlosser, or view the video on the USHS Web site.[42]

*   *   *

THERE IS SOMETHING ABOUT COWS I would like to understand. Chickens and pigs will gladly and easily become companion animals, treating us as if we mattered to them and bestowing upon us (often undeserved) friendship. This is rarely the case with cows. Why? Does the fault lie with us or with them? Or is it even a fault? Could it be that it is simply not within the nature of a cow to allow human intimacy?

It baffles me, because if any animal should remain aloof, it is the cat, not the more social cow. Cats are, of course, often aloof. But they are also, as most of my readers hardly need reminding, capable of great acts of friendship, even going so far, I have no doubt, as to sacrifice their lives for the sake of a loved human companion: an example of a cat who committed suicide to be near her human when he jumped out of a window comes to mind. This ability to become close to a member of another species is not, in fact, part of their nature. Unlike chickens, pigs, and cows, who all come from species that are

sociable (like us), cats descend from an ancestor that was soli-
tary. The African wildcat has no friends in nature. Our domestic cats do. So I have to assume (and this is my own thesis, not
shared by many scientists) that cats have, miraculously, benefited from their association with humans. I say miraculously,
because it is not often that domestication benefits the animal.
We are the ones who reap the profit, not them. But in the case
of cats—uniquely, I would say—giving up their nature as soli-
tary animals has actually been good for them.

For the other animals, being part of a larger group means
that it does not require any fundamental shift in nature for
them to adapt to us as companions. Pigs and chickens and, of
course, dogs are not doing anything extraordinary in allowing
us into their circle of intimate friends. They are designed to
want friendship and to benefit from it. Cows, too. Why, then,
is it so rare to read any account of a deep friendship between
a human and a cow? What do they know about us that pre-
cludes it? I don't know. But I do know that they have the most
intimate friendships among themselves, and that cows are as
capable as any other herd animal of forming strong personal
ties to another animal, whether blood-related or not.

To some extent, we are already receiving messages from a
world hidden to many of us. Rosamund Young lives on Kite's
Nest Farm in England, perhaps the most famous organic farm
in England. Rosamund has the same relationship with her
cows that most people have with their extended family. She
knows the names of all 132 of them; she knows who is related
to whom, and who likes whom as well. She could sit down
and write 132 biographies, and "each one would be completely
distinct from all the others," she told me. She also believes

that cows can teach us to relax. "That is why I like them," she explains. "They are much nicer than we are, more integrated, more whole. They pick up my mood very quickly and hate it, for example, when I am in a rush. They just don't believe in rushes."

We walked around her farm until evening, and as the sky began to darken, Rosamund said to me, "See how the cows settle, looking away from the lights of the valley and toward the moon." Rosamund finds her greatest happiness among cows. She has no doubt that cows feel all the major emotions that humans do. "Even worry?" I asked. "Especially worry," she replied. "They have so many different kinds of worry, ranging from the most mild, when a calf wanders out of sight, to the most extreme, when they think something terrible has happened to it." How about surprise? I asked, remembering that some philosophers claim animals cannot feel surprise because they cannot anticipate the future. "Well," she said, "how about this? My Welsh black cow had six black calves, and then one day she produced a pure white calf (she had been mated with a Charolais bull). She came round to our door and stared at us with a look that was easy to read: 'Are you sure it's mine?' "[43]

I was also able to pay a visit to New Zealand's largest organic dairy, Marphona Farms in Mangatawhiri, an hour from Auckland. On this 3,000-acre dairy farm live some 1,000 cows. I met the farm manager, a likable young man, Marcin Paloaka, from Poland (via Australia), who took me around the farm for three hours, showing me everything I asked to see. Unlike almost all dairy farms in the United States, the cows live outdoors all year. They are milked twice a day for approximately four minutes, once early in the morning and again in early afternoon.

Other than that, they spend the rest of their time grazing on a series of hilly grass paddocks of between two and five acres each. They eat the lush grass and are also fed a supplement of organic silage, barley, and a molasses treat.[44]

We were walking along the outside of one of these paddocks; about twenty-five cows were all bunched together, not eating and seemingly frozen. They were simply staring straight ahead into empty space. I could not figure out what they were doing, so I asked Marcin. "You know, to be honest," he told me, "I have no idea. Sometimes, I look at what cows do and I realize that they really are very mysterious beings. We just have no idea what it means or what might be going through their minds." Did he believe that they had minds? "Oh, absolutely. They are as complex as any other animal I know. They form friendships, sometimes in ways that are totally unpredictable. I really like cows." "Do you eat them?" I wondered. "Oh sure, everyone on this farm does. There are no vegetarians here." I told him I did not eat any animal product, and he simply nodded his head. "I can understand that," he said. "At least we allow the old girls to live out their lives on the farm. When they are no longer producing sufficient milk, we let them live on the pastures, eating and enjoying being with their friends. It seems only fair after what they give us."

To my surprise, Marcin is interested in pursuing homeopathy with the cows, and told me he has had astonishing results in terms of their health and general well-being. The farm takes about 3 gallons of milk a day from each cow, far less than a conventional dairy farm. Still, the life is hardly ideal. The cows are artificially impregnated, and when the calves are born, they are taken away almost immediately, to prevent the bond that normally forms between cow and calf. "That is just why we do it. We do not want this bond to develop, because then both cow and calf will suffer." The calves are not fed a milk replacer, but rather real cow's milk—another contrast with conventional dairy practice. The female calves are kept to add to the dairy herd. But the males are kept for a year or two at the most, then sold for meat.

But when we continued our visit to the calf sheds, I learned that some of the calves of both sexes fail to thrive. If their weight gain is marginal, for whatever reason, they are sold as pet food. In normal circumstances, the calves are kept inside until they weigh about 220 pounds, which happens usually around three to four months. Then they are kept outside, night and day. (The winters in New Zealand are fairly mild; summers, too, and the farm is planting more and more shade trees in the paddocks for the cows to shelter under.)

A woman in her fifties, Charmaine, was working in the calf pen when we arrived. There was a sign saying: LOVE FARMING, WE DO, with a picture of a young child hugging a vulnerable-looking calf, as if protecting it from any harm. As we spoke, Charmaine was being followed by a persistently affectionate calf no more than a few weeks old. His weight was marginal, but not enough to sell him off. Charmaine was going to bottle-feed him for the next three months. "You clearly like this little guy," I told her. "Does it ever bother you to think about what is going to happen to him?" "No." "Really?" "I couldn't work here if I let myself think about it." "But sometimes you still do?" "No, I don't go there." There was a pause, then she looked up at me and said: "There was one calf who had the most beautiful face. She was also very affectionate, loving, even. She liked to be touched. But she was very small and I knew she was going to be killed. When I went home on her last evening, she looked at me very intensely. For a long time. I could have sworn she knew something. That night, I could not get her out of my mind. To this day—and this was years ago—I cannot forget her. She was simply unforgettable."

Marcin listened, obviously uncomfortable, shifting from foot to foot. But he did not try to change the topic or move me away. He was himself a rather gentle man, and I wondered if he had chosen the right profession. I saw and learned a lot that afternoon, but I must admit I was relieved to leave. If you must drink milk, then surely this New Zealand farm is less involved in cruelty than most. There are very few grass-only dairies in the United States.[45] Cows that eat greens alone produce less milk, and their production can go way down in the winter, making it hard for farmers to make a profit.

*　*　*

I HAVE LONG BEEN IMPRESSED with the implications of a principle mandated in medicine: "informed consent." It may sound innocuous—how could anyone be against informed consent?—but it is actually quite complex and subversive if taken entirely seriously. In referring to the treatment of animals, the "consent" part is fairly easy and straightforward, although one can still raise the question of who is competent to consent and what happens when they are not (after all, none of the animals on farms ever consented to be there). It is the "informed" that can take us humans into deep and uncharted waters. When do we deem information to have been sufficient?

A reader could skim my section on veal calves and decide that it is sufficient to convince them to take the no-veal pledge. Others could read it differently. I am aware of the fact that telling people how to vote, what to wear, where to worship, and what to eat are losing propositions. None of us welcomes such advice. And yet, we have all been receiving it our entire lives: after all, what is growing up in a family about if not this very process of socialization (some would call it indoctrination) into the dominant culture, at least the one that dominates the family? Our parents tell us what to believe every moment of our early lives, which may partly explain why some people are allergic to hearing more of it as they turn into adults. Yet surely one part of becoming an adult is freeing ourselves from the prejudices instilled in us as children and forming our own views. How else do we explain that so many have changed their lifestyles, chosen their own religion or path in life?

For some reason, people who eat less and less meat are likely to give up eating cattle before they stop eating pigs.[46] Having known many pigs, I find this hard to understand. Although I have never lived with a pig, I have had the good fortune not only to read some wonderful accounts but also to have visited many animal sanctuaries and been introduced to the porcine companions of many a lucky human. To a person, their first comment is that if you have ever lived with and loved a dog, you will find living with a pig most familiar. Indeed, we often walked the hills as we talked, and behind in truly canine fashion would come one or several curious pigs wanting to join the fun. Wagging their tails, they would come when called by name just as quickly and surely as any family dog. Their intelligence has never been in doubt ("Dogs look up to you, cats look down on you, pigs is equal," said Winston Churchill). But I think only fairly recently has it become clear that pigs are fond of us, and given half a chance will make fast friends with any human who takes the trouble to treat them with belly-rubs, kind words, and a clean place to sleep next to them at night. If this thought bothers you, it is only because we have maligned pigs with myths that are false and defamatory for years. It speaks to their generosity that they forgive us as easily as they do.

Wild boars also clearly possess this quality. In his remarkable book *Mein Leben unter Wildschweinen* (*My Life with Wild Pigs*), Heinz Meynhardt writes of his acceptance into a herd of wild boars.[47] Were Meynhardt to have seen these boars only as quarry to be hunted, his detailed knowledge about their social relations, their child rearing, and other intimate aspects of their lives could never have been compiled. Extraordinarily sensitive to danger as boars must be to have survived centuries of active hunting, allowing a member of the enemy into their ranks is mysterious and humbling.

Something like 100 million pigs are killed each year in the United States and over 1 billion worldwide for food.[48] Ninety-seven percent of these pigs are raised, if that is the word, on corporate hog farms. These are intensive farms, which means that the pigs are confined indoors for their entire life: not only do most never see the sun, they never even see natural light; most barns are kept in a permanent twilight state—farmers claim this keeps them calm and avoids aggression. By nature, pigs are highly sociable and inquisitive, but there is no social behavior on these farms. As soon as a sow is pregnant (generally by artificial insemination at around seven months), she is put into a gestation crate, or sow stall, a metal cage about the size of the sow herself, just two feet wide, with concrete or metal slatted floors, and no nesting material.[49]

In these barren conditions, the sows go crazy. They bite the bars, or their own tails, and spend hour after hour shaking their heads. After four months, just before they give birth, they are transferred to a "farrowing" (birthing) crate. Again, the space is severely restricted: the pigs have barely enough room to stand up and in many they cannot turn around. They are not able to have any contact except for suckling with their piglets (up to twenty at a time, thanks to the miracle of modern breeding; under natural conditions they give birth to four or five piglets), frustrating one of the strongest instincts in a mother pig—to be with, protect, and have constant contact with her young. Researchers have shown that the behavior of the domestic sow and the wild boar when it comes to building a nest, or indeed, being a mother, has not undergone any change at all.[50] Any pig, wild or domesticated, when ready to give birth, chooses an isolated spot where she builds an elaborate nest of carefully selected twigs—wild pigs often travel many miles to find the ideal secluded spot. They give birth in the nest, changing it from night to night to avoid predators.

The nest is so constructed that if the sow lies on top of one of her piglets, the baby will simply drop through the nest to the ground and come back to the mother. There are no instances known of a wild pig accidentally smothering her young, though this is the excuse the industry gives for separating piglets from their mother.[51] Under the conditions of factory farming, pigs can do nothing to express their instinctual (and emotional) needs. They are prisoners. They paw, nose, and bite the bars in a vain attempt to build the nest nature has designed them to want.

Animal scientists have found elevated cortisol (stress hormone) levels in sows attempting to build nests in metal cages. High cortisol levels are correlated with greater stress in animals.[52] And the piglets born under these horrific conditions? They are not able to spend any time with their mother. Separated as they are by the bars of the cage, they lie in a small area called a "creep" that allows them to suckle from the mother without any other contact. They are prematurely weaned (at around three weeks), and both the sow and the piglets call for each other constantly. The baby pigs' tails are cut off, their needle (baby) teeth are cut, and the males are castrated, all without anesthesia, causing them intense physical pain and often leaving them with "phantom" pain for the rest of their lives.[53] The stress is so enormous that the sows are becoming increasingly anorexic (the psychology of anorexia in young breeding sows is becoming a serious topic for research).[54]

The piglets are then put into a metal cage or small pen, where they will attempt to suckle on one another. After a few more weeks, they are put into rearing pens, where they are intensively reared (that is, without any restrictions or anything that would distract them from eating), fed a high-protein diet to make them reach "slaughtering weight" as soon as possible, within about four months (pigs in the wild can live for ten years or more). Some females are kept for breeding stock, but most go to slaughter before they are six months old. Needless to say, the life of these pigs is as far removed from their natural behavior as it is possible to be. Pigs are among the most playful and exploratory of animals, spending the greater part of their day investigating their environment.[55] Meanwhile, the mother is immediately reinseminated, and begins the same cycle all over. She does so for three or four years, until she, like the hens and the cows, is "spent" and sent to slaughter.

The strange thing is that for all we do to pigs, they still seem to retain a certain fondness for our species. This capacity, call it even a talent, is not confined to the domesticated pig.

What struck me whenever I visited a farm was how much more sophisticated was the life the animals were capable of living than was assumed by those exploiting them. The more we are willing to see about their lives, the more we *will* see. Humans seem to take a perverse pleasure in attributing stupidity to animals when it is almost always entirely a question of human ignorance.

Consider the turkey. No Thanksgiving Day can pass without a series of silly jokes about turkeys appearing in newspapers nationwide, as if we had to make up for the gigantic one-day slaughter with slander about the lack of intelligence in turkeys. Despite the folklore, turkeys are not stupid and do not stand in the rain and drown. They have a "rain posture" that allows them to reduce their overall exposure to getting wet, by streamlining themselves. Occasionally, very young turkeys might drown because when they instinctively look up to see what is falling on them they can be harmed by the lack of a maternal wing to shelter them. In fact, turkeys, like chickens, can recognize and remember hundreds of individual flock members.[56]

To disabuse ourselves of foolish ideas about turkeys, we need only read the remarkable *Illumination in the Flatwoods: A Season with the Wild Turkey*, by Joe Hutto. In this book, Hutto uses his experience with wild turkeys to give us a most persuasive description of imprinting. Nearly two dozen eggs were hatched in his presence, and he became the leader of a flock of extraordinary birds. He lived among them for one year in the forests of Florida and learned more about turkeys than anyone else has ever recorded. He tells us, "I have never kept better company or known more fulfilling companionship." Hutto is driven, in spite of his scientist's training, to recognize that "in the most fundamental sense our similarities are greater than our differences." He considers himself privileged to be in their presence, feeling less desolate, less isolated, as he is "bathed in the warm glow of these extraordinary creatures."

A naturalist who has hunted wild turkeys all his life, Hutto affirms the turkeys' mental abilities: "As we leave the confines of my language and culture, these graceful creatures become in every way my superiors. More alert, sensitive, and aware, they are vastly more conscious than I. They are in many ways, in fact, simply more intelligent. Theirs is an intricate aptitude, a clear distillation of purpose and design that is beyond my ability to comprehend."

He describes his friendship with one particular bird, Turkey Boy:

Each time I joined him, he greeted me with his happy dance, a brief joyful display of ducking and dodging, with wings outstretched and a frisky shake of the head like a dog with water in his ears. Occasionally, he would jump at me and touch me lightly with his feet. His anticipation and enthusiasm made it difficult for me to disappoint him.

What draws Hutto to them, beyond their unusual intelligence is "observing the absolute joy that these birds experience in their lives . . . they are in love with being alive."[57]

Like many other birds, turkeys are sensitive to the death of another turkey. John James Audubon reported how after he had shot a turkey hen sitting on a fence, the males yelped in answer to her cries as the wounded bird sat there. "I looked over the log," he wrote in the fifth volume of his *Birds of America* (1827–39), "and saw about thirty fine cocks advancing rather cautiously towards the very spot where I lay concealed. They came so near that the light in their eyes could easily be perceived, when I fired one barrel, and killed three. The rest, instead of flying off, fell a strutting around their dead companions."[58] Karen Davis's passionate and compassionate *More Than a Meal* tells of how on occasion when a factory farm turkey has a convulsive heart attack, it causes other birds around him to die. The National Turkey Federation calls this "hysteria," and uses it as an example of the turkey's lack of intelligence. Davis, on the contrary, believes that "it indicates a sensibility in these birds that should awaken us to how terribly we treat them and make us stop it."[59]

Rarely is an animal as badly treated as turkeys on factory farms in the United States. According to an article in *Turkey World*, "Poults come in one side of the service room bright eyed and bushy tailed. They are squeezed, thrown down a slide onto a treadmill, someone picks them up and pulls the snood off their heads, clips three toes off each foot, debeaks them, puts them on another conveyor belt that delivers them to another carousel where they get a power injection, usually of antibiotic, that whacks them in the back of their necks. Essentially, they have been through major surgery. They have been traumatized. They don't look very good."[60]

*   *   *

No ANIMAL UNDER DOMESTICATION, with the possible exception of the cat, leads the life it was designed to lead by nature. All of the changes that humans have managed to create, mainly through selective breeding, are not intended for the benefit of the animal. We benefit; the animals suffer the consequences. Does this mean that if we care about animal suffering and about the quality of their lives, we need to give up eating all animal-derived food? I am afraid so. I see no other conclusion possible for me personally. Why "afraid"? Because I realize how alien this is to most people's upbringing and their habits of mind. We are not encouraged, on a daily basis, to pay careful attention to the animals we eat. On the contrary, the meat, dairy, and egg industries all actively encourage us to give thought to our own immediate interest (taste, for example, or cheap food) but not to the real suffering involved. They do so by deliberately withholding information and by cynically presenting us with idealized images of happy animals in beautiful landscapes, scenes of bucolic happiness that do not correspond to anything in the real world. The animals involved suffer agony because of our ignorance. The least we owe them is to lessen that ignorance.

Perhaps the time has arrived when we can begin to look at domesticated animals on our farms not as meals on our plates, but as companions on this journey on a fragile and endangered earth. Although they should fear us as their ultimate predator, many of them, given half a chance, miraculously form strong attachments to us. This appears to be especially true of pigs, chickens, turkeys, and rabbits. They seem to have an emotional generosity that makes allowances for our moral weakness, perhaps forgiving us in a gesture of compassion we would do well to emulate. Maybe the time is coming when we can turn to these farmed animals not as animals to be slaughtered for our table, but as distant family, who have some special, deep affinity with us and are only waiting for a signal that we are at last ready to live with them in a kind of harmony, one that brings benefit to all species.

I am aware that few readers will want to follow me directly into veganism. There is a site on the Web sponsored by the Johns Hopkins Bloomberg School of Public Health called "Meatless Mondays" that calls on people to do precisely that, to eat no meat once a week (www.meatlessmondays.com). That is a start, and a good one. Their point is that we can help prevent heart disease, stroke, cancer, and diabetes by 15 percent by choosing to have Meatless Mondays: "Diets high in saturated fat, found mainly in meat and high-fat dairy products, increase the risk of heart disease, diabetes, and stroke. What's more, a high-fat diet may increase the risk of certain types of cancer. These 'lifestyle diseases' are killing Americans and in 80–90 percent of cases, deaths are preventable. Our goal—consistent with recommendations made by the U.S. Dept. of Health and Human Services, the U.S. Dept. of Agriculture, and the American Heart Association—is to help Americans reduce consumption of saturated fat 15% by 2010. That works out to eliminating saturated fat one day a week."

My friend Michael Greger, the director of Public Health

and Animal Agriculture at the Humane Society of the United States, tells me that Americans consume about 22,000 animals in their lifetime. So, if people engaged in Meatless Mondays, they would probably save the lives of over 3,000 animals. I would add that if people care about the lives of animals but feel unable to become vegan or vegetarian, they should at least make certain that the animals they eat, or the products of those animals, come from animals who have been "humanely" raised. So animals and animal products from organic farms are better for our health. Asking about how chickens are kept when you buy eggs, or how the dairy cows live when buying milk, is a fine beginning. Actually visiting the farm where these products come from is always a good idea, and can be enlightening. I don't think I would have become a vegan without this kind of direct knowledge. Bear in mind this simple recent admonition from George Monbiot of *The Guardian*: "If you care about hunger, eat less meat."

Chapter
Three

THE FISHY BUSINESS
OF AQUACULTURE

*There is some five times more genetic diversity among
brown trout populations in Ireland alone than among
human populations throughout the world.*

—Andrew Ferguson, Queens University, Belfast

*It is simply not possible to produce fish on an industrial
scale in a sustainable way. You will never get it into ecological balance.*

—Wolfram Heise, director of the marine
conservation program at the Pumalin Project,
a private conservation initiative in Chile

LIKE MANY PEOPLE WHO WANT TO BECOME VEGETAR-
ian, my transformation took place gradually. I first gave up
red meat. Chicken took a bit longer. And fish took the longest. Why? I often wonder. Partly, I suppose, because humans

rarely identify with fish. They don't resemble us in any way. For instance, when I watch my son's rat eat with her delicate little paws holding the food as she nibbles away, her bright black eyes darting around to check for danger, I can easily see myself. It is no surprise to learn that we share so much of our DNA with other primates (up to 98 percent) and with other mammals, even mice (90 percent).[1] But we don't realize that we also share 85 percent of our genes with zebra fish.[2] They don't *look* like us, they don't *sound* like us, nor do they have facial expressions the way we and other animals do (who can recognize a sad fish?). For years, people believed that fish were not capable of suffering. After all, if they were, would they not cry out in pain?

I can remember once as a young boy, perhaps ten or eleven, I went on a fishing trip with my school. When I caught my first fish I was thrilled, but when I saw it writhing about, twisting on the hook, and then thrashing on the deck of the boat, whether in pain or sheer terror, I was horrified. Adults were amused by how naive I was, telling me that this was a mere reflex action on the part of the fish. Yet there was nothing obviously robotic in how the fish was reacting. How could I not imagine myself with a hook in my cheek being hauled into an element in which I could not breathe? I would panic—and that is what I saw in the eyes of that fish. I could not be talked out of it at the time, but I could be bribed. Later that afternoon, instead of each person being photographed with the fish he caught, we were randomly assigned fish. I was given a huge marlin, as big as I was, and I brought home the photograph as proof of my heroic deed. I did not admit that I had not caught this "monster" fish and basked in the positive comments I received over the next few weeks. But I never did forget the look in that little fish's eye, and to this day I have never fished again.

In my freshman year of college I read Izaak Walton's classic *The Compleat Angler,* published in 1653, and was enchanted by the language. But one of the most famous lines in the book disturbed me. Walton is talking of using a live frog as bait: "Use him as though you loved him, that is, harm him as little as you may possibly, that he may live the longer." But if you truly loved that frog, you would never use him in the first place, and he would have lived considerably longer. What's true for the bait is true for the fish.

Yet the myth that fish feel no pain continues. It's embedded in everyday language. We speak of fish as "cold-blooded," as if that were an emotional state. The phrase is part of our culture: think of Truman Capote's *In Cold Blood.* It can even be used in a profound sense. Consider the words of Elie Wiesel: "Cold-blooded murder and culture did not exclude each other. If the Holocaust proved anything, it is that a person can both love poems and kill children."[3] But in actual fact, "cold-blooded," when used to refer to animals such as reptiles and fish, simply means that they cannot control their body temperature. Animals in water depend on external sources like sunlight and streams to regulate their temperature, which fluctuates according to their environment. Humans do this through the autonomic nervous system—a gift from evolution, since the wildly varied temperature of an outdoor environment demanded this ability. We are able to maintain a constant body temperature by producing the heat that we need internally and without conscious thought. So we are self-regulating and fish are not. This can't be what bothers us.

The term "cold-blooded" probably first arose because of the medieval belief that there were four "humors" operating in our bodies: sanguine, choleric, phlegmatic, and melancholic, i.e., hot, cold, moist, or dry. Too hot, and you reacted with great emotion, "in the heat of the moment." Too cold, and you became calm, even overly calm (think of the French expression *sang-froid*, literally "cold blood," but which has come to mean to act without passion, even ruthlessly).

It is also a bit puzzling why we feel that something not like us deserves less respect, that its death is less troubling. Of course, we know the horrors of what Freud called *le narcissisme des petites différences*. Every tribe, every ethnicity, every religious and political group identifies members as being inside or outside its membership, even when the sense of belonging is entirely illusory. Philip Zimbardo's original prison experiments in 1974 demonstrated as much. He arbitrarily divided undergraduates at Stanford University into two groups, wardens and prisoners. But he had to stop the experiment after only six days because the wardens became sadistic and the prisoners depressed. This can produce hatred, of course, as Zimbardo showed (and to which he has devoted a new book),[4] but it can also act as a marker that easily devolves into indifference. Ethnocentrism involves both hatred and indifference. I think it would be a rare individual who "hates" fish. We are just indifferent to them and our taking of their lives for food.

Fish seem to pay us no attention, which isn't necessarily true. As a former scuba diver, I remember turning around after having an eerie feeling that I was being followed. Sure enough, behind me was a whole school of barracuda. "They are just curious," my instructor explained. There is little written about the curiosity of fish for humans. Freeman House in his lovely book *Totem Salmon* writes that "so powerful are the ties between humans and salmon that even in rivers and streams where salmon are still running—but in numbers severely diminished—the ghosts of salmon are rising. Salmon resides in the hearts of humans."[5] Salmon are such complex animals that they have imprinted themselves very deeply on the human psyche, especially in areas where salmon live. Many indigenous people of Canada and the Pacific Northwest have cultures that include songs, dances, visual arts, and legends based on the lives of salmon. But this affection is not reciprocal. Unlike a dog or a cat, in whose psyche we no doubt figure in myriad and subtle ways, it is unlikely that any salmon anywhere has ever thought of humans with affection. As far as I can see, salmon want nothing to do with us, and rightly so.

Patrick Bateson, at Cambridge University, pointed out that fish are complex, long-lived animals, who possess highly efficient mechanisms for avoiding injury. "For instance, some fish respond by flight when they encounter substances released from the damaged epidermal cells of fish similar to themselves," which certainly implies that they recognize injury and are aware that they, too, are subject to it. T. J. Hara, a Japanese scientist, first made this remarkable discovery in 1986.[6]

But until very recently if you asked people, including many scientists, whether fish experienced pain, the answer would be a flat no. This changed in 2003. The research was conducted by a team from the Roslin Institute and the University of Edinburgh, who injected bee venom into the lips of trout. The trout responded by rubbing their lips against the gravel of the tank, clear evidence that the response was not a reflex, but directly derived from the discomfort felt. Their gills beat faster; they could no longer solve simple problems; and they took considerable time before they would resume eating. Moreover, when given pain relief medication, they resumed normal activity. This work, said Dr. Lynn Sneddon, who led the research team, "fulfils the criteria for animal pain."[7] Considering that trout are caught by hooking their lips with a snare, it seems beyond doubt now that fishermen cause the fish they catch to suffer. Donald Broom, a scientific adviser to the British government, says bluntly: "The scientific literature is quite clear. Anatomically, physiologically and biologically, the pain system in fish is virtually the same as in birds and animals."[8]

The same team of scientists at the University of Edinburgh also discovered that fish have brains remarkably like our own. They found that the amygdala in fish is associated with emotions, as it is in humans. When this part of the forebrain is damaged, the fish lose their sense of fear, just as people with lesions in the amygdala do. One of the scientists, Victoria Braithwaite, went so far as to say she found it "curious that it has taken us so long even to bother to ask whether fish feel pain. Perhaps no one really wanted to know."[9] Why would we not want to know? Well, if you have convinced yourself that you eat fish precisely because you believe they do not suffer the way warm-blooded animals do, then information on this topic is going to be unwelcome. And even scientists find it difficult to go against centuries of prejudice masquerading as scientific fact.

There is a myth among many fishermen that fish have a very short memory, and cannot remember the pain a few hours or even a few minutes later. But there is no scientific evidence that fish have short memory spans. Culum Brown, a University of

Edinburgh biologist who is studying the evolution of cognition in fish, says, "Fish are more intelligent than they appear. In many areas, such as memory, their cognitive powers match or exceed those of 'higher' vertebrates, including non-human primates." Their long-term memories help fish keep track of complex social relationships. Their spatial memory—"equal in all respects to any other vertebrate"—allows them to create cognitive maps that guide them through their watery homes, using cues such as polarized light, sounds, smells (salmon have a better sense of smell even than dogs), and visual landmarks.[10] Nobody is yet certain precisely how salmon find their way back to their natal streams, but these enhanced abilities are clearly implied. We can denigrate these abilities by saying they are "instinctive," but it may well be that human abilities are equally instinctive. And instincts are amenable to education and experience, in fish and in humans.

Phil Gee, a psychologist from the University of Plymouth in England, proved that fish can distinguish between different times of day: he trained fish to collect food by pressing a lever at specific times of the day, and only at those times. He says that "fish have a memory span of at least three months," and they are "probably able to adapt to changes in their circumstances, like any other small animals and birds."[11] Italy's new laws against keeping goldfish in small glass bowls as being inherently cruel are based on these new findings.

Just to be sure, I checked with Professor Gee, who wrote me an e-mail in which he justified his view, saying:

I didn't set out to do a study of memory, but as the 3 second memory myth seems to be strongly embedded in the

collective consciousness of journalists, they always ask
the "is it true that?" question. My response is to explain
that they wouldn't have been able to learn the task in my
work on temporal discrimination (or any of the many
tasks trained by other researchers) if they had a 3 sec-
ond memory. I also made an off-the-cuff reference to the
longest interval tested being at least 3 months. Actually,
that was a cautious response to a question on a subject
that was peripheral to my work. Going back to my ref-
erences, the source I was drawing on actually showed
retention of a conditioned response of at least 374 days
in salmon."[12]

Some scientists claim that fish remember escape routes for up
to a year. I would not be surprised to learn that as we do more
research, we will discover that we have seriously underestimated
every aspect of their intelligence, memory, and social sophisti-
cation. Given that many fish live in complex societies, it would
not be surprising to learn that they have social abilities as well.
Researchers like Culum Brown report that boldness and shyness
are common traits in the population of young fish, just as they
are in any group of children. He was able to show experimentally that if the researcher repeatedly chased a fish with a net,
that tended to make the fish more bold, showing that boldness,
like shyness, is heavily influenced by life experiences.[13]

I have been fascinated by the fact that in many species of fish,
the males are good fathers. Some of them mouth-brood. The
males hold the eggs in their mouths, give birth to the fry there,
and carry them around for the first few weeks of life. When I
was living in Bali, we had a pond filled with large Japanese carp.

From a distance, I could see the father fish swimming on one side of the pond and his babies on the other. If I approached too quickly, and the father sensed danger, he would race to the side of the pond where his fry were, just as they would be racing in his direction. He would open his mouth very wide, and in would swim the fry. With his mouth closed, he would swim frantically about the pond searching for stragglers, and when he found them, he would suck them in. When I walked a sufficient distance away to convince the father his young were safe, he would open his mouth and out would swim the babies. I wondered how often he would perform this paternal duty, but did not have the heart to test him. I am sure I would have tired before he did; after all, for him it was a matter of life and death, for me merely a means of gratifying my curiosity.

Nor are other humans really as indifferent to fish as it may appear. The number of fish tanks in American households is enormous. There are an estimated 150 million pet fish in the United States (compared to almost 74 million pet dogs, 84 million pet cats, and 16 million birds), which translates to about 22 million households with aquariums.[14] What does it mean to have a fish as a pet? For some people with aquariums, it is no more than having a piece of the natural world—or rather, something that is meant to simulate the natural world in the background—that gives them a feeling of peace and tranquility. There is research evidence that Alzheimer's patients benefit from watching the brightly colored fish in an aquarium, probably more so than from watching television.[15] In a study conducted at Purdue University, an elderly Alzheimer's patient approached the researcher and asked her: "Hey, fish lady, how many fish are in this tank, six or eight?" The researcher was surprised by the question, but told her there were six fish in the tank. "Well, one time I counted six and one time I counted eight," the woman replied. The researcher added that "We were absolutely amazed, because we had no idea that this woman could talk, much less count."[16]

For those who study fish and the oceans in which they live, there is little on earth more fascinating. As the marine biologist Richard Ellis at the American Museum of Natural History in New York points out, "the life under the shimmering surface is more intricately woven than that of any rain forest. For all of recorded history, humans have used the ocean as a resource for food. There has always been the sense that the ocean was so big, so deep, and so vast, that it could never be exhausted. We would never have to worry about an end to its productivity. Mother Ocean we called her, and we were her dependents. How could she possibly let us down? But she has. Or rather, we have let her down. Today we are fishing in ways that nature never expected, and any numbers of fish species are now so vulnerable they are listed as critically endangered, not to mention those already gone extinct."[17] No wonder Ellis calls his latest book *The Empty Ocean*.

When President Jefferson sent off Meriwether Lewis and William Clark on their 8,000-mile trek across the West in 1804, they saw hundreds of pallid sturgeons, an ancient fish that has existed since the time of the dinosaurs; Topeka shiners, that look like streamlined goldfish; the Westlope cutthroat trout; the bull trout (really a char); six species of Pacific salmon and steelhead; and other fish that today are critically endangered (two subspecies of the cutthroat trout are already extinct).[18] Today, according to a 2007 report by the World Conservation Union, more than one third of the freshwater fish in Europe face extinction. Of the 522 freshwater fish, 200 species may well disappear from the planet soon, and 12 are already gone forever. Fish are disappearing even more quickly than Europe's birds or mammals.[19] It would appear, from a large variety of sources, that our oceans are increasingly fished out. The number of fish in the ocean does not grow in correspondence to the increasing number of people in the world who want to catch and eat them. For the ocean, it is a zero-sum game. But our population continues to increase, and more and more people want to eat at the top of the food chain—that is, they want meat, including fish.

In his excellent essay "The Cry of the Ocean," the journalist and writer Peter Steinhart notes: "Life on earth began in the moonpull and seawind of the oceans. Human blood still has the salinity of seawater. We are, ourselves, miniature oceans, dressed in skin and gone exploring the arid world that rose out of ancient seas. We haven't gone far: Half the world's population still lives within 50 miles of the coast." He points out that from 1980 to 1994, New England cod, haddock, and yellowtail flounder had declined 70 percent; South Atlantic grouper and snapper 80 percent; and Atlantic bluefin tuna 90 percent. More than two hundred separate salmon spawning runs had vanished from the Pacific Northwest. Steinhart adds that "we like to think of the oceans as so vast and ancient as to be above greed or vanity. . . . But we now have the technological capacity to do to fish exactly what we did to the buffalo and the passenger pigeon. We are reducing the oceans' productivity. We risk hunger, poverty, dislocation, and war. We destroy links to our evolutionary past and to the future."[20]

Since this article was published in 1994, the situation has

only gotten worse. Steinhart is not suggesting we stop eating fish, but as with factory farming, there is a problem here of gigantic proportions, and the solutions are not clear. I am aware that people will probably never completely abandon eating fish; fish are simply too readily available—or have been in the past. But some of us may well rethink our attitude to the native inhabitants of the oceans that were once our home too. At least that is my fond hope.

If not, the problem appears not only insoluble but also extraordinarily dangerous. Scientists estimate that the maximum amount of marine fish we can remove is 100 million metric tons.[21] But already we have gone beyond that figure. We may think that the ocean is inexhaustible. When we overfish tuna—or any other species of fish, for that matter—the effects on the ecosystem can be severe but not always immediately apparent. With the disappearance of a major predator, however, the marine ecosystem becomes oversimplified and the environment may change in ways that cannot be predicted. Food webs are delicate: if cod and mackerel are overfished, the Alaskan Stellar sea lion will starve (the population is already down by 80 percent). If we take too many plant-eating fish from a coral reef ecosystem, algae grows to dangerous levels, destroying other fish. The proliferating algae also prevent light from reaching the coral reefs, which depend on light, and so they and the plants that exist on them begin to disappear.

Equally dangerous is the so-called bycatch, a weasel word, designed to disguise the number of "non-targeted" fish caught up in nets along with the desired fish, and destroyed by accident, as it were. The bycatch is calculated to be one quarter of the global fish catch. Included are thousands of crabs, starfish, juvenile cod, sharks, and hundreds of other "unwanted" sea creatures, as well as many rare species. They are dumped back into the ocean, dead. The long lines also take and kill marine mammals, birds, and sea turtles. Purse seine nets catch dolphin, who die horribly of asphyxiation. Discarded gill nets kill marine mammals through what is known as "ghost-fishing." Trawls, of course, damage the seabed along which they are dragged.[22] These ships are huge now (the length of four football fields), and often weigh more than 8,000 tons; and their tow nets have openings 3,500 feet in circumference that can trawl at depths of 3,000 feet into the ocean. In an hour, they can haul as much as 200 tons of fish.[23] For every 3 tons of fish processed, 1 ton or more of other sea animals are killed. By any standards, this is strip-mining—mindless exploitation driven by greed and a "me first" attitude.

*   *   *

APART FROM BELIEVING THAT the oceans could never be emptied, for people who eat fish, there is a vague sense that the fish has a sporting chance of escape. After all, the fish may have lived a long life in the freedom of the ocean. Surely this is better than the life of a farm animal. Moreover, the fish may well have been the prey of another piscine predator long before humans came on the scene. We are just one more danger in their dangerous environment. So, we hang on to the comforting image of a man sitting on a pier fishing for his dinner. But the way fishing is practiced today involves no sport and no real concern for the welfare of the animals, or their and our ecosystem (the oceans). And indeed, as we shall see, our own health.

Today, farmed fish are becoming increasingly important to the diet of most people on the planet. Fish farming is the world's fastest growing sector of food production. According to an FAO (Food and Agriculture Organization of the United Nations) report, *The State of World Aquaculture—2006*, whereas in 1980, aquaculture accounted for 9 percent of fish consumed by humans, in 2006 that figure stood at 43 percent, and it is expected to climb. Essentially, there has been an 8 percent yearly growth since the 1980s. In 2001, 40 million tons of fish were farmed, almost one half of the entire fishery production of the world. From 1984 to 1996, aquaculture increased from about 13 percent to 35 percent of the capture fishery yield. The industry is increasing substantially—it is now worth $63 billion a year—and there may well come a point in the not too distant future when the oceans are fished out and all the fish eaten is from aquaculture.

The most common fish farmed are salmon—farm-raised outnumber wild by 85 to 1—with the main farms located in Chile, Norway, Scotland, and Canada. Today in Scotland—as in many North Atlantic countries—farmed salmon outnumber wild salmon by 300 or 400 to 1.[24] Other highly farmed fish are trout, cod, eel, halibut, sea bass, and turbot, as well as huge quantities (over 1 billion pounds a year imported into the United States) of shrimp. Most shrimp are "farmed" in tropical coastal areas, causing economic and social disasters in many nations—particularly Asia and Latin America—and posing serious health hazards for consumers.[25] How? Disease is rampant on many shrimp farms, which is not surprising given the crowded conditions there. Antibiotics are dumped into the farms by the ton. But they don't always prevent viruses from forming. White Spot, one of these viruses, destroyed many farms throughout Asia and Central America in the 1990s.[26] Some viruses survive freezing and show up on people's plates. (If you are wondering about the face on a shrimp, I have heard children compare them to sleeping babies.) The antibiotic chloramphenicol is banned in the United States for use in shrimp farms, but it is used by many countries that export shrimp. Aplastic anemia (a lethal blood disorder) has been linked to this antibiotic.[27]

Not much has been written for popular audiences about what fish farming is really like. One exception is Philip Lymbery's *In Too Deep*.[28] Little of what goes on in the industry is known to the general public, even that part of the public interested in being well informed. I had no idea, for example, of the way that commercially raised eels are killed. Living in New Zealand, I have always had a special affection for this remarkable animal. Partly this stems from the fact that the affection is often returned: wild eels are easily tamed and will, with time, come when they are called, allow themselves to be picked up, and even taken out of the water. They recognize people they know (generally children, who find them enchanting) and trust them. They can reach nearly ten feet long, and can live for almost a century. Eels lead mysterious lives. They breed somewhere in the tropical or subtropical Pacific Ocean east of Australia. The female breeds only once in her life, which may not be until she is sixty years old. To do so she makes her way to the ocean, traveling at night, and even crossing land. When she reaches the sea, she swims perhaps 3,600 miles to the place in the Pacific Ocean where she was originally hatched. Once she reaches her destination, she lays up to 20 million eggs. A mature male, who has also made the same trip, externally fertilizes the eggs. She dies. He dies. (Had she not given birth, the female eel could have lived another forty years.) Obviously, in order to make this extraordinary voyage, eels must be conscious of their surroundings. Nobody, today, doubts that they feel pain.

So, although I know that eels are widely eaten, I had not thought about how they ended up on someone's plate. The primary method in industry is to bathe them in dry salt, which gradually penetrates and desiccates their bodies. It is very hard to kill an eel. So by the time they are ready to be "gutted," most of them are still alive. Even after they are actually gutted, "a significant proportion is still alive after 30 minutes," according to industry accounts.[29] During that time they make strenuous efforts to escape, so we can assume they are experiencing absolute terror.

Fish farms try to convey an ecological or environmental image by claiming that they are not depleting oceans; the truth is that they too are dangerous in terms of the environment and human health. These have been neatly summed up in a recent article by David Barboza in *The New York Times*: "Industrial fish farming has destroyed mangrove forests in Thailand, Vietnam and China, heavily polluted waterways and radically altered the ecological balance of coastal areas, mostly through the discharge of wastewater. Aquaculture waste contains fish feces, rotting fish feed and residues of pesticides and veterinary drugs as well as other pollutants that were already mixed into the poor quality water supplied to farmers." The article concludes: "Currently, China's coastal fish farms face many of the same challenges as those on land. Waters there are heavily polluted by oil, lead, mercury, copper and other harsh substances.

Veterinary drugs dropped in shoreline waters may easily spread to neighboring aquaculture farms and affect species outside the cages, and while coastal waters are less polluted than those on land, aquaculture farms, with their intensive production cycles, are prone to be polluters."[30]

*   *   *

MOST PEOPLE WHEN THEY think of farmed fish tend to think of salmon. By the 1990s, farmed salmon dominated the Atlantic salmon market in the United States and Canada. In Europe, as we saw earlier, salmon farms now produce almost 100 times the catch of wild European salmon.

Like eels, salmon have an unusual life in that they can live in both fresh and salt water (they are anadromous). The young Pacific salmon (called parr) hatch in freshwater streams and live there for anywhere from a few weeks to several years, before making their way to the ocean. Their bodies undergo a physiological and chemical transformation (a metamorphosis called smoltification) that allows them to adapt their bodies to salt water. They turn silver, a color adaptation that allows them to live in the ocean. Thyroid hormones change their endocrine system for the same purpose. These changes are the subject of much research, because it is also at this time that salmon imprint to some property of their native tributary that later allows them to identify it when they return to spawn as adults. They then may swim several thousand miles, and stay in the ocean for up to ten years. Chinook salmon can travel more than 10,000 miles in the Pacific Ocean before they return to spawn.

But eventually all salmon begin their return journey into freshwater rivers and streams. Once there, the salmon stop eating and again undergo a radical transformation in both appearance and color, developing canine teeth and a hump on their backs. They reverse the process that allowed them to be superbly adapted to the ocean waters, and here the physiological changes begin a degenerative process. Swimming upstream, the salmon are nonetheless capable of vertical leaps of more than six feet. For a species in physical decline day by day, they achieve remarkable results: chinook and sockeye salmon from central Idaho, for example, travel over 900 miles and climb nearly 7,000 feet upstream from the Pacific Ocean as they return to spawn. They usually are able to return to the very same stream where they were born. How they find the stream is still a mystery (they could possibly use the stars and currents when traveling in the ocean toward the natal river), but scientists hypothesize either that it has to do with their ability to smell the different minerals specific to that one stream, or that they are reacting to the magnetic field of the earth.[31]

This stream is their spawning ground, and here males and females finally meet one another. The female digs a nest (known as a redd) with her tail, and then she and her partner align themselves next to one another for the spawning ritual. Their bodies quivering side by side, the female releases her orange eggs (from 2,500 to 7,000) at the same time that the male releases sperm (called milt). Of these, less than 2 percent will return to spawn; most fall prey to larger carnivorous fish in the ocean, or to birds, marine mammals, or even disease. Fertilization occurs in the water as the eggs drift down into the gravel at the bottom of the stream. The fish repeat this same ritual in multiple nesting areas—usually about seven. Covering the nests with gravel to protect them, they stand guard for a few days. Both the males and females die shortly thereafter (this is not true of Atlantic salmon, however, who often make the transition from stream to ocean several times over their lives). The eggs hatch in thirty to ninety days, and the cycle begins again.[32]

Needless to say, no kind of farm could possibly duplicate this natural cycle. Nor does any try. Just as in the wild, the life cycle on a farm begins with eggs. The salmon ripe for spawning are caught as they make their way back to their natal streams. One of the most common methods is to anesthetize the female by immersing her in a chemical solution such as Benzocaine. She is then killed and her eggs surgically removed. It could be argued that the female was at the point of death in any event, which is true, but not a great argument for killing an aged human female. The male salmon is not anesthetized while his abdomen is massaged to collect the milt. Sometimes he is killed immediately, but other times he will go through this procedure up to ten times before he is killed.[33]

The fertilized eggs are transferred to land-based freshwater incubator trays and placed in a trough with flowing water. When they grow to the size of a finger—hence the name "fingerling"—they are put into freshwater tanks, cages, ponds, or raceways. When the young salmon reach six inches, at between one and two years, they become "smolts," and at the point when they would normally migrate to sea, they are transferred to sea farms. The rest of their life is spent in a cage, suspended in seawater, where most of these majestic fish, genetically programmed to swim the oceans, are doomed to swim in their own feces and a toxic brew of chemicals, dyes, pesticides, and pellets composed of smaller wild-caught fish. One of the world's experts on organic farming, Lawrence Woodward, CEO of Elm Farm Research Centre in Newbury and a former head of the United Kingdom's Soil Association, says that "Caged salmon have no relationship to the aquatic environment, other than that the cage is suspended in water . . . this is not a living ecological system."[34]

A typical sea cage measures 12–20 meters square, and can be between 5–20 meters (15 to 60 feet) deep. They are basically just giant nets, suspended from floating platforms in the ocean.[35] Each contains between 5,000 and 70,000 salmon. Here they spend the next one to two years until they reach a weight of between 2 and 10 pounds. To reach the required size, the fish have been used to almost constant feeding. Then they are normally starved for about seven to ten days in order to empty the gut and minimize the risk of the flesh becoming contaminated when gutted. The salmon are hauled to the surface from depths of up to 60 feet, where they will experience three times the atmospheric pressure at the surface. They are then slaughtered, sometimes manually by a handheld club known as a "priest," or else by placing the fish in a seawater bath saturated with carbon dioxide from which they make desperate attempts to escape (it can take up to nine minutes or more for unconsciousness to end the suffering).[36]

Salmon in the wild can live for sixteen years. It is odd, when you think about it, that fish are wildlife. We rarely think of them that way. There is no animal in the wild that we hunt to the same extent that we hunt fish. The scale is so great that Carl Safina, co-founder and president of Blue Ocean Institute, an international non-profit conservation organization, calls it "pure folly." What kind of life can they possibly lead in these crowded, unnatural conditions? As far as I know (I've been unable to get a response from the industry spokespersons I've contacted), there is no environmental enrichment at any salmon farm in North America, the United Kingdom, or elsewhere that I have heard about. That these animals are very much like bored zoo inhabitants is obvious, but the implications are not taken into account. The large schools of salmon, who spend their time ceaselessly swimming in circles around the cage, are similar to big cats pacing in small zoo pens. They are subject to predators, such as seals, who can lunge at the cage netting and bite at the confined fish, who have no ability to escape. The farmers in turn become enraged at the seals eating "their" fish and often shoot at them from boats, to the tune of thousands of dead seals a year. Some mammalian predators are also killed by getting caught in the nets and drowning.

It bears repeating that salmon spend almost their entire lives swimming freely through the oceans. Before they return to spawn, it is unlikely that they would have met a single other salmon. The aggression they show under the artificial conditions of the sea cages is entirely an artifact that we have created. Sian Griffiths of Glasgow University has done research showing that salmon can smell their siblings and are far less aggressive to fish they are related to than other salmon. Dr. Griffiths writes: "We are starting to see quite a lot of evidence that fish are able to make quite complex decisions. It's interesting work—fish can decide when to leave and when to join a shoal or leave a shoal, things much more complicated than we thought."[37]

But these farmed fish are not able to swim anywhere, except in useless circles, and the extraordinary fitness that wild salmon demonstrate is only a memory for them. Of course, they are not able to engage in their normal hunting behavior. Salmon are carnivores, and spend a great deal of their time hunting other fish. But in the nets, they eat what they are fed. Sometimes they are fed ground-up fish bycatch, grains, plant oils (which can be dangerous to people at risk of heart attacks),[38] and sometimes wheat flour, but they are never allowed to capture their own food. In China, according to David Pimentel, one of the world's leading experts on agriculture and the environment, the fact that the aquaculture is both high-impact and high-product means that fish are going to be fed "agricultural residues, hog manure and sewage."[39] Such feed is economical: some species of fish, Pimentel tells us, need less than one third the amount of food in terms of "yield" compared to beef. He feels that aquaculture, which is a $30 billion industry worldwide, is valuable in producing protein and recycling waste.[40] His hesitation has to do with the damage to the environment.

Indeed, concerns are being raised more and more frequently about the effects of fish farming on the environment. The David Suzuki Foundation, an environmental organization based in Vancouver, British Columbia, is very worried, noting: "Every day British Columbia's aquaculture industry dumps the same amount of raw sewage into the ocean as a city of half a million people. High concentrations of fish waste and drugs [used in the feed], along with drug-resistant microbes, pass through net cages to settle and destroy life on the ocean floor. Much of it drifts throughout the marine environment, contaminating shellfish beds and other habitats and spreads disease up the food chain."[41]

Most salmon farms—even, surprisingly, organic farms—give the fish a dye to create the pink coloring natural to wild salmon, which they would normally obtain from eating crustaceans and shrimp.[42] At least this is true today, in 2008. Even the U.S. Institute for Agriculture and Trade Policy has a campaign called "Go Wild," showing a picture of a salmon with the words FARMED SALMON DYED FOR YOU displayed prominently in front of a sad-looking fish.

The carotenoids (the pigments responsible for the colors of many plants, fruits, and flowers) added are astaxanthin and canthaxanthin (E161$_g$), made in a synthetic form from petrochemicals. Without these colorings, the flesh of farmed salmon would look an unappetizing muddy gray. True, astaxanthin is a natural pigment that wild salmon obtain by eating krill (tiny, shrimplike crustaceans), which in turn get the pigment from feeding on algae. But the synthetic version of astaxanthin differs from the one that occurs in nature and functions differently in the bodies of salmon and possibly human bodies as well.[43] There is also some concern about the safety of canthaxanthin. Marion Burros wrote about this in *The New York Times* on May 28, 2003: "European Union officials are reducing the permissible levels of canthaxanthin in fish and poultry from 80 parts per million per kilogram of feed—the levels permitted in this country—to 25 parts per million because there is some concern that high levels may cause retinal damage. In Canada the permissible level is 30 parts per million."[44]

The U.S. government now mandates that the words "coloring added" appear on any farmed salmon. The farmed fish industry assures us there are no negative effects. In 2003, the European Commission issued a report setting out all the scientific evidence linking canthaxanthin to retinal damage in the human eye.[45] It noted that since 1982, the levels of artificial colorings in the flesh of farmed salmon have more than trebled. As Don Staniford, director of the Salmon Farm Protest Group in Scotland, put it: "Farmed salmon is getting pinker—chemical companies are getting richer."[46] But if there are questions about the carotenoids, there seems to be no question that the huge amount of antibiotics being fed to farmed salmon may not be good for people. According to the David Suzuki Foundation, because farmed salmon are subject to disease and parasites to a greater degree than free-living salmon, powerful antibiotics and other drugs are poured directly into the net cages. These are the same antibiotics used to control human diseases and could easily lead to a rise in "superbugs" that are drug-resistant. There is thus a risk to the wider marine ecosystem, as well to workers on the fish farms, not to mention consumers.[47]

Studies in England and Canada in 2001 found that a small sample taken from farmed salmon had significantly higher levels of toxic dioxins, furans (a colorless, odorless liquid), and PCBs, with PCB levels about ten times higher in the farmed fish.[48] The researchers concluded that regular consumption of farmed salmon could lead to toxin intakes above the tolerable weekly intake for these chemicals—especially for PCBs, and especially for children under five and pregnant women.[49]

Most people who eat farmed fish are simply not aware of these issues: they are surprised when you tell them that the pleasing pink has been artificially created and that they could be ingesting antibiotics when they eat salmon. We have been so primed to believe that eating fish is good for us that scientific articles in scholarly journals just don't make it into the national consciousness. (I do recognize that there is also a scientific stream which takes the opposite point of view. I simply urge you to look at both sides.) In my opinion, there is more and more evidence all pointing in the same direction.

Some of the many fish who escape every season may be diseased and could pass on these diseases to their wild cousins. In 1998, more than 1 million diseased farm salmon in New Brunswick had to be slaughtered in their cages to prevent the spread of infectious salmon anemia (ISA). By mid-1998, the Scotish government had forced the closure of 40 percent of its salmon farms because of outbreaks of ISA. Norwegian taxpayers have paid $100 million to contain diseases spread from farmed fish to wild stocks over the last few years. In Norway, there are approximately five hundred salmon populations; more than forty of them have now been infected with a microscopic organism, the parasite *Gyrodactylus salaries*. In order to prevent the further spread of the parasites to rivers and hatcheries, Norwegian authorities have undertaken what they call a rotenone treatment program, that is, the total poisoning of rivers to kill all fish, infected as well as uninfected.[50]

Many diseases practically unknown in wild salmon are occurring more and more frequently in their caged cousins. Bleeding cataracts have led to blindness; in addition, farmed salmon suffer from bacterial kidney disease, infectious salmon anemia, and other diseases that are rarely known to affect wild salmon. Mortality rates of nearly 30 percent are not unheard of.[51]

These are not the only problems: salmon farms are often infested with sea lice.[52] To control them, Nuvan was used throughout the 1980s and 1990s. The makers of Nuvan (also called Aquagard) label their product with the skull-and-crossbones symbol for poison because it consists of 50 percent dichlorvos, a nerve toxin, and a carcinogenic organophosphate that is red-listed by the European Commission and considered one of the most toxic pesticides in the world. In 1998, a scientific paper linked dichlorvos use on salmon farms to testicular cancer.[53] It was still being used in some Scottish salmon farms as late as 2004, and even though it is banned, the Scottish Environmental Protection Agency issued twenty "exceptional" licenses in 2004. But sea lice are determined creatures and can build up resistance to dichlorvos.

Other toxic chemicals known to be used in salmon farming include cypermethrin, a carcinogenic neuro-poison known to kill lobsters in the larval stage, which can also destroy all insect life within a radius of seven miles;[54] teflubenzuron, a hazardous marine pollutant, 90 percent of which is excreted by the salmon into the sea and has an adverse effect on crabs, shrimp, and lobsters;[55] ivermectin, a neurotoxin that is not permitted by the manufacturer to be used in an aquatic environment because of its devastating effects;[56] emamectin benzoate, which is toxic to fish, birds, and mammals;[57] and malachite green, a carcinogenic chemical contaminant.[58]

That is not the end of the list. For example, formalin is a preservative and disinfectant, commonly used in fish farming worldwide, and approved in Britain by the government's Pesticides Safety Directorate.[59] Yet formalin is a solution of 37 percent formaldehyde gas dissolved in water, and as such it is a known human carcinogen. After reading about these hazards for a while, I feel I have entered a danger zone: my paranoia quotient rises with every article I read. I have given but a taste here. Considering that most people eat fish as a "health" product, they ought to know that they may in fact be consuming a package of dangerous toxins. Moreover, how can we know what regulations are in force, or enforced, in fish farms in Asia and other parts of the world? The Chinese produce about 70 percent of the farmed fish in the world, destroying much of their remaining mangrove forests in the process. There is contamination by sewage, industrial waste, and agricultural runoff that includes such pollutants as copper, DDT, heavy metals, mercury, and flame retardants. This, too, was discussed in Barboza's article in *The New York Times*.[60]

Then there is the fact that fish in the United States escape during storms and from damage to the pens or during transfers. Not being imprinted with any particular home stream, they have bred with local salmon. This has a negative impact on the genetic integrity of wild salmon and impoverishes the gene pool. Sometimes these salmon outcompete local wild salmon for food, displace them, or even eat them.[61] A National Research Council committee estimated that 180,000 fish escape from salmon farms in Maine each year— about 100 times the number of wild Atlantic salmon left in New England.[62] Nobody has ever asked, and perhaps we will never know, what these escaped fish feel. Do they feel like war orphans who suddenly find themselves free in a strange city? This could easily be the stuff of humor, but the truth is, we have no idea whatsoever of how fish under these circumstances view their world and their lives. It could be a lot more complex than we, in our ignorance, assume. What are the consequences that through breeding these fish may have lost the ability to avoid predators?

• • •

FARMS EXIST FOR OTHER KINDS of fish as well, including the great bluefin tuna, which are caught elsewhere and "ranched" in pens in the Mediterranean—not surprising when you consider that a single fish can be worth hundreds of thousands of dollars. Because they are in such demand for sushi and sashimi, numbers of these majestic fish that normally live for forty years, can reach 10 feet, and weigh over 1,000 pounds, one of the most wide-ranging animals on our planet (they can travel up to 7,000 miles in a few months), have plummeted 90 percent since the 1970s. Soon wild fish may live on only in memory.[63] In Mediterranean fish farms, in order to feed these giants, there is an immense tonnage of smaller fish vacuumed up to fatten the captured bluefin. The nets used for this purpose also take and kill countless other sea creatures—unwanted fish, turtles, and seabirds killed as "bycatch."

More common is the intensive farming of trout. Unlike salmon, trout are reared in fresh water, usually in raceways or rectangular earth ponds with a continuous flow of fast-moving water, which, because of the oxygenation, allows the fish to be kept at high stocking densities. There can be as many as thirty young trout, each about one foot long, in the equivalent of a bathtub of water. Normal behavior is naturally precluded. Are they stressed? They could hardly be otherwise: they fight, they have fin injuries, and they are susceptible to disease and to attack from parasites.[64] By any standard, these fish are suffering.

* * *

TWO ALTERNATIVES TO INTENSIVE salmon farming exist: one is organic fish farming. The fish themselves cannot be genetically engineered; no artificial ingredients or colorants can be used in the feed; there are lower stocking densities; and no chemical pesticide treatments can be used for parasite control. Instead, cleaner fish (wrasse) are used to clean the sea lice from the salmon. The wrasse themselves suffer: many die as they are being transported; others are eaten by the larger salmon; and some do not find enough lice for their own diet. The slaughter methods are also more stringent, with greater emphasis placed on welfare considerations, even though the salmon are starved for seven to ten days before slaughter just as conventionally raised salmon are. Britain's leading organic farming body, the Soil Association, sees promise but has reservations. From the point of view of the fish themselves, the stumbling block is the cage. What kind of life, we can legitimately ask, can fish used to traveling thousands of miles and finding their own preferred food possibly have in an artificial pen with thousands of unwanted cage mates being fed artificial pellets?

A small movement within organic salmon farming known as ecological aquaculture has started to gain momentum.[65] From an ecological point of view this is a vast improvement, since it uses sustainable, organic aquaculture principles and is more in line with what the consumer thinks of when the word "organic" is used. For example, whereas organic fish farming can use "exotic" fish not local to the environment, ecological aquaculture uses only native species. Moreover, ecological aquacultural businesses are not owned by large transnational companies. So they are sensitive to concerns of the neighborhood, making sure they put back money into the local economy and employ people from the area. The word "organic" as applied to fish farms is often a misnomer, and at least that is not true for ecological aquaculture. There is still little room for the feelings of the fish, however.[66]

When I finally had the opportunity to visit a salmon farm, it was similar to one of these aquacultural farms. I had previously contacted several salmon farms without any luck. From my research I knew what I could expect to find but nonetheless wished to verify it with my own eyes. Try as I might, though, I was not able to gain access to a commercial salmon farm; all my requests were flatly rejected with no reason given. Then I had occasion to visit the town of Takaka in Golden Bay on the South Island of New Zealand, where I learned that there were two salmon farms. I called them both. One told me that under no circumstances could I visit or see the operation. But, to my delight, the other said I was most welcome. I soon discovered why.

This was no ordinary salmon farm. I drove to the end of the lush Anatoki Valley, located in the native bush of the Kahurangi National Park. I could hear the rushing waters of New Zealand's steepest river, the Anatoki. It was winter, and I was the only person there apart from the owners, Jan and Gerda Dissel from Holland. They welcomed me and told me I was free to wander about as much as I liked. There were lawns of deep green grass. I walked over to a huge pond, at least two acres in size. I found out that it had 1,500,000 liters—almost 400,000 gallons—of crystal clear water in it. I could see juvenile Chinook salmon swimming lazily by. Off the main lake were several small tributary streams that led into the giant fern forest bordering the property and where more salmon were swimming. All my expectations were reversed; these 50,000 fish were not crammed into cages, nor were they confined in a pen and forced to swim aimlessly in circles. The water was so clean that I could see the sandy bottom of the lake. At one end of the lake water was pouring in from the Anatoki, and at the other end it was returning to the river from the lake.

The Department of Conservation visits the site every two weeks to test the quality of the water. The farm receives the highest grade. How did they manage to keep it so clean? There were strategically placed nets around the lake and streams. Local farmers and gardeners were encouraged to scoop out the fish droppings and use them as fertilizer. The demand was greater than the supply, and as a result the water was always immaculate.

Did these fish get "harvested" (killed)? Of course. This was no fish sanctuary (I know of none, alas) but a commercial enterprise. How come, then, the fish were leading what looked like an ideal life in comparison with the lives of commercially farmed salmon? Why was this salmon farm so different from all the others I knew about? Because it is not a true commercial enterprise but a tourist attraction. In the summer people come, rent fishing poles, sit along the grassy banks of the small island in the middle of the lake, and catch salmon. They take their catch to the main building, and the fish are returned in ten minutes, smoked and ready for eating at one of the picnic tables. This was how 85 percent of the salmon at the farm ended their lives. The other 15 percent were sold to local restaurants.

The welfare of the fish was much on the minds of the owners. There were several signs warning sternly against catch and release, on the grounds that to do so hurt and stressed (read traumatized) the fish, who would then die a slow and painful death. Far better to be caught and killed at once. Eating Anatoki's salmon is infinitely preferable to eating salmon from a typical salmon farm, not one of which, it would seem, wants us to see what kind of life the salmon are forced to live there. I was grateful to have found at least one salmon farm that did not follow the commercial model. It made me wonder, too, if this was not a model that could be followed by others. If the fish must be killed, why not make their life a bit more pleasant beforehand? Is it impossible for us to put ourselves into the mind of salmon and ask what we would prefer? Anatoki Farm is a bit of a fantasy, but it is not Disneyland for fish. They die. But at least until that moment, their lives are not ones of unremitting horror.

The second alternative is known as free-range fish ranching. This is on the increase and attracting attention worldwide. The young fish are reared in a river—ideally one far removed from streams where any wild salmon congregate (to avoid genetic dilution). They are kept under captive conditions in hatcheries (where chemicals to control disease might still be used) until they are ready to migrate to sea as juveniles. Then, instead of going into cages or pens, they are released into the ocean, again far from any wild salmon streams. The fish imprint on the river where they were born ("home"), and when they are mature, they return to this very river, where they are easily captured and killed. Under natural conditions, fewer than 10 percent of salmon return to their natal river. For ranched salmon, the figure is at least 10 percent, and sometimes even higher: Iceland reports return figures of 15 percent; 12–40 percent in Sweden, and 6 percent in Scotland and Ireland. Already twenty-seven countries are involved in ranching, with Japan and Alaska leading the way.[67]

The moral arguments against sea ranching are rather weak if we consider that the salmon are captured when they are near their natural life span in any event. The quality of life they lead before capture is incomparably better than for farmed salmon, since they live completely free lives (if you do not consider their earliest time in the hatchery—a few years or so until they can survive in the ocean) until they return to the river as adults. Since anybody can catch the salmon before they return to the river, there is always an economic risk for the private rancher.[68]

Is it better to raise salmon in this way rather than by intensive farming? Absolutely. It is the same with any farmed animal: the more freedom, the better. The more natural their lives and the food they eat, the better for them and for us. If you are going to eat fish, you would be doing yourself and the planet a favor to limit yourself to wild and free range. You could also decide to buy only fish that are listed in Environmental Defense Fund's "Best and Worst Seafood" or the Blue Ocean Institute's "Guide to Ocean Friendly Seafood."[69]

Would I myself be willing to eat salmon ranched in this way? In the end I do not feel entitled to take the lives and eat the flesh of any fish since I don't need to do so to survive, so

I have an easy solution: Stop eating fish altogether. This may well be the only way we can continue to enjoy our oceans as we have known them. In John Hersey's *Blues,* his book about the majestic bluefish, he defended fishing for sustenance while mourning the unhinged global slaughter that shreds fragile webs of ocean life. "We'd better marvel while we can."[70]

In 2006, *The Guardian Weekly* reported that the United Nations was afraid that humankind's exploitation of the deep seas and oceans was "rapidly passing the point of no return." The United Nations stated that in 2005, some 85 million tonnes of wild fish were pulled from the global oceans; 100 million sharks and related species were butchered for their fins; some 250,000 turtles became tangled in fishing gear; and 300,000 albatrosses were killed by illegal longline fishing.[71] Isn't it time that we rethink our attitude toward living, breathing, sentient animals who live in the sea? Maybe it is not enough to worry about what kind of fish we are eating, or what kind of life they led before we consumed them. Maybe it is time to think that we should not be farming, or catching, or harming, or eating any fish. If we simply left them and their home alone, maybe we could swim in their pure blue ocean with a clearer conscience—inhabitants as we all are of the same marvelous but endangered planet, without which none of us can survive.

Chapter Four

DENIAL

About suffering they were never wrong,
The Old Masters: how well they understood
Its human position; how it takes place
While someone else is eating or opening a window or
just walking dully along...

—W. H. Auden, *Musée des Beaux Arts*

At the moment our human world is based on the suffering
and destruction of millions of non-humans. To perceive
this and to do something to change it in personal and
public ways is to undergo a change of perception akin to
a religious conversion. Nothing can ever be seen in quite
the same way again because once you have admitted
the terror and pain of other species you will, unless you
resist conversion, be always aware of the endless permu-
tations of suffering that support our society.

—Arthur Conan Doyle

IN AN EARLIER CHAPTER, I SPOKE OF THE "EUREKA" moment when many people suddenly become vegetarian or vegan. But there is also a more profound version of this experience, when we suddenly realize that we have been disengaged or, as we like to say today, "in denial." What brings this about? It could be a more enlightened friend who talks to you about why they made the change. It could be a good animal documentary. It could be a book like *Charlotte's Web:* some children when they hear E. B. White's book read out loud determine never to eat another farm animal. It could even be a children's film, *Babe* or *Chicken Run* or *The Shark's Tale*. Amy Cherry, my editor, tells me, "When I was growing up, along with bologna and salami we had tongue sandwiches, which I loved. I had no idea why it was called tongue, as I had no idea why salami was called salami. At some point when I was probably around eight years old, someone told me—probably one of my brothers—that tongue came from a cow's tongue. I refused to believe him and continued to eat tongue for at least another year. And then I just realized one day that tongue was a tongue. Maybe I had actually seen one in a supermarket or butcher's shop. Whatever it was, I could no longer deal with that reality and haven't touched it since. But that was my first 'face on the plate' moment."

It seems appropriate that it often requires a child to remind us of the obvious. There is an anecdote that the famous professor of moral philosophy at Cambridge, G. E. Anscombe, once was serving lunch to Ludwig Wittgenstein in the garden of her home. Wittgenstein, as was his wont, ate in silence. Uncomfortable, Anscombe, to break the silence, said, "Isn't it interesting, Ludwig, that when children hear words like 'can you pass me a leg,' or 'I'll have the neck or the thigh," they can suddenly recognize that a chicken, as an animal, is being talked about, and become disgusted?" Wittgenstein's reply was, "No, Elizabeth, that is *not* interesting." (Odd, when you think that Wittgenstein was a vegetarian.) But Wittgenstein was wrong for a change. It *is* interesting. It is interesting precisely because the child is noticing what the adult is attempting to disguise, that we are talking about the body parts of an animal who was recently alive. There *is* betrayal involved here, and the child knows it. The noted chef Bill Buford in his book *Heat* concurs: "People don't want to know what meat is. For my neighbour (and my friends, and me, too, for most of my life) meat wasn't meat. It was an abstraction. People don't think of animal when they use the word [meat]."[1]

I find it interesting and suggestive that scholars who study food habits have pointed out that virtually all food-related "disgust entities" (as they call them) are of animal origin. People may dislike broccoli, but nobody is ever disgusted by the thought of eating it. Could it be that the disgust is in fact a displacement? I am thinking of an early disgust (which many children share) at the very thought of ingesting a corpse that was once a living being. In time we overcome this, as we increasingly swallow the prevailing attitudes toward food in our culture; but some may be left with a lingering feeling of guilt.

I sympathize with the deniers, for I have a similar reaction and hence a similar problem. I call myself a vegan, but really I should say, to be more honest, that I am "veganish"—or an aspiring vegan or nearly vegan or mostly vegan, or even a vegan manqué. Because when I find that something has been made with butter or eggs, even though I would not knowingly order these products, I sometimes let it go. Perhaps I am being polite to a host, or I'm at a restaurant and the diners are showing impatience, or in some other situation in which it would strike others as rude to make a fuss. So all I do is shrug. But I would not under any circumstances let it pass and eat the meat. What is the difference? I have a visceral reaction to meat, but not to butter or cheese or milk chocolate. Perhaps because of the disguise: it is hard to eat a chocolate chip cookie and think "suffering." Some might call this benign or healthy denial, but I can't.

A psychologist friend told me recently that some denial is indeed healthy, and even necessary for survival. Granted. But is not facing the suffering involved in meat one of them? I think not. I am sixty-eight: I have three children, ages thirty-four, twelve, and seven. If I allowed myself to think that I will not live to see the two younger ones as complete adults, I would become unbearably sad. From time to time, I do think about it, but only very rarely. Most of the time I keep it in permanent forgetfulness. Denial of our own mortality need not be pathological. Denial of someone else's can be. If I were to define "healthy" or "benign" denial, I would have to say that it's the kind of denial that does not involve the suffering of another. We should bear in mind the *bon mot* of François de La Rochefoucauld, the cynical observer of Louis XIV's court, when he said that "man has an infinite capacity for enduring the suffering of others." We find it easiest to sympathize over our own suffering. We are willing to extend this to our loved ones, a child, a parent, a beloved, a friend, but rarely beyond. But to remain indifferent to the suffering of any other living creature is never benign and rarely healthy.

In a recent article in *The New York Times* it was pointed out that Tamara Murphy, the chef at Brasa in Seattle, took delivery of eleven freshly killed piglets last Friday, destined for dishes of pork belly with braised greens and paprika-rubbed roasted chops. "I don't name them," said Ms. Murphy, who wrote a weekly blog in 2006, chronicling the short lives of some of the piglets earmarked for her restaurant from Whistling Train Farm. "They are being raised for food, and there is a respectful distance I need to keep," she said. Ms. Murphy visited the piglets weekly, starting the day after their birth, and accompanied them to the slaughterhouse before serving them in a dinner that was called a "Celebration of the Life of a Pig." The hardest part of the slaughter was the betrayal," she said. "The pigs get in the trailer because they trust you, they get out of the trailer because they trust you, they go into the pen because they trust you."[2] Although she calls it by its proper name, "betrayal," I found the article hard to fathom. When I showed it to the noted feminist legal scholar Catharine MacKinnon, she said it seemed to her denial to a remarkable degree to call extermination a celebration of the life of the exterminated.

Murphy may agree with some agricultural ethicists who believe that if animals could lead comfortable lives and die completely free of fear and pain, raising and killing them would not pose an ethical problem. Some writers have proposed the idea of an unwritten "domestic contract" between humans and our domesticated species that includes killing. This is now a popular view. Many intelligent and well-meaning people believe that domestication is a two-way street. The author John Coetzee wrote to me, saying, "I see eggs and cheese as a kind of rent that such animals pay us for feeding them and giving them a home."

A popular London chef, Hugh Fearnley-Whittingstall, has gone so far as to claim: "Of all the creatures whose lives we affect, none are more deeply dependent on us for their success as species and for their individual health and well-being than the animals we raise to kill for meat. I'm talking about common domestic livestock—poultry, pigs, cows, sheep and goats. We control almost every aspect of their lives. . . . We have done so for hundreds of thousands of years, to the point where their dependence on us is in their nature—evolutionarily hard-wired."[3]

Are we so blinded by our own needs that we can no longer recognize pure self-interest? A contract cannot be made by one party, and death is not usually the time when your rental agreement expires. Furthermore, farm animals have not been domesticated for hundreds of thousands of years, but for a mere 10,000, hardly enough time for there to have been any change in their evolutionary nature. They are hard-wired not to be domesticated animals but to be the creatures they actually are. Given half a chance, these animals quickly revert to their true nature. Long ago, Darwin noted that when pigs escape from farms they quickly revert to being wild, even to the extent of acquiring the stripes on their skin in a single generation that they lost during domestication. Chickens can be seen thriving on the roads outside towns throughout the world.

* * *

THE CONSCIENCE OF THE SEATTLE CHEF is at work, and that is a good thing. People clearly no longer like to think that a being suffered for their appetite. We want to see this as a two-way street, but it is really a dead end. There is no benefit for the animal in domestication, something that needs to be regularly pointed out since we so often forget it. As the geographer and historian Alfred Crosby put it, domestication as a new way of living was "at its base a matter of the direct control and exploitation of many species for the sake of one: *Homo sapiens.*"[4]

People justify this narrowing of the range of our empathy by invoking a certain uniqueness of the human animal. We are the only animal who cares about killing members of another species (all of us, to one degree or another, care—whether it is about farm animals or wild animals or animals killed by other animals). Cows are unlikely to spend time agonizing over humans ruthlessly slaughtered in East Timor during the Indonesian occupation. True; but then, they had nothing to do with it. In fact, cows don't ruthlessly kill anyone. And, in a further blow to our narcissism, the East Timorese generally don't agonize over the ruthless slaughter of pigs or cows or chickens on their island. Wherein lies our superiority?

If we have the capacity to imagine the suffering of an animal, we also have the power to refuse to allow ourselves to think about that suffering. Endowed with this ability, we more often than not neglect to bring our empathy into play. This is a form of denial, as is, too, the refusal to recognize the complexity of the animal we ingest. We refuse to acknowledge, in a complete breakdown of our capacity for empathy, that they are entitled to the full happiness of which they are capable. So when the philosopher Roger Scruton, in an essay entitled "A Carnivore's Credo," gives a bucolic and wholly unrealistic sketch of farms today with cows who, at the end of an idyllic life, are "instantly dispatched by a humane killer," he is able to make the fantastic statement that these cattle are treated "as well as cattle can be treated, and such animals are as happy as their nature allows."[5] Such a presumption to know the "nature" of any animal, human or not, allows Scruton, a philosopher, to end his essay with these bizarre words: "Duty requires us, therefore, to eat our friends." Eating one's friends would seem to negate any meaning of the word "friends." To reach this conclusion, we have to turn away from any suggestion that farm animals are emotionally complicated beings. The only way to come to this conclusion is through deep denial.

Scruton points out that farm animals are not honorary members of our moral human community the way our "pets" are. We could make yet another distinction: there are companion animals (a better expression than pets), and there are farmed animals (a more accurate expression than farm animals), and finally there is wildlife. We have more compassion for both companion animals and wildlife than for domestic animals destined to be eaten. Is this not the very heart—and a dark heart at that—of denial?

When I talk to people about this, they sometimes say to me, "But these animals would not even exist were it not for the fact that we humans need something they have." Michael Pollan made a similar statement when we had lunch in Berkeley, and I have seen it often referred to. Even the animal rights hard-liner Peter Singer, in *The Way We Eat* (coauthored with Jim Mason), can't condemn "the view that it is ethical to eat animals who have lived good lives and would not have existed at all."[6]

When thinking about arguments for animals, it is important to translate back into human terms. Of course we are not identical to domesticated animals, but we are similar enough so that we can conduct simple thought experiments: If some-body told you that your child was going to be "sacrificed" at an early age, would you still be willing to have children? In all honesty, we must also ask ourselves if we really believe that we bring farmed animals into existence for their sake, and not in order to eat them or exploit their bodies in other ways. Are we thinking about them or about us? Are we taking into account the miserable life they are most likely going to lead?

Denial is similarly at work in the comments by one of the world's leading ethicists about fish farming. R. M. Hare, the Oxford philosopher, in "Why I Am Only a Demi-Vegetarian," writes:

> In our village there is a trout farm. The fish start their lives in moderately commodious ponds and have what I guess is a pleasant life for fish, with plenty to eat. In due course they are lifted out in buckets and put immediately into tanks in the farm buildings. Purchasers select their fish, which is killed by being banged smartly on the head and handed to the customer. I am fairly certain that, if given the choice, I would prefer the life, all told, of such a fish to that of almost any fish in the wild, and to non-existence.[7]

Once again, a professional philosopher refuses to engage his heart at the same time as his head, and leaves behind his imagi-native faculty, the very thing that is supposed to raise humans above the beasts. Would anyone ever use the words "smartly banging on the head" for a human or companion animal as a preferred way of death? This is denial as whitewashing.

Denial is such an easy weapon that we are bound to see it misused. Every vegetarian at some point has been told that the carrot he is eating screams just beyond range of his hearing. James Lovelock, the inventor of the modern notion of "Gaia," offers a more sophisticated version of this retort: "It is surprising how few [people] seem aware that plants dislike being eaten and will go to extraordinary lengths to deter, disable, or even kill any animal or invertebrate trying to eat them."[8] (Examples in the plant world abound: the odorous suite of sulfur compounds in garlic; uncooked caper, the seed capsule of the euphorbia family, can cause disabling pain; chewing on the yew plant can kill humans and animals.) While true, no serious scientist suggests that plants feel pain in anything resembling the degree that humans and animals do. They have no central nervous system; they do not run away; they are not part of a community bound by ties of friendships and loyalties; and they have no visible emotions with which we can empathize. We may well be wrong, but so far no serious research has ever been done to suggest otherwise (in spite of the fanciful conclusions of books like *The Secret Life of Plants*). The future may prove me wrong. But until such time, to compare plant suffering with the suffering of humans and animals seems morally irresponsible. In fact, I do not believe the rebuke is meant seriously.

We all maintain a remarkable capacity to avoid hearing about atrocities committed by our own side, or by our own species, especially if those atrocities can be hidden from view. It has been said that denial is one of the most powerful forces in the universe. I had the bad idea, many years ago, of approaching families eating at a large steakhouse that was adjacent to a feedlot, and asking them whether they were aware of the presence of the feedlot and how it made them feel about their dinner. I had asked permission of the manager of the restaurant, but after trying a few tables and getting some unprintable responses, both he and I realized we had made a mistake. What I was hoping for was just a bit of clarification. "Would you mind, sir, if I read to you some words of the New England sage Ralph Waldo Emerson? 'You have just dined, and however scrupulously the slaughterhouse is concealed in the graceful distance of miles, there is complicity.' " It was not, in spite of the extraordinary aptitude of the quote, my finest moment.

What did I expect? I guess a long conversation about the nature of empathy. What, I wanted to ask my hapless diner, prevents you from feeling it? Is it denial pure and simple? The conversation could have branched out from there. I could have quoted the substance (though not the text, since it appeared years later) of a letter that appeared in *The Guardian Weekly* by Dr. Jeph Mathias from Manali, India: "If David Irving gets three years for denying the Holocaust, what do the rest of us deserve, who live in denial of today's atrocities? Global warming, species extinctions and millions of people dying of poverty in a wealthy world are not fairytales."[9]

I felt I was onto something: willed ignorance is surely just one more form of denial. Think about Kazuo Ishiguro's novel *Never Let Me Go*, on the complexities of adolescent friendship, loyalties, and love. The emotions of these adolescents are those of all other adolescents, yet there is something special about these young boys and girls. They all live in what appears to be a giant summer camp, but one with a mysterious, hospital-like atmosphere. Is it an orphanage? Only slowly do we realize that something far more sinister is at work here: these healthy children are being farmed for their body parts. Gradually, long before they reach adulthood, all their major organs, their kidneys, their corneas, and other vital organs will be taken from them, until they are given a "peaceful" death. We are told nothing about the kind of (future?) society that permits such hidden cruelty, but we can guess that denial is its primary characteristic. Still, I read many reviews, searching in vain for the obvious parallel. For it sounds familiar. Isn't this just what we do to farmed animals? They, too, are raised for their body parts. And yet, perhaps because it is so familiar, we do not even see this, or comment or think about it or appear to care.

Consider how difficult it has been for the greatest minds of Western culture to break free from what I like to call "pseudospeciation"—seeing the world in terms of "us" and "them." Aristotle's theory of natural slavery is a good example. Some men are born, he said, to be slaves. *Like animals*. They are both owned, are both property. According to Aristotle, this is because both animals and slaves lack *logos*, that is, speech, as opposed to noise.

A natural slave is a barbarian, and a barbarian does not speak Greek, he speaks a language of pure noises: *barbaros*. The etymology is onomatopoeic—people who do not speak, but make sounds like *blah blah blah*. This seems astounding coming from Aristotle, the father of modern science. Consider another bona fide founder of modern science, Charles Darwin. For Darwin, Fuegian Indians (as he described them in the tenth chapter of *The Voyage of the Beagle)* were not quite human. He saw them, rather, as the missing link between apes and humans. The proof is once again in their language: "The language of these people, according to our notions, scarcely deserves to be called articulate. Captain Cook has compared it to a man clearing his throat, but certainly no European ever cleared his throat with so many hoarse, guttural, and clicking sounds." But as Bruce Chatwin was later to point out, Darwin was unaware that a young Fuegian spoke as many words as Shakespeare ever wrote.[10]

Of course, our vision is much improved with hindsight. We are, to be sure, judging Aristotle and Darwin by our own more "enlightened" times. But this exercise in refusal to see commonality is a special kind of insensateness, which affects us all, always. Think what would have happened if another person with less condescension had "discovered" (odd word, if you think about it from their point of view) those Fuegian Indians. Maybe the world would be a better place now.

And so, all of us despair from time to time. How could we not? Henry Feingold, the historian, attempted to answer the question of why so few people during the Second World War did anything to help the Jews even when they knew Jews were being annihilated in an unprecedented way and in unprecedented numbers.[11] Why, he asks, were the Allies so indifferent? The Roosevelt administration offered no safe haven between the years 1938 and 1941, which it could easily have done. There were no threats of retribution. The Allies did not bomb the railroad lines leading to the concentration camps, and Britain proposed a White Paper limiting migration to Palestine at the worst moment of the refugee crisis.[12] The Pope failed to use his great moral power against the Nazis. The International Red Cross showed little daring in interpreting its role vis-à-vis the persecution of the Jews, even going so far in 1944 as to commend the Nazis for a model city near Prague built just for Jews known as Terezin. (Though it would not have taken much intelligence to see through the sham. Of the approximately 140,000 Jews sent there between 1941, when it opened, and 1945, when it was liberated by the Russians, only about 10 percent were still alive.) Single words or phrases are enough to conjure up similar scenes in our imagination, replete with horror and long-term denial: Gulag; Killing Fields; Srebrenica; Rwanda; Darfur.

The list is nearly endless. Feingold concludes: "Underlying the response of Jewish victims and witnesses at the time is an assumption about the world order so pervasive that we tend to forget that it is there at all. Jews believed then that there existed somewhere in the world, whether in the Oval Office or the Vatican or Downing Street, a spirit of civilization whose moral concern could be mobilized to save the Jews." That was a delusion. As one witness, Alexander Donat, put it: "We fell victims to our faith in mankind, our belief that humanity had set limits to the degradation and persecution of one's fellow man."[13] Is it, then, a historian of the Holocaust could ask, the least bit surprising that we eat animals without giving a second thought to the suffering that must be involved? It isn't. But perhaps an investigation of the underlying mechanisms for maintaining ignorance will be useful to understanding both cases.

Ernest Becker, the author of *The Denial of Death* (1973), may be right that the greatest denial is of our own inevitable death (best captured by the Catholic liturgical prayer known as the Office of the Dead, which contains the memorable line, *Timor mortis conturbat me*—fear of death disturbs me). In a book that I find dated by its incessant references to forgotten articles in the psychoanalytic literature, there are three incandescent pages (all it really takes) on the denial of death.

Becker's argument is that the fear of death is natural; universal across cultures; present in everyone; and the basic fear that influences all other fears. William James called death "the worm at the core" of man's pretensions to happiness. It could well be that deep depression is often but a disguised recognition of a looming end to every effort, every love, every thought. Equally important would be our denial of the significance of death to other members of our species. If we are horrified at the prospect that our life will, in a few short years, be over, we must bear in mind that this same fear and same horror affects all members of our species.

But if the denial of our own death is the example of the most profound form of denial, the *ur*-denial we might call it (one that may be necessary to continue living), then I would nominate another denial as possibly even more ubiquitous: denial of the deaths of other animals for our food. When this denial is brought to our attention, we call into play an entire series of clichés to justify killing animals for food. In fact, resorting to clichés is itself a first line of defense, a means of *not* thinking about the issues. Here is a partial list: (1) humans are omnivores; always have been, always will be. (2) It tastes good. (3) We need meat to live in a healthy manner. (4) Animals eat each other, so why shouldn't we? (5) Everyone does it. (6) I was raised that way. (7) To refuse to eat meat is to make yourself a social outcast.

There is a kernel of truth in all of these comments. I don't believe any of them, but I do understand their force. But there is this one big difference between death and killing animals: nobody disputes the denial of death. While we don't think about it every day, we are aware that we don't face it. Everyone is basically on the same page. Not so with animals. Why the difference? Well, for one thing, you can't do anything about death, but we can stop killing animals. What is amazing about all these defense mechanisms is how powerfully they work just below the surface of our awareness. Freud went so far as to say that all defense mechanisms work at the unconscious level. I don't believe that is true when it comes to killing animals: it is not that we don't know, but that we don't want to know, or we may even know that we are avoiding knowing. Avoidance is not unconscious; it is simply pushed to the back of the mind.

As we saw, nearly everyone in a recent survey said they cared about animal suffering. And just about everyone has, at some point in his or her life, wondered, Why am I eating this flesh? (Or am I being too sanguine here?) True, we have been doing so for thousands of years. True, too, that the retort so often heard from vegetarians is that we also had slavery for thousands of years. But in all fairness, there is a difference: slavery is universally condemned. It took a long time, but there is nobody left to defend it today.

There are, however, many reasonable, intelligent, and compassionate people who eat meat. Indeed, speaking from a purely statistical viewpoint, more compassionate people eat meat than do not. Although the arguments against slavery have been so compelling that all right-thinking people are now of one mind, this is obviously not true of vegetarianism. Why the disparity? For one thing, in the case of slavery, not everyone enjoyed or benefited from its practice. In fact, most people were far removed (which is not to say that people did not benefit from colonialism even when not directly involved). So the stake was less obviously personal. Eating meat or animal products is very personal. It is something some people do as often as twice every day, nearly every day of their lives. Asking somebody to give up something this familiar, this intimate, this central to his or her sense of self is inordinately hard. Consider some parallels for a moment: If we were urged, for good reasons, to stop driving, stop shopping, stop having sex, never read another newspaper, stop taking showers, stop using e-mail or drinking coffee, or abandon some of the other basic mainstays of our life, we would also object vociferously, or reach for a convenient defense mechanism.

* * *

DENIAL IN THE LARGEST SENSE in which we so often use it today is simply a specific psychic defense against an overwhelming reality. Or perhaps it is rather a manner of living, some might even say a technique for survival, indeed, *the* defense mechanism of the twenty-first century. The history of the word might shed some light on how it operates in our present reality. It is impossible to read any newspaper without either coming across the direct use of the word "denial" or the use of the concept on a daily basis. In fact, the only way to read the paper every day about all the hunger, misery, and atrocities in the world and still keep living the way we do is by taking refuge in denial.

Here are just a few recent news stories that refer to the concept of denial:

The New York Times on June 4, 2008, published an op-ed piece titled "The Science of Denial" about how the Bush administration has done everything possible to avoid addressing climate change, essentially by indulging itself in massive denial.

Neal Peirce in a recent *Seattle Times* column discussed the Southwestern and Southeastern droughts, as well as the Western "flame zone," where mega-fires are increasingly the norm, in order to reflect on our seemingly willful "myopia about the future" in the context of global warming.

Former Federal Reserve chairman Alan Greenspan says in his memoir: "I am saddened that it is politically inconvenient to acknowledge what everyone knows: The Iraq War is largely about oil."[14] "Politically inconvenient" is another euphemism for denial.

Why has the concept of denial moved to the forefront of our consciousness? Because it is, with its twin, "repression," at the very center of twentieth- and twenty-first-century psychology, just another way of saying with T. S. Eliot that "human kind / Cannot stand very much reality."

We all need protective devices. The defense mechanism has moved from being a device, related to castration fears and penis envy (two ideas which play little role in modern thinking, but which were central to Freud and his many followers until fairly recently), to assuming a much larger role in people's consciousness.

It has become something of a cliché to announce: "As a society, we are in massive denial about this," which can refer to just about anything the writer happens to believe and you may not. So, when it comes to how the meat that reaches our table got there, I like to believe that those who eat meat are in massive denial.

But is this truly a case of denial, or something less grand? We need to sort out our terminology here. Perhaps it is best to begin at the origin: Sigmund Freud. "Denial" is usually understood as the unconscious turning away from reality. That is, we are not aware that we are not facing up to something—denying that we are angry, for example, or that we are jealous. The reason that denial played such an important role in Freud's psychological theories is that for Freud, repression was the very cornerstone of psychoanalysis. No repression, no neurosis, no therapy, no profession. It was also, let me be the first to admit, an enormous step forward compared to the psychology Freud inherited in Vienna during his time. Michel Foucault in *The History of Sexuality* remarks that "repression operated as . . . an injunction to silence . . . an admission that there was nothing to say about such things, nothing to see, and nothing to know."[15] If this is true, then Freud's attempt to replace this kind of repression or denial with something closer to what we regard as modern-day common sense (or "insight," as the analysts like to call it) was surely revolutionary. What did Freud himself say?

In a paper entitled "Moral Responsibility for Dreams" (1925), Freud in one of the great throwaway lines in the history of psychology asks: "Must a man be held responsible for his own dreams?" This is followed by one of his more profound witticisms: "Whom else would you hold responsible?" "What else" Freud asks, "is one to do with them?" Unless the dream is inspired by alien spirits, it is a part of my own being, he insists. He is not referring to trivial content, either: he says explicitly that he is referring to dream content that he describes as "immoral, incestuous, perverse, murderous and sadistic lusts."[16]

Freud goes on to say that if we do not assume responsibility for our evil thoughts in a dream, then we "deny" both thought and action, for dreams contain both. Of course, Freud is not saying that we need to feel guilty for every ugly image in our dream life, but he does seem to be saying that we must recognize that these images come from us and that turning away from our own dreams is a psychological error. We must own the feelings and thoughts in our dreams as belonging to us, not to some external power. If we take nothing away from Freud's now much disputed dream theory but this idea, we have gained something.

In that same year, 1925, Freud returns to denial: "We know how children react to their first impressions of the absence of a penis [in a little girl]. They disavow the fact, and believe that they *do* see a penis."[17] We already see here the dilemma with which I began this chapter: one person's denial is another person's indifference. But who would not recognize a strong tendency to deny the face on our plate? If children react with disgust to their first encounter with the "other" at dinnertime, it is only because they have not yet been introduced to denial. It will come in short order.

In an unfinished "Outline of Psycho-Analysis," written in 1938, the year before he died, Freud explains that we attempt to detach ourselves from reality by the use of denial. It is here that Freud recognizes that denial is simply a part of repression in general. The reality of our food—that is, the reality that there is a face, indeed, a person there in the widest sense—must be repressed into our unconscious to allow us to go on eating. Vegans often report that they eat with a clear conscience for the first time in their lives when they refuse to consume any animal product.

According to Freud, we deny an idea and then repress the

feelings that accompany that idea. It is not clear from various accounts in his work whether both or only one of these actions is unconscious. But Freud has in mind important matters (beyond the penis), and that is why, I believe, the notion of denial has stayed with us from his time until the present, and why it is still useful, indeed, indispensable. The *feelings* that accompany eating another being are stronger—much stronger—than the accompanying thoughts. And it was Freud who first introduced us to the concept that feelings can be unconscious, even if this sounds like a contradiction. If the *idea* of eating a sentient being is conscious, the *feelings* of disgust, of horror, of guilt, may lie beneath our consciousness; in other words, we may well remain unaware that we have such feelings. Thus, a psychoanalysis of the act of eating is entirely possible; why is it missing?

Although Freud wrote about repression as the very cornerstone of psychoanalysis, the popularization of the concept is due to his daughter Anna Freud and her book *The Ego and the Mechanisms of Defense* (1933). The problem is that the popularization was not always based on the best information. Here is a dilemma: because her book was written to justify fantasy as opposed to reality, the work obscures the very topic it is meant to illuminate. In fact, in my opinion the book itself is an act of denial. Here is an example: Anna Freud has a section on infantile amnesia and the Oedipus complex. She wants to understand why, among all animal species, only the human infant falls in love with one or both of her parents. She writes: "The tiny human being is similar to a newborn animal in many respects, though worse off in some ways than the animal young. The latter are dependent on their mothers for only a short period, *at most a few weeks.* After that they evolve into independent creatures who can manage without further care."[18] In other words, because a girl is so dependent on her parents, she falls in love with them. Then, years later, she *imagines* that they have sexually abused her as a way of expressing her own erotic feelings for them, but without actually owning those feelings or even acknowledging them as real. In a stunning reversal, psychoanalysis claimed that the fantasy is true while the event is not. Here Anna Freud supports the standard view, prevailing for over a hundred years, that the account of abuse given by a woman is nothing more than a fantasy that derives from her many years of dependence.

This is where animals and denial enter the picture: apart from the major glaring error about the incidence and prevalence of child abuse in Freud's time (denial or ignorance or a combination of some as yet undiscovered source of not knowing?), Anna Freud's views of animals are misplaced. We now know that a nine-year-old elephant calf still spends half her time within five yards of her mother's side, five to six years after weaning. And some species of female whales will nurse their calves for as much as twenty-five years.

We train children from a young age by providing them with picture books about idyllic farms where the humans live in harmony with the animals and where we do not even obliquely refer to eating them. Children are given McNuggets or fish fingers to eat, which don't look like animals at all. The children are trained to disassociate. They eat in a kind of trance of denial. And when, one day, the veil drops and they become aware, for the first time, of what they are actually eating, they have been known to react with the same horror we reserve for cannibalism. After all, being carnivorous is just cannibalism extended to another species.

What should we call something that we deliberately choose not to know about? And what do we call it when an entire society takes this path? Consider slaughterhouses. They are remote from our homes and remote from our awareness. The "family farm" conveys an image of a good life for human and other animals alike. I doubt such a place ever existed anywhere except the human imagination. After all, how ideal could a place be when its raison d'être is to kill the occupants? And these occupants, the animals on the farm, did not choose to be there.

*   *   *

IF THESE THEORETICAL ARGUMENTS hold for the family farm, how much more so for factory farms? In chapter Two, I detailed the horrors of factory farming. As long ago as 1906, Upton Sinclair in his novel *The Jungle* wrote this searing passage: "The shriek was followed by another, louder and yet more agonizing, for once started upon that journey, the hog never came back. One by one the men hooked up the hogs and slit their throats. There was a line of hogs with squeals and lifeblood ebbing away. Until at last each vanished into a huge vat of boiling water (some still alive). The hogs were so innocent. They came so very trustingly. They were so very human in their protests. They had done nothing to deserve it."[19] Upton Sinclair was able to dispense with denial. Or rather, he must have had recourse to some other form of defense, for he continued to eat meat.

The horror of all this, and the absurdity, has been well captured by David Coats in his *Old MacDonald's Factory Farm*:

Isn't man an amazing animal? He kills wildlife—birds, kangaroos, deer, and all kinds of cats, coyotes, beavers, groundhogs, mice, foxes and dingoes—by the million in order to protect his domestic animals and their feed. Then he kills domestic animals by the billion and eats them. This in turn kills man by the million, because eating all those animals leads to degenerative—and fatal— health conditions like heart disease, kidney disease, and cancer. So then man tortures and kills millions more animals to look for cures for these diseases. Elsewhere, millions of other human beings are being killed by hunger and malnutrition because food they could eat is being used to fatten domestic animals.[20]

The kind of denial referred to above is the one we employ when it is in our interest, that is, when it leads to less guilt, less cognitive dissonance for us. We are concerned with our own suffering, not the animals' suffering. Denial is a convenient overarching mechanism. But we employ other defenses as well: most simply, we just avoid thinking about something. This surely explains some of the unpopularity of the person who insists we pay attention. We are all to some extent guilty here: I did not want to visit a slaughterhouse, for example, while writing this book. I am sure I would have learned something I could not learn from a book, but I assumed it would be so painful that I simply could not bring myself to witness it. Even the remarkably astute slogan: "We must not refuse to see with our eyes what they must endure with their bodies" was insufficient to persuade me.

We also distance ourselves, sometimes literally: "nimby,"

"not in my backyard," is surely a partial explanation for why it is illegal to kill a pig in your own yard within city limits (aside from health concerns). Few people, it would seem, want to be reminded that the pig is there for a reason and that reason involves slaughter. When we see animal suffering, some people simply walk away. For others, the distancing mechanism is more psychological: they never connect the face on their plate with a single animal's death. Food comes so disguised it often requires a conscious effort of the imagination to put the face back onto the meat.

When the underlying reality is particularly unpleasant, we minimize—numbing ourselves to the actual extent of the real story. We say, "Things can't possibly be as bad as people tell us," because we don't want them to be that bad. This is a form of magical thinking, a way of shutting our eyes. Surely if things were *that* bad, somebody would do something about it.

Withdrawal can take the form of removing our interest (another horror story about furry pets, yawn, yawn); or our wandering attention (understandably, since we are besieged by other equally pressing images of horror). Of course this reaction can be genuine: not everyone need become an activist in the cause to end animal suffering. And becoming a vegetarian may seem like going too far. In fact, it is not such a difficult step and could be legitimately seen as the very best form of activism.

Among my happiest memories of my twenty years of living in Berkeley are lunches at the upstairs café of Chez Panisse. It is considered by many to be America's finest restaurant, and is widely regarded as one of the best restaurants in the world. Alice Waters, the founder of Chez Panisse, along with her many other virtues, is responsible for making American eaters aware of the value of fresh, local, and organic food. Chez Panisse always has one vegetarian option (alas, rarely a vegan one), but I am glad to say that when I interviewed Alice Waters for this book, she told me that they are serving less and less meat there, and she feels this is compatible with good and healthy eating.

The classic psychological defense of "splitting" is another form of minimization. We can say that there are good farms and bad farms, and refuse to have anything to do with the latter. But it is still a defense mechanism, because we have split something in two that belongs as one: the animal who provides the food. Whether she comes from a good farm or a bad farm, her life is still taken from her long before she is ready. We rationalize her death by claiming that she had a good life and we are therefore guiltless and entitled to eat her.

Other times we use the awkward defense of "reversal." Instead of concerning ourselves with the suffering of the animals, we claim that it is we who are the ones who suffer by having to keep these animals fed and safe. We act put upon. We become testy. We make fun of animal rights activists. Sometimes we even make fun of the animals themselves. Notoriously, in the footage taken by the Humane Society of cruelty in slaughterhouses, we saw men mocking the animals they were torturing. (Humans do this to one another as well, as we know from Abu Ghraib and other torture centers.) The psychology of such behavior is worth an entire book. It is odd, when you think about it, that some people may hurt animals or other people as a way of dealing with their own terror of being hurt, or as a means of running away from their feelings of responsibility and guilt.

In severe cases, we can even dissociate. I think of children who understandably do not want to recognize the animal on their plate as the animal they were playing with earlier in the day. Children who raise animals for 4-H Clubs and have to see them led off to slaughter have a variety of reactions, many involving some kind of denial—whether by turning away and walking off or by believing the animal is going to a different home rather than to its death.[21] The psychologically healthy reaction of mourning the animal who was their friend is not encouraged by adults, primarily, I think, because it raises uncomfortable questions that are difficult for any adult to answer honestly. "Dad, I thought you raised me to show compassion to those more unfortunate than we are, or for those who suffer?" There is no good answer to this good-faith question.

You could argue over whether the denial is conscious, preconscious, or unconscious, or when it begins to shade into "disguisal" (a parallel to denial), as when we disguise what we eat either literally (in packaging) or with euphemisms—pork, bacon, or sausage, not pig; beef, steak, or hamburger, not cow; mutton, not sheep; venison, not deer; veal, not calf; and perhaps most notoriously, pâté de foie gras, not diseased goose liver. Temple Grandin, who designs slaughterhouses for the meat industry, goes so far as to speak of euthanasia, as if in murdering animals we are engaging in an act of mercy.

As with child sexual abuse, why did society take so long to acknowledge it? We don't really know, but slowly some things are becoming clear: children, much like animals, simply do not have equality when it comes to matters of this importance. Some of the men who abuse children do so simply because they can. Others are despots and tyrants in the only place they have total power: their homes. Some of the perpetrators are honored members of society—professors, judges, legislators. They hold great power outside the home. It is in their interest to have society regard these accusations as baseless lies. All of the perpetrators, whatever their rank in society, depend upon societal denial. In the parallel with factory farming, the benefit is even more widespread. Hence, the denial is even more firmly rooted. For not only does industry profit; so do all the consumers who eat meat. It is in nobody's interest to acknowledge the reality, the suffering, the horrible lives, and the savage deaths of the animals, except for the animals themselves and their few, but growing, number of advocates.

In the past, some animal scientists have engaged in a kind of willed ignorance, falsely claiming that animals feel nothing. This position became increasingly less tenable as more research became available, but there were still the objections that what animals feel may well be beyond our understanding, and hence outside the realm of our possible empathy. Yet one need not know all the details of what another person suffers to know that they *do* suffer. More and more, people are giving animals too the benefit of the doubt. Could we not at least maintain that while they feel pain (perhaps even more keenly than we do), they do not reflect about the pain, and hence avoid the kind of suffering that comes from contemplation, self-awareness, or memory? This is an unlikely source of comfort: we need only observe how dogs avoid a person who has been unkind to them to recognize that the memory of pain is critical to their very survival. Indeed, this *must* be true from an evolutionary standpoint for all animals.

If somebody chooses to eat meat, fish, or an animal product

without engaging in denial, there is little to be said. My job, as a writer, is finished the minute somebody engages with what I have written. My duty is to inform as accurately and as vividly as possible. It is only when the curtain of denial has been torn aside that we are free to make the choices each of us must make for ourselves.

We must remove ourselves from whatever blind hides our vision, and look out at the horizon to face what we see there. We owe animals no less. We also owe ourselves no less, it turns out. That is the topic of my last chapter.

A DAY IN THE LIFE
OF A VEGAN

*I don't understand why asking people to eat a well-
balanced vegetarian diet is considered drastic while it
is medically conservative to cut people open or put them
on powerful cholesterol-lowering drugs.*

—Dean Ornish, MD

WHAT YOU HAVE READ SO FAR MAY HAVE OPENED YOU
up to try eating less meat, becoming vegetarian, or even going
vegan. If it has, you have an extra reward: the choice you have
just made is of direct benefit to your own health.

Let me explain. I have had a recent disconcerting experience: a test showed I had parasites in my body. I took three
heavy-duty antiparasitics for ten days. I expected not to have
any reaction at all. Instead, I immediately felt nauseated, tired,
lethargic, uninterested in food (or sex), and only wanted to stay
in bed. This lasted for the entire duration of the treatment. I
am glad I did it. Not only because I rid myself of parasites;

more important, I gained sympathy for people who have to suffer these debilitating symptoms on a constant basis.

Poor health affects just about every one of us. I have been a blessed innocent. Vegetarian for most of my life, I have never really experienced illness. Now at sixty-eight, several years vegan, I find that I have never been healthier: I weigh less than I did at thirty; I am stronger than I was at forty; I have fewer colds or minor illnesses than at fifty; and in my entire life I have experienced no major illness of any kind. I have never, I am glad to say, been to a hospital except as a visitor. I exercise every day: lifting weights, running, swimming, kayaking, or riding my bike. I expect to live, illness-free, into my nineties. (Good thing I am not superstitious!)

So, knowing what it was like to feel badly all day has been illuminating. Of course, in this case, I knew the cause. But if I did not, I believe I would devote all my energy to finding out. I am not alone. Most people who feel ill would spend as much time as they could searching for a solution (although by that time, they may not have the necessary energy—better to search while we are still healthy). As you know, you could go online now and spend the next couple of months reading material. You could compile (as I have) a small medical library. And you might still be confused, because many of the experts so often contradict one another. But in fact the findings are not all that confusing; it just takes time to sort them out. By time, I mean it can take years to see what lasts and what falls away. Sometimes, even though science recognizes the errors, it can take the public considerably longer.

The Atkins Diet (and its progeny, the South Beach Diet and the Zone Diet, to name only two obvious culprits) has not disappeared from public interest (though it has from medical interest) in spite of the fact that the founder, the cardiologist Robert Atkins, developed cardiomyopathy and suffered cardiac arrest before he died in 2003 at seventy-three, and in 2005 the company filed for chapter 11. Atkins weighed over 200 pounds at the time of his death. Indeed, millions of Americans are still on carb-restrictive diets, eating meat, cheese, and eggs, and eschewing bread, pasta, and many fruits and vegetables.[1] So many diets are like this that there is an entire book-publishing industry specializing in books against particular diets, and even against the very idea of diets—though not nearly as large as the book publishing industry that specializes in diet books.

Why, then, do I say it is not all that confusing? Because if one looks at the science, and at the writers who are science-based and have nothing at stake, there does seem to be some sort of consensus: it is beneficial to eat more fruits and vegetables, fewer animal products (especially any kind of processed meat and some would add dairy), more whole grain rice and other cereals; to buy organic food whenever possible; to avoid refined or highly processed foods (such as white bread where the nutritious plant kernel, including the fiber-rich bran and the nutrient-rich germ, have been stripped away during milling), white rice equally denuded of its nutrients and vitamins, and white pasta; to avoid pastries and soft drinks; to drink filtered tap water; and to exercise every day. The standard professional organizations—the World Health Organization, the American Cancer Institute, the American Heart Association, and the American Dietetics Association—all find agreement here.

To some extent, the Food Guide Pyramids from unbiased scientific bodies demonstrate this received wisdom. But this is not the case for the mother of all food pyramids, the U.S. Department of Agriculture (USDA) Food Pyramid. It has been refined to MyPyramid, a personalized eating plan devised by USDA, but has been criticized by some leading experts as deeply flawed and heavily influenced by various food industries. The reason is surely because the panel that writes the dietary guidelines must include various experts from medicine, and that is fine. What is not so fine is that these experts are subject to intense lobbying from the National Dairy Council (some are paid consultants with obvious financial conflicts of interest; others have direct ties to the meat, dairy, and egg industry), the American Meat Institute, the Soft Drink Association, and other groups whose sole interest is the bottom line. As Marion Nestle, professor of nutrition and chair of the Department of Nutrition and Food Studies at New York University, put it: "Why do we have a milk group? Because we have a National Dairy Council. Why do we have a meat group? Because we have an extremely powerful meat lobby." How likely, then, is it that the very best science will turn up in the recommendations? Not very, for this is at bottom a political process.[2]

You can easily build your own pyramid, especially once you have finished reading this chapter. Or you could find some excellent ones online, for example, the one offered by the Physicians Committee for Responsible Medicine (www.pcrm.org). If you want to include some meat and dairy products, then the Harvard School of Public Health is probably a good source for you (http://www.hsph.harvard.edu/nutritionsource/what-should-you-eat/pyramid). If you want to move toward lowering the meat in your diet, a good summary (and guideline) is the statement by the world's largest association of nutrition professionals, the American Dietetic Association: "Vegetarian diets offer a number of nutritional benefits, including lower levels of saturated fat, cholesterol, and animal protein as well as higher levels of carbohydrates, fiber, magnesium, potassium, folate, and antioxidants such as vitamins C and E and phytochemicals. Vegetarians have been reported to have lower body mass indices than non-vegetarians, as well as lower rates of death from ischemic heart disease; vegetarians also show lower blood cholesterol levels; lower blood pressure; and lower rates of hypertension, type 2 diabetes, and prostate and colon cancer."[3]

Why am I so sure about the science? Because it seems that a consensus is building: the American Medical Association (hardly known for its progressive positions) and the America Dietetic Association (ditto) both agree that one can be perfectly healthy as a vegetarian or vegan (with certain caveats, i.e., taking a vitamin B-12 supplement). The American Heart Association and the American Cancer Society have endorsed plant-based diets to help prevent disease and satisfy nutritional requirements. After all, meat, dairy, and eggs contribute 100 percent of the cholesterol in all diets, and the great majority of the saturated fat, which, as my friend Michael Greger, MD, at the Humane Society of the United States, tells me has no known nutritional benefit and no minimum safe intake levels.

Animal products are the only foods that contain cholesterol (except for trace amounts in plant foods). There is some debate as to whether the saturated fat found in organic virgin coconut oil is good for you, as my wife Leila and I believe, or not, as Michael Greger maintains. Coconuts have been a staple of diets in South Asia for millennia and in my opinion there is

no purer drink in the world than pure young coconut water.[4]
As Marion Nestle put it: "There's no question that largely
vegetarian diets are as healthy as you can get. The evidence
is so strong and overwhelming and produced over such a long
period of time that it's no longer debatable." She adds, "My
number-one reason for eating a plant-rich diet is that it tastes
good. I feel deprived if my meal doesn't have lots of vegetables
in it."[5] Medical doctors and researchers who specialize in this
area and who have large and varied clinical practices are unani-
mous in praising the health benefits of what they call, reasonably, a whole foods, plant-based, or a plant-centered diet.[6]

As a longtime researcher and somebody familiar with
claims from one medical field (psychiatry), I am accustomed
to looking at evidence with what I hope is a lack of bias and
have found strong support for plant-based diets. Neal Barnard, the founder of the Physicians Committee for Responsible Medicine, told me after reading this chapter in draft form:
"I do think you can be quite confident that a meatless diet is
dramatically better than a diet including meat, particularly
from the standpoint of cardiovascular risk and cancer risk,
and that a dairy-free diet is a good way to reduce prostate
cancer risk, among other issues."[7] The benefits of a whole
grain diet are also increasingly recognized. Whole grains
contain fiber-rich bran and nutrient-rich germ. There is little doubt, now, that whole grains protect against cancer. A
2001 "meta-analysis" looking at all the studies done to date of
whole grains and cancer risk showed a protective association
for colorectal cancers; gastric cancer; hormone-related cancers
(breast, prostate, ovarian, and uterine); and pancreatic cancer.[8]
Research also shows benefits against coronary heart disease,

type 1 diabetes (related to cow's milk), multiple sclerosis, and other autoimmune diseases.[9]

Such a diet is also important for the healthy maintenance of our kidneys, bones, eyes, and brains.[10] But in the United States today, 98 percent of the wheat consumed is in the form of white flour. It's surprisingly easy to make the important changes we need to make to improve our health: a plant-centered diet— let's just call it vegan for short—consisting primarily of organic fruits and vegetables, along with unprocessed, unrefined, natural whole grains, the way we were designed to eat. Not just physicians but all of us should remember that the Hippocratic Oath, "Do no harm," extends to the environment surrounding us, to our animal cousins, and to our own precious bodies.

I have become persuaded that our concern should not only be illness but wellness. Many people become vegan because they were ill and learned that eliminating animal products can help them grow well again. But it is a good idea to give the food we eat serious thought *before* we become ill, so that we remain healthy. We need to differentiate between people who are seriously ill and turn to a plant-based diet to cure themselves, and those people who turn to a plant-based diet to remain healthy. The literature mostly deals with the former, but many people in the latter category eagerly follow this research. Nor is there any hard-and-fast line dividing the two approaches: after all, if a plant-based diet is capable of helping to prevent certain types of cancer, coronary artery disease, high blood pressure, diabetes, obesity, gallstones, kidney stones (that's why there is a rumor that NASA wants the next generation of astronauts to be vegetarian), kidney disease, and the many other diseases of affluence in the Western world, and there appears to be no downside, beyond social inconvenience, I can see no reason why anybody would not want to at least try this diet.

So, I do not feel I am missing out on much by becoming a vegan. Certainly, my health has improved immeasurably. I feel younger, lighter, and happier. And, as I said earlier, I am stronger now than I have ever been. For a man of sixty-eight to be able to bench-press 200 pounds is no small matter. Need I add that many of America's great athletes have been vegan? There was a time when to be vegetarian (never mind vegan) was considered "unmanly" and a sure sign of physical weakness. That is no longer the case. Carl Lewis, who won nine Olympic Gold Medals, was vegan, and Dave Scott, the six-time Ironman Champion, was a vegetarian during the 1980s, the time of his victories. One of the great tennis players of all time, Martina Navratilova, was and remains a vegan. One of the best ultramarathoners in the world, Scott Jurek, won the Athens-to-Sparta race (152 miles); he was only the second person in the history of the race to win it in less than twenty-three hours (he ran less than nine-minute miles the entire race) as a vegan. The first time he ran the Badwater Ultramarathon, Jurek shattered the course record by more than half an hour, and a full two hours ahead of his closest competitor. Not bad for a man who ate no animal products. The vegan author John Robbins is over sixty and still has a six-pack stomach.

Part of the reason people think of vegetarians or vegans as weak is because they are under a common misunderstanding about protein. According to the World Health Organization, a thirty-year-old requires about 21 grams of total protein and amino acids for every 1,000 calories. In fact, that amount is very easy to obtain from a normal vegan or vegetarian diet. If we look at any recognized chart giving the protein and amino acid contents of common foods (grams per 1,000 calories), we find that broccoli comes in at 106 grams, spinach at 129, lentils at 77, tofu at 106, soy milk at 83, and mung beans at 96 (all beans—black beans and pinto beans, peas and lentils both brown and green, are good, and of course whole grains are a great source of protein).[11] So, if you simply ate a diet containing some of these items, you would generously cover your protein requirement.

Many people believe that vegans and vegetarians cannot get all the nutrients they need from plant food and that meat is essential to any optimally healthy diet. With good attention to diet and with the exception of vitamin B-12 (about which more later), you can eat nutritiously. Broccoli, Brussels sprouts, leafy green vegetables like kale and collards, and carrots all contain calcium. Fruits are rich in fiber and vitamins. (All those books that talk about choosing a diet based on bright colors in fruits and vegetables are correct. The vivid colors are not just to delight our eye; they are signals of antioxidants and nutrients that are wonderfully healthy for you.)[12] Beans, peas, and lentils all contain fiber, protein, iron, calcium, zinc, and B vitamins. Grains are rich in fiber and complex carbohydrates. Tofu, made from soybean, also contains many of the nutrients found in meat and takes on the flavors of various healthy sauces better than any meat. Vegans don't have to worry about high cholesterol. I was present when Dr. Caldwell Esselstyn (who was for many years a renowned surgeon at the Cleveland Clinic) took the blood test for cholesterol—his LDL or low-density lipoprotein, known as "bad" cholesterol, was so low it did not show up on the machine at all!

My wife is a pediatrician who follows the technical research on nutrition very closely. She does so for three reasons. First, her medical specialty as a pediatrician is working with children on the autistic spectrum, including children with Asperger's syndrome, using a biomedical approach. This treatment avoids all psychiatric drugs, concentrating instead on changing the children's diets—taking them off gluten, and all dairy products (especially cow's milk), and giving them supplements such as zinc, iron, the B group of vitamins, magnesium, omega-3 fatty acids, and other naturally occurring substances. (What each child needs specifically is determined by taking standard blood tests to see what is missing in their bodies.) It has been her clinical experience to see amazing turnarounds: children who just a few months or even weeks earlier were banging their heads in desperation, unable to attend school, not speaking, and making almost no eye contact, are suddenly different people. She has received many letters of gratitude from the parents. Pediatricians have been reluctant to acknowledge the benefits of such a diet, hardly standard issue knowledge in medical school, but slowly more and more of them are coming around.

We have two young children of our own, and as a specialist in children's health, Leila feels an obligation to make certain that Ilan and Manu are eating food that is as healthy as possible. She knows that according to the American Dietetics Association, there is no need to introduce any meats, eggs, or dairy products into a toddler or child's diet (I explain below that the most famous U.S. pediatrician of all time, Benjamin Spock, recommended that kids be raised without any meat or dairy products). Well-planned vegan and vegetarian diets not only provide all the nutrients necessary to support growth; they also promote good health in childhood and start disease prevention early. Finally, Leila cares about our health since we are going to be responsible for our children for many years to come. She is especially eager to make certain that as I approach my seventies, I am vigorous, disease-free, and athletic enough to enjoy the kind of life people her age, twenty-five years younger than me, enjoy. I'm a lucky guy! Through Leila, I have access to the very latest and most reliable research on matters of diet and health. As a voracious reader, I have read widely in the literature and am eager to share what I have gleaned. So what I present here is not just my own idiosyncratic tidbits picked up over the years, but reliable research and evidence-based medical nutrition.

Having said that, I must add that just about everything I have to say in this chapter is plain common sense. You don't really need advanced degrees in biochemistry or medicine to know how to eat well and healthily. Why then, you may wonder, have not more people adopted the vegan way? That is a good question and not easy to answer, but I suspect it has something to do with exposure. You will remember my earlier comments in chapter Two on the lives animals lead and the value of informed consent. It applies here as well. You need the correct information before you can consent to what you put into your body. As a child, I was lucky that my mother, Diana (still with us at ninety), was what our more relaxed relatives called a health nut or a pure food fanatic. To my mind there is nothing nutty about health or fanatical about wanting pure food. But in the 1940s, such concerns were more unusual than they are today.

· · ·

SOME OF MY FONDEST MEMORIES have to do with going on Saturday with my mother and sister Linda to the Los Angeles Farmers Market. I especially liked getting a drink made of fresh coconut milk mixed with fresh carrot juice. Seeing all those fresh fruits and vegetables brought there by local farmers gave me a taste for outdoor markets that I have never lost. When I was fourteen we moved to Hawaii, and I still remember the many roadside stalls piled high with produce from the farms behind the roads. It was cheap, healthy, pesticide-free food. Today, wherever I am, I gravitate to outdoor markets. In France, Italy, Spain, and Germany, in fact, throughout most of Europe, such markets, which have always been abundant, are marvelous to visit even as a tourist. If this tradition was lost for some time in America, it is now making a mighty comeback. There are more and more green and farmers' markets throughout the States—some 4,300 at last count.

There is no controversy about my first rule of healthy eating: Eat as many fruits and vegetables as you possibly can. However many you eat now, eat more tomorrow. That is why I patronize these outdoor markets: you are benefitting your own health and you are supporting local farmers. My second rule is also not terribly controversial: in these markets, and everywhere else for that matter, I look first for the freshest organic produce. True, it costs more, but it tastes so much better and is so healthy for you. In order for farmers to use the term "organic," the farmer has to conform to strict federal guidelines.[13] The seeds must be organic, the soil must be waste- and pesticide-free; no chemical fertilizers are permitted; no toxins of any kind can be part of growing organic produce. When you think about genetically modified foods, and the unknown effects to our health from radiation, neurotoxins, hormones, and steroids, you can see why somebody who wanted to protect his or her family's health would choose, if they can afford it, organic.[14] The Organic Consumers Association has predicted that by 2020, most food in U.S grocery stores will be organic.

If you take the trouble to read the label on just about any commercial insecticide or herbicide (together called pesticides) in common use, you will be absolutely appalled. The scholars who write for the *Journal of Pesticide Reform* recognize that there is no such thing as a "safe" pesticide, because pesticides are by their very nature designed to kill.[15] Many are neurotoxins, obviously a serious issue for children and their growing brains. For example, 2,4-D—banned in Sweden since 1977—is a component of Agent Orange. Probably the most common herbicide used by lawn companies, it is present in many pesticides and fertilizers found in stores under names that sound harmless, such as granular weed and feed products, and is used in agricultural production. The Sierra Club of Canada published a report in 2005 insisting 2,4-D be discontinued. To investigate pesticide use further, go to the Web site of the Agency for Toxic Substances and Disease Registry of the U.S. Department of Health and Human Services to find out about what is commonly sprayed onto our foods.

My third rule is closely related to my previous two: Become a locavore, eating as close to the origin of the food itself as possible. I confess that I am a new convert here. Reading Gary Paul Nabhan's book *Coming Home to Eat* first alerted me to this issue.[18] Then my wife kept remarking how little sense it makes that so much of what we eat on a daily basis must travel so far because we insist on eating out of season, expecting strawberries in winter or buying grapes flown in from Chile.

In a planet overheating by the day, carrying food on planes or ships for vast distances to please jaded palates should stop.

Many people recognized this long ago. I am by no means a purist here (bananas are rarely local, but as I write this I am in Queensland, Australia, where they are grown locally, and let me tell you, there's nothing quite like a banana picked ripe off the plant). Few people are; but it is still a good rule of thumb. Think about what is in season, learn the variety that exists at that time in your local area, and then see if you can make these foods your everyday choices, with just a few exceptions for the sheer pleasure of it.

Alas, not everyone has access to outdoor markets, so my next advice is to visit your local small independent grocery. Nearly every town in America has a health food store with local produce, and food co-ops are not just a carryover from the sixties, but very much alive and thriving. We do well to patronize them as much for the employee benefits as for the fresh food. Much of this food is organic, too.

How can anyone resist Whole Foods? I say this not because John Mackey, the CEO, is nearly vegan, although I find that very appealing. Instead, it's because shopping in most Whole Foods stores is an aesthetically satisfying experience. They are often stunning to look at (one I know has a waterfall in the center of the market), and they offer such a seemingly limitless variety of food. They are attempting, too, to become more responsive to their communities, seeking out local farmers, opening their parking lots to farmers' markets on Sundays, and offering some farmers low-interest loans. I like the number of Fair Trade items (their dark chocolate bars are sublime— remember, dark chocolate is vegan, and because of the higher cocoa content, it is better for your health). You will discover a true *embarras de richesses* at Whole Foods, things you never knew existed (though you will have to forget my third rule to enjoy them), such as the unique mangosteen from Bali, kiwanos (horned melons from New Zealand—not delicious, but fun to look at), Ugli citrus fruit (definitely not beautiful but very tasty).

I think my absolute favorite food, as a good California boy, is either artichokes or avocadoes—how can you not love a fruit tree that in a single season can give you more than 2,000 tasty avocados? I love that you find so many different varieties of them at Whole Foods, including the baby variety of both. I am very lazy when it comes to making food, so I often go for the small drums of ready-made fresh guacamole, along with a tub of salsa (the more coriander it has, a wonder food, the better). I am always astonished at how the free market in America encourages growth you might never expect: ten different kinds of soy cheese; twenty different kinds of soy yogurt; one hundred different kinds of meat substitutes. Also, Mackey explained to me that Whole Foods is attempting to raise the bar on animal welfare, and have HSUS and PETA (People for the Ethical Treatment of Animals) consulting.

You could visit one of the reasonably priced Trader Joe's spreading nationally: they have some wonderful products (for my sake, try the tofu ravioli—you won't regret it), much of it organic and vegetarian, and they sell almost nothing with coloring or preservatives.

And today, even Wal-Mart has organic food (though this makes many people, including me, a bit nervous). Safeway, too, sells organic produce and a wide range of meat, cheese, butter, and yogurt substitutes. Soy milk is available everywhere, and brown rice milk made with chickpea protein is my new favorite dairy substitute, ideal for cereals, coffee, and tea.

I know what some of you are thinking. I have thought it myself: Whoa, wait a minute. Vegan, huh? Then how come you need to create a meat look-alike, or a yogurt look-alike, or a cheese look-alike? Why, I bet you even brag that people cannot tell the difference: give an omnivore a soy yogurt next to a milk yogurt and in a blind test, he can't even tell the difference, right? (Right!) It is true, there are substitutes for just about everything. But it is, I agree, just a tad odd that we make a Tofurkey, soy-based, to resemble the real bird, when what we want to get away from after all is the real bird. Why remind ourselves? Habit, I suppose—or some nostalgia for the foods of our childhood.[19] It will disappear, I predict, soon enough. I don't see the great harm. Meanwhile, tofu products and meat and cheese substitutes taste better and better every year, as the demand for them grows.

But there is a far more urgent issue. And a word of caution is necessary here. Vegans and vegetarians—well, actually, everyone—need to learn how to read labels so that they can learn what is actually in their food. It is no good going into a health food section of your local market and coming out with something you could have had in any fast food restaurant. The philosophy is not complicated, and requires no esoteric knowledge or skills. Once again, ordinary common sense is our best guide: food is best when it is less processed. You don't want artificial coloring in your food. You don't want tons of sugar (run when you see the words "corn syrup" in a list of ingredients) added to your drinks or food. You don't want any more salt (sodium) in your diet. (Like me, you probably already eat too much.)

I said it was all just common sense. But that is something of an exaggeration. These labels are written in such a way that we, the naive consumer, have no clue what they are talking about, and after a few tries basically give up and trust to their goodwill. Big mistake. These companies are not there for our health; they are interested in their own financial health. They use numbers, in my opinion because numbers are confusing; they don't carry any meaning for us. How are we to know that E621 refers to MSG (processed-free glumatic acid or monosodium glutamate), a substance that affects many people adversely? The Truth in Labeling Campaign has asked the Food and Drug Administration to require manufacturers to identify ingredients that contain monosodium glutamate by specifying MSG on a product's label—but so far without success.

Because labels are so hard to understand, you might want to choose a book that will teach you how to read a label. I heard a lovely, funny lecture by the nutrition researcher Jeff Novick, which is easily available for download on the Web, and you can find any number of sites that give simple instructions.[20] My wife never lets me bring anything into the house unless I assure her that I've read the label. It's hard, but I'm learning.

But how processed is processed, and how can we always know what is involved? Take soy. I practically live on tofu (always organic, non-GMO). I love it. Recently, I spent a few days at a wonderful animal sanctuary in Vacaville, California, Animal Place, with the founder, Kim Sturla, and the author and lawyer Jim Mason, both superb vegan cooks. They taught me how to marinate tofu in garlic, soy sauce, lemon, and olive oil for a few hours before frying it in a pan coated with extra virgin organic coconut oil—one of the healthiest oils you can use for cooking, primarily because it is heat-resistant (since it is saturated, it is not prone to oxidation and does not denaturate).[21] It is not hydrogenated, hence contains no trans fats. (Because of their link to heart disease, I suggest you take trans fats out of your diet. The New York City Board of Health has banned them entirely from all 20,000 restaurants in the city.)[22] Coconut oil also has a long shelf life and can be kept in the cupboard. I like the taste, too, since one can detect the coconut.

Soy is full of essential amino acids, a good source of B vitamins and of protein. John Robbins has pointed out that in 2000, the Nutrition Committee of the American Heart Association published a major statement in *Circulation*, officially recommending the inclusion of 25 grams or more of soy protein, with its associated phytochemicals intact (i.e., not in the form of an isolated soy protein supplement), in the daily diet as a means of promoting heart health. This recommendation is consistent with the FDA's recent ruling allowing soy protein products to carry the health claim: "25 grams/day of soy protein, as part of a diet low in saturated fat and cholesterol, may reduce the risk of heart disease."[23]

However, it is true that there is soy and there is soy. The more processed the soy, the less healthy. Organic tofu, eaten in moderation (hard for me), is never risky, and organic soy milk (always get the kind made from whole soy beans, not from powder or soy protein) contains protective phytochemicals that could well protect us against chronic diseases such as heart disease and osteoporosis. Miso (a potent probiotic), tempeh (fermented soy beancake with a nutty, mushroomlike taste), and the fermented soy sauce tamari (or shoyu), though processed and with a high salt content, really do make tofu and vegetables taste great. Edamame, the green immature vegetable soybean that is so tasty when boiled in salty water and eaten as a snack, isn't processed at all. However, isolated soy protein (SPI, the leftover byproduct of creating soy oil, often by using aluminum tanks), textured vegetable protein (TVP), and hydrolyzed soy protein, found in many of the "fake" meats served in Chinese restaurants and bought in supermarkets, taste great, and are a good source of protein, but they are not healthy. (On the other hand, no animal was harmed in the making of those products.) They are made from genetically modified commercial soy beans, not whole soybeans, are not fermented, and have none of the benefits of the more traditional soy products, since most of the nutrients have been processed out.

As usual, my wife said it best when she sent me off to our local supermarket the other day. Not entirely confident of my newly minted skills in label reading, she gave me a simple piece of advice, devised to avoid disaster: "Honey, stick to the perimeter." She wanted me to do most of my shopping on the outer circle, avoiding the center where the food containing the most processing is to be found. It is hard to resist the siren call of all those exotic-looking packages, but I'm convinced that she is right.

•   •   •

I AM NOT A GREAT COOK; I am not even a passionate amateur cook. So, depending on where I am, I love to let others do the cooking for me, especially if there is a really good vegetarian or vegan restaurant in the neighborhood. If you live in any of the large American cities—New York, Los Angeles, Chicago, Seattle, San Francisco—or even smaller towns like Portland, Santa Fe, or San Antonio, you have a choice of excellent restaurants serving or specializing in vegetarian or vegan food. Years ago I ate at Greens, in San Francisco, long before I was vegan, and I had no idea there were so many delicious dishes that contained no meat. It was an eye-opener then. Today, when you are in San Francisco, I suggest you go to Millennium. But bring along an omnivore friend who is a skeptic, and then observe the look on his face.

Even if you live where there are none of these restaurants, you will almost certainly have access to my favorite vegetarian food: burritos, to be found in all taquerias throughout America (though not, strangely enough, in Mexico). If you are lucky, they might even serve brown rice instead of white. Want to know why? Beriberi, caused by the lack of a minute quantity of the chemical thiamin, or vitamin B-1 in the diet, was considered a mysterious disease, with weakness, loss of feeling in the feet and legs, then swelling from fluid retention, and finally heart failure. In Javanese prisons, white rice was the staple food, and beriberi was the result. Chickens in Java when fed by chance on white rice lost the use of their legs (polyneuritis). Hmm. When fed brown rice, where the grain still contained its bran and germ, they returned to health. For thousands of years, rice was eaten in this natural state, which we call brown rice. When brown rice is polished to become white, it leeches all the nutrients out of a highly nutrient-rich food.[24]

Surprisingly, though, wherever in the world people make their main meal out of rice, they prefer white rice if available. Does it taste better? Is it a status symbol? Is it because it has a longer shelf life? It is certainly not in their best health interest, yet we find this to be the case in India, China, Japan, Vietnam, and Indonesia—in short, everywhere that rice is the staple food. White rice has only been available for the last few hundred years, beginning about 1700 in Japan. It simply never occurred even to the most observant that wealthy Japanese were falling ill, while the poor rickshaw boys who carried them around remained immune because of the different rice they routinely ate. The more milled, the more thoroughly washed, the less thiamin and the more disease. Chickens knew this instinctually (and will refuse white rice unless starving); humans had to learn it from chickens.

The taqueria with brown rice might also have whole wheat tortillas. Hey, what is this thing you have for brown? It's simple: part of the same philosophy I mentioned earlier, our main health squeeze: natural is best; the less processed the less refined, the better. True of rice, bread, tortillas, and especially true of sugar. Not many people have thought about it, but white sugar is awful stuff compared to natural sugar. Almost all the sugar we eat in the United States comes from sugarcane. The juice that is squeezed out of the tall grasslike plants is one of the most delicious-tasting substances there is. I drank it in India on a very hot day, with lime and ice, knowing full well that I would suffer almost immediately. I felt I had no choice: it was 100 degrees in the shade (in Pune) and the sight of this green liquid drink was irresistible. I had four glasses.

When this molasseslike liquid is heated, it turns into what we call natural sugar. To make it white, a common procedure is to use charred cow bones (which the large companies call, deceptively, "natural" charcoal; vegetable carbon is also frequently used) to filter the golden or darker cane sugar.[25] (There is an ion exchange system, used by at least one large company in the United States to give sugar its white color. The plant cost over $30 million to build, and most sugar producers consider it prohibitively expensive.) Organic sugar, by law, is not permitted to use bone char, so some vegetarians who use sugar choose organic sugar. I prefer the taste of Canadian organic maple syrup, but I use it somewhat reluctantly. It is vegan all right, but I read how the syrup is collected by giving the tree an actual wound that can take years to heal. (Maybe I am becoming more and more anthropomorphic in my old age, but this definitely makes me uncomfortable.) Stevia, made from the sweet leaves of a South American shrub that was widely used by the Guarani tribes of Paraguay and Brazil, is thirty to forty times sweeter than sugar. And there are any number of plant sweeteners in the health food stores these days, such as blue agave nectar from the Mexican lilylike succulent, and brown rice syrup, that are entirely vegan and very tasty. If you are making a protein shake with bananas and almonds, little tastes better than Moroccan Medjool dates.

By the way, what I have been writing about here explains why so many of the very best scientific studies are unable to show any great advantage for a vegan diet over a vegetarian diet or even one that contains meat. I am thinking in particular of the single largest and most respectable scientific study ever undertaken in this area, the European Prospective Investigation of Cancer (EPIC), which started in 1992. It involves over 500,000 people in the United Kingdom and eight other European countries, and looks at the relationship between diet, lifestyle, and cancer. Tim Key, one of the main researchers, could not find the differences we all expected. The problem is that a vegetarian or a vegan can be a junk food addict just as easily as a person who eats only at McDonald's. Eat too many vegan cupcakes, too much soy ice cream and yummy dark chocolate, and you will rapidly become obese—especially if you decide to forego walking in the hills, cycling to town, swimming in the ocean, or jogging around your neighborhood. You can eat only canned meat substitutes and find yourself getting weaker and weaker. You can avoid fresh fruits and vegetables and never think about omega-3 fatty acids, until you become ill. (You could smoke and drink, too.) You could drink five cups of coffee a day, and stay in your room reading vegan books all day without getting the vitamin D you need from the sun. You could say to hell with B-12, and take no supplements at all. You could do all these things, and become unhealthy pretty quickly.

If you participated in Tim Key's study, you would skew the results. In other words, you can be just as unhealthy as a vegan as you can as somebody who eats meat and pays no attention to his or her health. But if you eat vegan for your health as well as for the environment and the animals, then it is possible to say, from a purely scientific and nutritional point of view, that there is no healthier diet than a vegan one.

Well, almost. Recently, I have become aware of a further step. I am not referring to a raw food diet. I think raw food is great; I love it. I ate at Café Gratitude in Berkeley (there are now four of them) and it was terrific. Raw food diets and raw food restaurants are becoming increasingly popular. My wonderful friend Marti Kheel, co-founder of Feminists for Animal Rights, has been a raw foodist for many years and she looks half her age. She made me the most delicious breakfast I think I have ever tasted, with raw almonds, buckwheat, fruit, coconut flakes, and fresh almond milk she made herself—it was pure delight. She sings the praises of such a diet for one's health with great conviction and erudition. But I am not yet persuaded that from a purely health point of view it is superior to a good and varied vegan diet.

No, I was referring to a gluten-free diet. Let me explain. Many friends tell me they feel so invigorated and healthy when they eat little or no gluten (or at least, no wheat). We are not talking about people with celiac disease, who cannot tolerate gluten, nor even about the 80 percent of people suffering this disease who have not yet been diagnosed. I mean ordinary people who seem to have sensitivity to foods containing gluten. The theory behind this is simple: some foods with gluten tend to be much more highly processed and this system of processing came late in human development. Our immune systems are not yet in tune with it. Also, we eat too much wheat. We maybe have bread for breakfast, a sandwich at lunch, and wheat pasta for dinner. Even if whole meal, this is still in excess of what we need.

It made sense to try a gluten-free diet, and I decided I would do so for a few months to see if indeed I felt more energetic and healthier. At sixty-eight, there are a lot of odd-sounding ideas you are willing to try to feel younger. I liked the results; but to be honest, I could not really tell if I was just responding to the extra attention I was giving to eating (a version of the much maligned placebo effect) or whether it was simply the result of cutting out so much bread. I love good bread (staff of life, and so on), but I am sure it is not a healthy thing to eat in quantity. At the very least, it puts on weight. So I lost some weight, and I felt great. But there was a cost: being gluten-free takes a lot of attention. It's amazing how many foods contain gluten.

That made eating in restaurants hard, although not necessarily shopping, since so many supermarkets now have sections devoted to gluten-free foods because of the prevalence of gluten or wheat sensitivity.[26]

I have some respect for the notion that our bodies have not really had time to adjust to the way we eat today; that they are still attuned to eating as we did during our evolutionary history—before the advent of agriculture, only 10,000 years ago, and long before the Industrial Revolution of only 200 years ago—back when we were still hunter-gatherers. *The Paleolithic Prescription* popularized this view.[27] In many ways, the authors propose something similar to the Mediterranean diet: low fat, low cholesterol, lots of exercise, little alcohol, no smoking, and little caffeine.[28] So, although I am very partial to cereal and grains, Leila is wondering if we should not cut down on these as well.[29]

You can see the problem. Once you get started thinking about these things, it's hard to know where to stop! In fact, though, most of the difficulties appear to be such only because we are not used to eating in new ways. Most of us are naturally conservative when it comes to something as familiar as the way we eat. But the minute we make changes, and those changes become more familiar, *and* they bring benefits, it is surprising how easy it can be. Critics of any change like to say that we are so bombarded with contradictory dietary advice that we should simply ignore all of it and do as we have always done. This is ridiculous. If you have always eaten badly, nothing but unhealthy foods, clearly something needs to happen to awaken you. In November 2007, the World Cancer Research Fund conducted a study that used analysis from 7,000 cancer studies from around the world. Their conclusion was that bacon is such a cancer risk it should be avoided entirely. The study also suggested a link between red meat consumption and bowel cancer, and recommended that people should cut back their intake to 500 grams a week.[30]

We can develop a different strategy to novelty: Embrace it. This is how I responded when I read an important new article by the medical researcher Gary Fraser, showing that eating a handful of nuts every day can protect us from a great variety of illnesses.[31] I was delighted, and immediately added nuts to my diet. Why not? The science was sound, the nuts were great. My favorites are almonds (tamari roasted), walnuts, sunflower seeds, and pistachios, but I like all nuts, especially eaten with organic raisins.

•   •   •

LET ME ILLUSTRATE HOW EASY all of this can be by going through my typical day. I like to start with freshly squeezed organic orange juice, or, even better, a shake with fresh fruits. I take my supplements with it because Leila believes in them and has convinced me. Many of the physicians I respect do not recommend supplements, because they believe you should get everything you need from the food you eat. The one exception, for everyone on a vegan diet, is vitamin B-12. Vegetarians get B-12 from animal products such as cheese, milk, and eggs, and omnivores get it from meat. Vegans have to get it either through a supplement (including nutritional yeast), or by drinking soy or rice milk that has been fortified with the vitamin. The other supplement to add to a vegan diet is omega-3 fatty acids, which have gotten a lot of good press recently, and justly so: they boost the immune system, they can help reverse heart disease, they fight degenerative disease in general, and promote healthy skin. Leila loves them. She grinds up flax seeds. But flax seeds do not contain the long-chain omega-3 fatty acids DHA and EPA, which *are* found in wild salmon and other wild fish, but these fish are also a source of methyl mercury. So I take a supplement with algae-derived DHA, making it vegan.

I love cappuccino, and we have a machine to make it. But I have read enough literature to be skeptical of the health value of caffeine. I think it is best avoided (or at least no more than one coffee a day). Years ago I had some hypertension of the eye; when my optician in Berkeley told me to go off caffeine as an experiment, I did so, and got a lower reading immediately. But when I am working on a book, it is almost impossible for me not to have some organic black tea or a latte. I froth up the rice milk made with chickpeas, and it looks just like a professional latte. Friends, who gag at the idea, admit they can hardly tell it is not milk. Soy milk is fine, too, though I have a tendency to eat so much soy (mostly in the form of tofu) that I was glad to find a less fatty substitute that tastes great.

But milk makes a body feel good, you tell me. I don't think so. I never thought so. And then I read a fascinating little book called *Don't Drink Your Milk*, by one of the great pediatricians of America, the late Frank Oski, for many years professor and chair of the Department of Pediatrics at the Johns Hopkins University School of Medicine, physician-in-chief at the Johns Hopkins Children's Center, and no vegan, I might add.[32] Even Benjamin Spock, the most influential U.S. pediatrician of all time, wrote in the seventh edition of his *Baby & Child Care* (second only to the Bible in number of copies sold), the last edition before he died, that children should be raised without exposure to meat and dairy: "I no longer recommend dairy products after the age of 2 years. Other calcium sources offer many advantages that dairy products do not have."[33]

There is no argument I can think of for cow's milk. As Frank Oski put it, all the fortified versions of soy and rice milks contain more than enough calcium, as well as vitamin D and protein, and have advantages over dairy milk, for example, supplemental iron. Michael Greger says: "Soy milk is only deficient in blood pus, antibiotics, artery-clogging fat, and cholesterol." It is worth noting that in Japan before the introduction of dairy products, there was no osteoporosis at all. In fact, in general, the countries where people consume the least amount of dairy have the lowest rates of osteoporosis.

Back to my breakfast: If they are in season, I always buy a fresh papaya. I got used to eating them in Hawaii and have never lost the taste for this remarkable fruit, so rich in nutrients and antioxidants like beta carotene and vitamin C, as well as potassium. I usually have cooked organic oats with rice or soy milk. If I am not eating cooked oats, I will make a mixture of cereals, using brown rice puffs, corn puffs, and organic muesli, with fresh fruit. I use frozen organic mixed berries when fresh berries are not in season. I don't always succeed in avoiding the muesli made with honey, even though most vegans don't eat honey. Well, it is an animal product (even if a healthy and tasty one). Bees make it for themselves, not for us; we just rob the hive. And the large honey producers, the factory bee farms, often kill off the bees in winter because it is cheaper to replace them in spring than to feed them and keep them disease-free over the cold months. How's that for gratitude? Even though, from a philosophical point of view, I can see good reason to stay away from honey, it is still not high on my list of "cruel foods." On the days when I don't have cereal, hot or cold, for breakfast, I like to put organic almond butter on a slice of rye bread (no wheat!) with raspberry or another jam. Almond butter is tasty and healthy, too. As you can see, making breakfast is fast and easy.

My lunch is equally effortless. It has to be when you are as cooking-challenged as I am. I tend to make my favorite food in the world at least two or three times a week: a salad. I was fed salads my entire childhood, and it still remains the food I eat most often. I was glad to learn recently that there is new research showing enormous benefits to eating greens. I always add avocado, for me the very heart of a salad. Organic avocados really do taste better (they have that nutty flavor) than conventional ones. I include tomatoes and cucumber, using a mesclun mix, or any mix of baby lettuces. I add cilantro, because I love it. My dressing is made with extra virgin olive oil, lemon, sea salt, and fresh garlic, which I add to just about everything. I switch around by using good French Dijon mustard and balsamic vinegar. I often add a squirt of Bragg Liquid Aminos, derived from soy beans and purified water, a kind of (healthier?—alas it contains quite a bit of sodium) tamari sauce.

As for salt, I definitely eat more than I should. Most of the vegan health specialists I spoke to are opposed to any use of sodium, because it is the equivalent of using white sugar. But once you have tasted *fleur de sel,* which is now readily available in all large or specialized supermarkets, it is hard to avoid using it. Enough garlic (you can never use too much) can compensate. I eat my salad with bread, olives, and Italian artichoke hearts. (I could write a whole chapter on these; suffice it to say they are sublime. The best ones are tiny, and come from Italy in jars of olive oil—very expensive, so a rare treat.) This standard lunch is very quick to make—less than ten minutes—and very satisfying. I vary it with an avocado sandwich, basically the same meal on top of bread, with a nice olive or artichoke spread, topped with sun-dried tomatoes and fresh red onion. If I am feeling up to it and have a few more minutes, I might make falafel balls, hummus (I like anything made with chickpeas, as you can see), and a tahini sauce with olive oil, salt, and garlic.

I generally don't have dessert with lunch, but when fresh figs are in season, I eat them, as well as Fuyu persimmons that have become so popular recently. (Eaten like an apple, when they are hard, as opposed to the Hachiya, just as good, but the Hachiya ones need to be very soft, as soft as jelly basically. Imagine, there are 2,000 different varieties of persimmon!) Watermelon in season is also a favorite of our whole family, especially since once in Berkeley our boys saw a truck that had a sign on it: WATERMELON, MAGICAL FRUIT: YOU EAT IT, YOU DRINK IT, YOU WASH YOUR FACE IN IT. You can guess why I wish they'd never seen that sign.

If I'm feeling very lazy, I will stop by my local Korean sushi stand. I urged the vendor to try using brown rice. He was reluctant (it is not traditional), but brown rice double-avocado sushi has become his best-selling item. Remember to ask for the ginger that is not colored (nothing with artificial coloring is ever good). Whenever guests come to the beach for a meal, I always make a salad with the sushi, and they are amazed at how delicious vegan food can be.

Dinner is more challenging for me, but not for Leila. If I lived in California again, I would have, as I always did every single night, fresh artichokes, with a sauce of lemon, oil, and salt. Alas, there are rarely artichokes in Auckland (nearly reason enough to return to California). A simple meal I make is to put as many vegetables as I can—potato, garlic cloves, sweet potato, carrots, broccoli, and so on—into a large baking dish, sprinkle liberally with extra virgin olive oil and a bit of iodized salt, and then bake at a high temperature for 45 minutes or so. They are just as good a day later, so I always make plenty. I have also learned to make brown rice (described earlier). I fry a yellow onion in extra virgin organic coconut oil. I add fermented tamari sauce, cooked chickpeas, or cooked brown or green lentils.

When I lived in India, I learned to love raita, made of cucumbers and yogurt, so now I simply substitute soy yogurt, which improves all the time. I use a sweet mango chutney (Patak makes a great one) and my favorite Indian spice of all: Patak's mild (or medium) mango relish or mango pickle. I really could eat this dish every day—and when I'm alone in the house, I do. Leila grills fresh mushrooms to go with it, and grates up carrots and beet with a garlic sauce. Some friends brought us Trader Joe's rice pasta the other day, and the kids are now crazy for it. I also learned to make a mean gazpacho with fresh tomatoes, and I love it on summer evenings.

Soup, somebody explained to me, is foolproof: I put whatever vegetables are around in a pot of water with fried onions and garlic, all the nice spices I can find, and just let it cook for hours. One of my favorites, and definitely our young son Manu's favorite, starts with round rice-paper rolls (you can find them in any store that sells Chinese food—they are incredibly cheap). You simply drop them for a few seconds into a pan filled with warm water and they make the perfect soft pocket. Inside you put cilantro, bean sprouts, a bit of brown rice or brown rice noodles, tofu, grated carrots, bits of lettuce, and any other vegetables. Add some sweet chili sauce and wrap everything up. I will be amazed if any child does not like the result.

If this all sounds overly simple to you, I confess that I often reach for the phone—Indian takeout, Thai takeout—or call the local taqueria. But Leila objects: fresh is always better, healthier, less expensive, less hard on the environment, and better-tasting, she says. Leila also goes for complex dishes. I love it when she makes vegan lasagna, using soft tofu instead of mozzarella, and whole wheat pasta. She makes amazing polenta or couscous dishes and experiments with different curries. We use some of the vast resources on the Internet. There are great recipes available for free these days; you hardly need to buy a cookbook any longer, although there is a growing shelf of good vegan cookbooks, our personal favorite being *The Candle Café Cookbook*.[34]

· · ·

I HAVE ONLY SLOWLY COME to my current philosophy of food and eating. I was raised a vegetarian, and when I was in junior high school, I started an anti-hunting club. My friends and I would take our BB guns, go into the forests of the Hollywood Hills, and shoot above the tree branches to scare away the birds when we knew hunters were preparing to kill them. I remained a strict vegetarian until I went to Harvard. There, my best friend, the late Bimal Krishna Matilal, later a professor of Indian philosophy at Oxford, and I began the slippery slope of including tuna in our diet, because we were unprepared for living on our own (at the Center for the Study of World Religions) and too ignorant to engage in creative cooking. It was a devolution rather than evolution, and we both knew it at the time. Sooner or later, we vowed, we would return to our vegetarian roots.

That moment came for me when I did the research for my book *When Elephants Weep.* How could I see so clearly the deep emotional affinity between animals and humans, and still continue to eat the former? But I balked at taking the final step, at recognizing how much suffering goes into dairy and eggs. It was not until I did the research that went into *The Pig Who Sang to the Moon* that I saw there could be no further excuses. I finally took the plunge, and my wife and I are now vegans, along with one seven-year-old vegan son, Manu, and a twelve-year-old vegetarian son, Ilan.

The rules for what Jews, Christians, and Muslims can and cannot eat come from the Bible, the Koran, and the religious oral tradition. There is, if one searches hard enough, some rationale behind the various proscriptions, but mostly the answer is "because the Bible tells me so." I am not terribly sympathetic, except for "You shall not cook a kid in its mother's milk" (Ex. 23:19; Deut. 14:21), because I can understand the horror behind the observation. The other day I compared notes with a friend who is a Jewish neurosurgeon who keeps kosher

at home. We encountered some of the same difficulties in finding restaurants, in going to the homes of friends, attending
functions, or going to parties, but the reasons were different.
His choices were dictated not by his own feelings, observa-
tions, and research, but by what foods are certified as kosher
by the Rabbinate. The foods I eat depend on my own ethics, a
sense of what is healthy, and what I feel is good for our planet.
If somebody tried to modify my diet by the tenet of tradition,
I would be perplexed. Which tradition? There are so many. For
all the restrictions imposed by a vegan diet, I actually feel freer.
I can happily eat (and I do) at many ethnic restaurants—Thai,
Malaysian, Chinese, Mexican, Korean, and Japanese.

I do not even think of being vegan as a restriction at all;
rather, it is a shift. If somebody says to me, "Ah, but you can't
have a delicious cheesecake," my answer is that I can do so, but
I choose not to (or I eat the version with soy cream cheese). In
this sense, everyone is restricted in diet. "I'll pass on the sheep's
eyes, thank you very much." "Sorry, no bull testicles tonight for
me." "I won't try the chocolate ants, but thanks for thinking
of me." When we consider how many delicious, healthy vegetables exist, and how few omnivores consume them regularly,
we realize that becoming vegan opens up a whole new world of
taste and health, surely an advantage.

I don't think that eating small amounts of meat occasionally
is a risk to one's health. But it does not strike me, after spending considerable time with the literature on both sides, that it
is of any benefit, either. Given that each bite of meat involves
the killing of an animal who did not need to die, I think there
can be no question that striving to eat only plant-based foods
makes good sense. It is also important to recognize that eating

well is not about giving certain foods up so much as it is about eating fresh, healthy, local food, that is minimally processed and organic whenever possible. If it can come straight out of your own garden, all the better. Fresh air, exercise, sunshine, and plenty of fruits and vegetables is the default position for our species: we evolved to live this way.

NOTES

Introduction THE GOLD STANDARD IS GREEN

1. Norman and John Buffalo Mailer, *The Big Empty: Dialogues on Politics, Sex, God, Boxing, Morality, Myth, Poker and Bad Conscience in America* (New York: Avalon Books, 2006), p. 146.
2. Charles Darwin, *The Descent of Man and Selection in Relation to Sex,* Elibron Classics (Boston: Adamant Media Corporation, 2000; orig. pub. 1871), p. 597.
3. *Woman the Gatherer,* ed. Frances Dahlberg (New Haven, CT: Yale University Press, 1981). See esp. chap. 1 by Adrienne L. Zihlman, "Woman as Shapers of the Human Adaptation." A more recent book along similar lines is J. M. Adovasio, Olga Soffer, and Jake Page, *The Invisible Sex: Uncovering the True Roles of Women in Prehistory* (New York: HarperCollins, 2007).
4. See Richard Leakey, *The Origin of Humankind* (New York: HarperCollins, 1996).
5. Donna Hart and Robert W. Sussman, *Man the Hunted: Primates, Predators, and Human Evolution* (New York: Westview Press, 2005).
6. For more information, see the section on meat eating in Richard W. Bulliet, *Hunters, Herders, and Hamburgers: The Past and Future of Human-Animal Relationships* (New York: Columbia University Press, 2005), pp. 54–63.

7. J. P. Strong, ed., *Atherosclerosis in Primates* (Basel: Karger, 1976). See also J. P. Strong, D. A. Eggen, and S. K. Jirge, "Atherosclerotic lesions in baboons by feeding an atherogenic diet for four years," *Experimental and Molecular Pathology*, 24 (1976), pp. 320–32.

8. A useful summary of all the arguments can be found at http:// www.naturalhub.com/. See also Lewis Binford, *In Pursuit of the Past: Decoding the Archeological Record* (Berkeley: University of California Press, 2002). A good recent critique of "the man as carnivore" theory is J. F. O'Connell, K. Hawkes, and K. D. Lupo, "Male strategies and Plio-Pleistocene archeology," *Journal of Human Evolution*, 43 (2002), pp. 831–72. See too the excellent summary of the issues in Kristen Hawkes, J. F. O'Connell, and Nicholas G. Blurton Jones, "Human Life Histories: Primate Trade-Offs, Grandmothering, Socioecology, and the Fossil Record," in *Primate Life Histories and Socioecology*, ed. Peter M. Kappeler and Michael E. Pereira (Chicago: University of Chicago Press, 2003), pp. 204–27. I am grateful to Professor Hawkes for providing me with these sources.

9. It is not entirely clear how often this happens, nor how much of what Jane Goodall saw could have been the result of the somewhat artificial conditions of her research station, where the animals were often given food.

10. Oswald Spengler, *The Decline of the West,* trans. Charles Francis Atkinson, abridged edn. (New York: Vintage, 2006).

11. Some might dispute that we really have free choice when it comes to what we eat. N. W. Pirie, in *Food Resources Conventional and Novel* (New York: Penguin, 1969), says: "People have never had freedom of choice in nutrition. With the best of intentions their parents misled them in their youth and, with more questionable motives, advertisers misled them in adult life."

12. See Shannen L. Robson, "Breast milk, diet, and large human brains," *Current Anthropology*, vol. 45, no. 3 (June 2004), pp. 419–42.

13. Gary L. Francione, *Introduction to Animal Rights: Your Child or the Dog?* (Philadelphia: Temple University Press, 2000), p. 16.

14. George Orwell, *The Road to Wigan Pier* (1937; The Complete Works of George Orwell, 2003), chap. 1, http://www.george-orwell .org/The_Road_to_Wigan_Pier/index.html (emphasis added).

15. For books on Jainism in general, see Padmanabh S. Jaini, *The Jaina*

Path of Purification (Berkeley: University of California Press, 1979); Paul Dundas, *The Jains* (New York: Routledge, 2002); John E. Cort, *Jains in the World: Religious Values and Ideology in India* (New York: Oxford University Press, 2001); and Michael Tobias, *Life Force: The World of Jainism* (Fremont, CA: Jain Publishing Co., 1991). In "Beitraege zur Geschichte von Vegetarismus und Rinderverehrung in Indien" (published in *Abhandlungen der Geistes-und sozialwis-senschaftlichen Klasse,* no. 6 [Wiesbaden, Ger.: Franz Steiner Verlag, 1961], pp. 559–625), possibly the best article about the history of vegetarianism in ancient India, Ludwig Alsdorf quotes an interesting and unusual verse from the ancient (500 BC) Hindu text known as *Manavadharmasastra (The Laws of Manu,* verse 51; cited by Alsdorf on page 577). It says that the following people are equally to blame for the killing of an animal: the butcher of the animal, the person who sells the meat, the person who buys the meat, the cook who prepares it, the waiter who serves it, and finally the consumer who eats the meat.

16. For a translation of this text, see Olle Qvarnstrom, *The Yogasastra of Hemachandra: A Twelfth Century Handbook on Svetambara Jainism,* Harvard Oriental Series, vol. 60 (Cambridge, MA: Harvard University Press, 2002).

Chapter One THE ONLY WORLD WE HAVE

1. The editors of *World Watch* magazine, published by the Worldwatch Institute on June 15, 2004 (vol. 17, no. 4). Aside from the books and articles directly cited, the following could be consulted with profit: Vaclav Smil, *Feeding the World: A Challenge for the Twenty-First Century* (Cambridge, MA: MIT Press, 2000). See too his article, "Eating meat: Evolution, patterns, and consequences," *Population Development Review,* 28 (2002), available for download as a PDF file at http://home.cc.umanitoba.ca/~vsmil/publications_pdf.html. Also Worldwatch Institute, "Meat: Now it's not personal." *World Watch* (July–August, 2004). Valuable is chap. 16, "Are Vegans Better for the Environment?" in Peter Singer and Jim Mason, *The Way We Eat: Why Our Food Choices Matter* (New York: Rodale Press,

2006). And finally, *The Fatal Harvest Reader: The Tragedy of Industrial Agriculture,* ed. Andrew Kimbrell (Washington, DC: Island Press, 2002).

2. Richard Lewontin, Steven Rose, and Leon J. Kamin, *Not in Our Genes* (New York: Pantheon, 1985), p. 100.

3. See www.peclimate.org, and also the fine article by Anna Lappé, "There's a Homegrown Way to Address Climate Change," *Seattle Post-Intelligencer,* March 13, 2008; also available from Common Dreams News Center.

4. See www.organicagcentre.ca/ResearchDatabase/res_livestock_cow methane.asp.

5. Global Forum for Health Research Forum 8, Mexico City, November 2004; Danielle Nierenberg and Leah Garcés of Worldwatch Institute; and World Society for the Protection of Animals, "Industrial Animal Agriculture—The Next Global Health Crisis?"

6. The National Resources Defense Council gives all the alarming figures, easily accessible at www.nrdc.org.

7. The technical details with statistics, figures, and calculations can be found on the Web site of the EPA: www.epa.org.

8. Margaret McCasland, Nancy M. Trautmann, and Keith S. Porter of the Center for Environmental Research, and Robert J. Wagenet of the Department of Agronomy at Cornell University, "Nitrate: Health effects in drinking water." Available at http://pmep.cce.cor nell.edu/facts-slides-self/facts/nit-heef-grw85.html.

9. According to Daniel Grossman of NPR's *Living on Earth,* "It was the largest outbreak of waterborne disease in modern American history."

10. See Robbin Marks's useful *Cesspools of Shame: How Factory Farm Lagoons and Sprayfields Threaten Environmental and Public Health,* Natural Resources Defense Council and the Clean Water Network (July 2001).

11. The executive summary of "Spills and Kills: Manure Pollution and America's Livestock Feedlots"—a report by the Clean Water Network, the Izaak Walton League of America, and the Natural Resources Defense Council in August 2000—concludes that "spills and dumping of manure and other waste products occurred over one thousand times at feedlots in the ten surveyed states between

1995 and 1998. Over 13 million fish were killed in more than two hundred of the spills." See http://www.cleanwaternetwork.org.

12. "NOAA Forecasts Larger Than Normal 'Dead Zone' for Gulf This Summer," *NOAA News Online,* July 24, 2006. Hypoxia, or reduced oxygen levels, in the Gulf of Mexico due to rising nutrient loads, especially nitrogen (think manure, fertilizer), makes it the second largest dead zone in the world. Fish flee, and any sea life that cannot move away eventually dies.

13. Consumers Union SWRO, "Animal Factories: Pollution and Health Threats to Rural Texas" (May 2000). See too G. Hamscher, et al., "Antibiotics in dust originating from a pig-fattening farm: A new source of health hazard for farmers?" *Environmental Health Perspectives,* vol. 108, no. 3 (2000), pp. 233–38. See also M. Mellon, et al., *Hogging It: Estimates of Antimicrobial Abuse in Livestock* (Cambridge, MA: Union of Concerned Scientists, 2001). Finally, D. Cole, et al., "Concentrated swine feeding operations and public health: A review of occupational and community health effects," *Environmental Health Perspectives,* 113 (2005), pp. 137–42.

14. For scientific facts on air pollution, see http://www.greenfacts.org/air-pollution/particulate-matter-pm/index.htm.

15. Polly Walker, et al., "Public health implications of meat production and consumption," *Public Health Nutrition,* vol. 8, no. 4 (2005), pp. 348–56.

16. Bonnie Powell puts it well: "The meat industry in this country is broken from start to finish. We take ruminants and feed them grain their stomachs weren't designed to eat, treating them like garbage disposals for our industrial leftovers; implant steroids so they'll grow faster; feed them antibiotics so they can survive the poor diets and crowded feedlot conditions; then ship them to slaughterhouses where they are killed and processed at speeds that practically beg for bacterial contamination and worker injuries." Found at http://www.commondreams.org/archive/2008/02/18/7121/.

17. Enza R. Campagnolo, et al., "Antimicrobial residues in animal waste and water resources proximal to large-scale swine and poultry feeding operations," *Science of the Total Environment,* 299 (2002), pp. 89–95.

18. See T. Colburn, et al., "Developmental effects of endocrine disrupting chemical on wildlife and humans," *Environmental Health Perspectives,* 101 (1993), pp. 378–84.

19. P. Sampat, "Groundwater shock: The polluting of the world's major freshwater stores," *World Watch* (January–February 2000), pp. 10–22.

20. T. Kendall, et al., "A control study of the physical and mental health of residents living near a large-scale swine operation," *Journal of Agricultural Safety and Health,* 3 (1997), pp. 13–26. See also S. Schiffman, et al., "The effect of environmental odors emanating from commercial swine operations on the mood of nearby residents," *Brain Research Bulletin,* 37 (1995), pp. 369–75.

21. Quoted in the fine new book by Dr. Michael Greger, *Bird Flu: A Virus of Our Own Hatching* (New York: Lantern Books, 2006), p. 93.

22. Ibid., p. 358.

23. A. J. McMichael, "Environmental and social influences on emerging infectious diseases: Past, present, and future," *Philosophical Transactions of the Royal Society of London,* 359 (2004), pp. 1049–58. See also S. Schrag and P. Wiener, "Emerging infectious disease: What are the relative roles of ecology and evolution?" *Trends in Ecology and Evolution,* 10 (1995), pp. 319–24.

24. As determined by a 1996 University of California at Davis study found on the Web at http://vric.ucdavis.edu/issues/bulletinboard/counties/riverside/leaflettuce.pdf.

25. I have just finished reading a remarkable book by Maude Barlow (author of *Blue Gold*) called *Blue Covenant: The Global Water Crisis and the Coming Battle for the Right to Water* (New York: The New Press, 2007). Barlow, a recipient of Sweden's Right Livelihood Award (the "Alternative Nobel"), is founder of the Blue Planet Project (www.blueplanetproject.net), which demands water justice based on every individual's right to water. I highly recommend this book to everyone interested in our environment and the problems discussed in this section.

26. R. Goodland and D. Pimentel, "Sustainability and Integrity in the Agriculture Sector," in D. Pimentel, L. Westra, and R. F. Noss, eds., *Ecological Integrity: Integrating Environment, Conservation and Health* (Washington, DC: Island Press, 2000).

27. David Pimentel, *Journal of Clinical Nutrition,* 2003, 78 (suppl.), 660s-3S. The most reliable and widely accepted water estimate to produce a pound of beef is the figure of 2,500 gallons/pound, but the figure is sometimes as high as 12,009 gallons per pound (by contrast, potatoes take 60 gallons per pound, wheat 108, corn 168, rice 229, soybeans 240). *Newsweek* once put it more graphically by saying that "the water that goes into a 1,000 pound steer would float a destroyer." A kilogram of beef causes more greenhouse gas and other pollution than driving for three hours while leaving all the lights on at home, a recent Japanese study has found. There is some controversy about the exact figures, but even the most conservative estimates are still strongly in favor of growing plants directly for human consumption.

28. Derek M. Brown, "Pfiesteria: How the meat industry destroys waterways," *Good Medicine* magazine, Physicians Committee for Responsible Medicine, vol. 7, no. 1 (Winter 1998), available at http://www.pcrm.org/magazine/GM98Winter/GM98Win1.html.

29. T. Shields and J. Warwick, MD, "Counties Awash in Pollution-Causing Nutrients," *The Washington Post,* October 3, 1997. See too D. L. Corell, T. E. Jordan, and D. E. Weller, "Livestock and Pasture Land Effects on the Water Quality of Chesapeake Bay Watershed Streams," in K. Steele, ed., *Animal Waste and Land-Water Interface* (New York: Lewis Publishers, 1995), pp. 107–17.

30. J. M. Burkholder and H. B. Glasgow, "Insidious effects of toxic estuarine dinoflagellate on fish survival and human health," *Journal of Toxicology and Environmental Health,* 46 (1995), pp. 501–22. See also Corell, et al., "Livestock and Pasture Land Effects," pp. 107–17.

31. See the Sierra Club, December 27, 2001: "Animal factory manure discharge tests at 1,900 times state maximum *E. coli* levels," cited in the 2005 booklet *Industrial Animal Agriculture: The Next Global Health Crisis?* World Society for the Protection of Animals (WSPA), written by Danielle Nierenberg of Worldwatch Institute and Leah Garcés of WSPA.

32. http://www.waterquality.crc.org.au/hsarch/HS22a.htm; there were also six deaths—see http://www.sierraclub.org/factoryfarms/resources/comphealthstudies.pdf.

33. Quoted in Walker, "Public health implications of meat production and consumption," p. 350.

34. David Pimentel, et al., "Water resources: Agriculture, the environment, and society. An assessment of the status of water resources," *BioScience,* vol. 47, no. 2 (February 1997).

35. In all fairness it must be acknowledged that according to no less an authority than Lester Brown, "It is widely assumed that moving from animal protein to high-quality proteins from plant sources, such as beans or tofu made from soybeans, is more land-efficient. But this is not always the case. For example, as noted earlier, with poultry it takes just over 2 kilograms of grain to produce 1 kilogram of additional live weight. For catfish, it is less than 2 kilograms of grain per kilogram of weight gain. An acre of land in Iowa can thus produce 140 bushels of corn or 35 bushels of the much lower-yielding soybean. Feeding the corn to chickens or catfish can yield more high-quality protein than growing soybeans and consuming them directly, say as tofu" (Lester R. Brown: *Plan B 2.0: Rescuing a Planet Under Stress and a Civilization in Trouble* (New York: W. W. Norton, 2006), pp. 178–79).

This is a valid point. And indeed, chicken is quickly becoming the meat of choice for many people concerned with the health of the environment, perhaps even because of the influence of Brown. But we must also take into account the fact that what chickens are being fed by commercial firms bears almost no resemblance to their natural food, as people who buy their eggs from organic local farmers know well. And there are many problems with aquaculture (discussed in chapter 3). The ethical concerns are left out of the equation as well, but that is really not Brown's point, and I think we have to concede that he makes good sense. If our *only* concern were efficiency of production, he might well be entirely correct. But if we factor in human health and the health of the chickens, we could still make a case for tofu. Moreover, David Pimentel, who is not a vegetarian, notes, "Animal agriculture is a leading consumer of water resources in the United States. Grain-fed beef production takes 100,000 liters of water for every kilogram of food. Raising broiler chickens takes 3,500 liters of water to make a kilogram of meat. In comparison, soybean production uses 2,000 liters for kilogram of food produced; rice, 1,912; wheat, 900; and potatoes, 500 liters." This data is from 1997, and the figure of 43,000 I quoted above seems to be the latest figure.

36. Retrieved at http://www.nytimes.com/2007/07/31/opinion/31tue4 .html. Note, too, the quote from Philip Fradkin, of the National Audubon Society, certainly not a pro-vegetarian organization: "The impact of countless hooves and mouths over the years has done more to alter the type of vegetation and land forms of the West than all the water projects, strip mines, power plants, freeways, and subdivision developments combined"—Editorial from *The New York Times* (July 31, 2007).

37. David Pimentel, "Livestock production and energy use," in R. Matsumura, ed., *Encyclopedia of Energy*, 6 vols. (San Diego, CA: Elsevier, 2004), pp. 671–76.

38. Lester R. Brown, *Plan B 3. 0: Mobilizing to Save Civilization*, updated and expanded edn. (New York: W. W. Norton, 2008), p. 173.

39. Another significant problem of monoculture and monocrops is soil degradation—"For each pound of red meat, poultry, eggs and milk, farm fields lose about five pounds of prime dirt." See the outstanding article by Joan Dye Gussow, from the Program in Nutrition at Columbia University, "Ecology and vegetarian considerations: Does environmental responsibility demand the elimination of livestock?" *American Journal of Clinical Nutrition*, 59 (1994) (suppl): 1110S-62.

40. Plants for a Future is a vegan-organic project in Cornwall that researches edible and otherwise useful plant crops for sustainable cultivation. Their online database currently features over 7,300 such species that can be grown within the United Kingdom—see www .pfaf.org. The Vegan Organic Network also has useful information on these issues at www.veganorganic.net.

41. We have to remember that the soil on U.S. cropland is eroding ten times faster than sustainable soil replacement. David Pimentel has calculated that it takes 500 years to replace one inch of lost soil—David and Marcia Pimentel, "Land, water and energy versus the ideal U.S population." See www.pg.org/forum_series/ forum0205.html.

42. David Pimentel, "Population and its discontents," *World Watch* magazine (September–October 2004).

43. Penny Livingston, director of the Permaculture Institute of Northern California (http://www.ecotecture.com/library_eco/interviews/livingston_p_2a.html), says that you could feed this many people on half an acre, "because you start thinking in terms of cubic feet instead of square feet. You can start trellising, for example. One of the methods of increasing your production is going vertical. It is called 'stacking.' Permaculturalists think in terms of multiple canopies. . . . You have all these different layers, then you pattern your garden to allow the sun to come in as you need it. So you might create little meadow areas where you can grow cantaloupes or tomatoes or something that needs really hot sun."

44. See Jules Pretty's fine book *Agri-Culture: Reconnecting People, Land and Nature* (Sterling, VA: Earthscan, 2002). Three other books that I have found useful are Dana L. Jackson and Laura L. Jackson, eds., *The Farm as Natural Habitat: Reconnecting Food Systems with Ecosystems* (Washington, DC: Island Press, 2002); Daniel Imhoff and Jo Ann Baumgartner, eds., *Farming and the Fate of Wild Nature: Essays in Conservation-Based Agriculture* (Healdsburg, CA: Watershed Media, 2006); and Jules Pretty, ed., *The Earthscan Reader in Sustainable Agriculture* (Sterling, VA: Earthscan, 2005).

But I believe it all began in 1940, with the publication of *An Agricultural Testament* by Sir Albert Howard, who has been credited with the "invention" of organic soil preservation (London: Oxford University Press, 1940). Who can disagree with his conclusion (p. 224): "The prophet is always at the mercy of events; nevertheless, I venture to conclude this book with the forecast that at least half the illnesses of mankind will disappear once our food supplies are raised from fertile soil and consumed in a fresh condition"? Nor can I leave unmentioned the remarkable work by Masanobu Fukuoka, who used natural farming methods including the incorporation of weeds to get greater yields than any of the more conventional chemically based methods: See his *The One-Straw Revolution: An Introduction to Natural Farming* (Emmaus, PA: Rodale Press, 1978). Fukuoka speaks of young people living in his orchard who eat brown rice and unpolished barley, millet, and buckwheat, together with the seasonal plants and semiwild vegetables, and who are remarkably healthy. He adds: "If 22 bushels (1,300 pounds) of rice and 22 bushels of winter grain are harvested from a quarter acre field such as one of these, then the field will support five to ten people each investing an average of less than one hour of labor per day. But if the field were turned over to pasturage, or if the grain were fed to cattle, only one person could be supported per quarter acre" (p. 103). See the splendid interview with him about applying natural farming techniques in Africa, "Greening the desert," *Sustainable Habitat* (Autumn 1986), p. 37. Jules Dervaes, a permaculture gardener in Los Angeles, has transformed a 1/5-acre city lot into a permaculture garden of Eden. Growing over 350 different edible and useful plants, he and his family produce 3 tons of organic fruits and vegetables annually on their small lot, as reported in the *Los Angeles Times* (www .worldchanging.com).

45. Apart from the Pretty book, several sites show similar results. See, e.g., http://www.fao.org/docrep/006/Y3951E/y3951e08.htm, showcasing eleven positive cases.

46. See Jules N. Pretty: *Regenerating Agriculture* (Washington, DC: Joseph Henry Press, 1995). Also his *The Earthscan Reader in Sustainable Agriculture*. For an interview with Peter Kenmore, see http://www.learner.org/channel/courses/envsci/scientist/transcripts/ kenmore.html.

47. Pretty, *Agri-Culture,* p. 93.

48. "Smithsonian Researchers Show Amazonian Deforestation Accelerating," *Science Daily,* January 15, 2002.

49. The most important document here is the widely cited 400-page report *Livestock's Long Shadow,* which was released in November 2006 by the United Nations Food and Agriculture Organization. It can be found on many places on the Web by simply typing in the title.

50. These are the words of Sir Nicolas Stern from the Stern Report of 2006. See too Daniel Howden, "Deforestation: The Hidden Cause of Global Warming," in *The Independent,* May 14, 2007.

51. For example, Julian Borger, "Feed The World? We Are Fighting a Losing Battle, UN Admits," in *The Guardian,* February 26, 2008, points out that India and China are demanding more and more

meat, which, because it yields greater profits, takes up land normally used for fruits and vegetables.

52. 2003–7 Precautional Moratorium on CAFOs, APHA, 2003 Policy
Statement (www.apha.org).

53. *State of Food Insecurity in the World 2006:* Food and Agriculture
Organization of the United Nations. See also WHO, *Malnutrition,*
at http://www.who.int/water_sanitation_health/diseases/malnutri
tion/en/, and Rome Declaration on Food Security, *World Food Sum-
mit,* November 13–16, 1996 (Rome: FAO, 1997). See D. Pimentel
and A. Wilson, "World population, agriculture and malnutrition,"
World Watch magazine (September–October 2004), pp. 22–25.

54. "In 1993 the EPA estimated that over two billion pounds of pesticide-
active ingredients a year are applied throughout the United States,"
says Jay Feldman, director of the National Coalition Against the
Misuse of Pesticides, in Washington, DC. The agriculture industry
accounted for 84 percent of this pesticide use. The situation appears
not to have changed significantly in more recent years.

55. See Walker's important invited paper, "Public health implications
of meat production and consumption," *Public Health Nutrition,* 8
(2005), pp. 348–56.

56. "Our estimates of 24.6 million pounds in animal agriculture and
3 million pounds in human medicine suggests that 8 times more
antimicrobials are used for nontherapeutic purposes in the three
major livestock sectors than in human medicine"—Executive summary from the Union of Concerned Scientists' report "Hogging It:
Estimates of Antimicrobial Abuse in Livestock" (January 2001).

57. John Krebs, "The second Silent Spring?" *Nature,* 400 (August 1999),
pp. 611–12.

58. A single cow can belch out anywhere from 25 to 130 gallons of
methane a day. See the recent editorial in the *Los Angeles Times,*
"Killer Cow Emissions. Livestock are a leading source of greenhouse
gases. Why isn't anyone raising a stink?" October 15, 2007, at http://
www.latimes.com/news/opinion/la-ed-methane15Oct15,0,1365993
.story?coll=la-tot-opinion&track=ntothtml. The July 2005 issue of
Physics World states: "The animals we eat emit 21 percent of all the
CO_2 that can be attributed to human activity." Animal agriculture
produces more than 100 million tons of methane a year.

59. The report is readily available on the net, notably at www.virtual centre.org/en/library/key_pub/longshad/A0701E00.htm#sum.

60. The 700-page Stern Review, "The Economics of Climate Change," which reaches similar conclusions, is even more widely accepted: http://www.hm-treasury.gov.uk/independent_reviews/stern_review.

61. Eshel and Martin's paper "Diet, Energy and Global Warming" was published in *Earth Interactions,* vol. 10, no. 9 (2006); it is easily accessible on the Web at http://geosci.uchicago.edu/~gidon/papers/ nutri/nutri.html. This site also contains discussions of the paper in various journals and newspapers.

62. Telephone conversation with the author, January 12, 2008.

63. British government: http://www.direct.gov.uk/en/Environmentand greenerliving/Greenershopping/DG_064434.

64. In an e-mail leaked to a vegetarian campaign group, *Viva,* an EPA official expressed sympathy for the green benefits of a vegan diet. The official said the government may in future recommend eating less meat as one of the "key environmental behaviour changes" needed to combat climate change. See http://uk.reuters.com/article/ scienceNews/idUKL3044053120070530.

Chapter Two THE LIVES THEY LEAD

1. There are so many good Web sites where information on all aspects of this topic can be found that it is hard to single out just a few. But I would recommend http://www.ari-online.org/pages/ europe_8_batteryhens.html, from Animal Rights International, and in particular the marvelous, rich in information and heart Web site of United Poultry Concerns, founded by Karen Davis: www.upc-online.org.

2. A remarkable short story by James Agee, "A Mother's Tale," from 1952 begins with these unforgettable lines, when a young calf first notices the trains carrying cattle to the slaughterhouse: "The calf ran up the hill as fast as he could and stopped sharp. 'Mama!' he cried, all out of breath. 'What is it! What are they doing! Where are they going!' " See *The Collected Short Prose of James Agee,* ed. Robert Fitzgerald (Boston: Houghton Mifflin, 1968).

3. Bertrand Russell, *The Conquest of Happiness* (New York: Routledge, 2006; orig. pub. 1930), p. 15; Roger Scruton, *Animal Rights and Wrongs* (London: Demos, 1996), p. 141.

4. Ruth Harrison, "Case Study: Farm Animals," in R. J. Berry, ed., *Environmental Dilemmas: Ethics and Decisions* (London: Chapman & Hall, 1993), p. 118. The quote is part of Harrison's explanation for how she came to write the pioneering book *Animal Machines: The New Factory Farming Industry* (New York: Ballantine, 1966; orig. pub. London: Vincent Stuart, 1964).

5. F. W. R. Brambell, *Report of the Technical Committee to Enquire into the Welfare of Animals Kept Under Intensive Livestock Husbandry Systems, 1965.* Command Paper No. 2836 (London: Her Majesty's Stationery Office, 1965).

6. This quote comes from the original 1965 Brambell Report. It can be found online at the UPC debeaking factsheet: www.upc-online.org. The site notes that in 1990, Michael Gentle and his associates at the Institute of Animal Physiology and Genetics Research in Edinburgh showed that experimentally debeaked chickens demonstrated chronic pain and suffering after the operation—"Behavioral evidence for persistent pain following partial beak amputation in chickens," *Applied Animal Behavior Science,* 27 (1990), pp. 149–57.

7. I. Duncan, G. Slee, E. Seawright, and J. Breward, "Behavioural consequences of partial beak amputation (beak trimming) in poultry," *British Poultry Science,* 30 (1989), pp. 379–88. The leading author, Dr. Ian Duncan, is from Guelph University's Department of Animal and Poultry Science and an authority on chickens.

8. The researchers at the *Institute of Animal Physiology and Genetics Research* in Edinburgh found that hens would be prepared to walk nearly a mile in order to reach a nest box to lay in. See "The life of a battery hen compared with the life of a pet hen," http://greenfield.fortunecity.com/hummingbird/285/battery.html.

9. Good information on chicken behavior can be found in the books and articles listed in Recommended Reading. See too the information on chickens on the Web site of United Poultry Concerns—http://www.upc-online.org/chickens/chickensbro.html, and the Humane Society of the United States—http://www.hsus.org/farm/resources/animals/chickens/.

10. Marian Stamp Dawkins: *Through Our Eyes Only?—The Search for Animal Consciousness* (London: W. H. Freeman, 1993).

11. Quoted in "Animals Are Sentient Beings: Konrad Lorenz on Instinct and Modern Factory Farming," *Der Spiegel,* November 17, 1980, p. 264. See too the Humane Society of the United States site, where they cite other scientists and experts on laying hen welfare at http://www.hsus.org/web-files/PDF/farm/HSUS-Synopsis-of-Expert-Opinions-on-Battery-Cages-and-Hen-Welfare.pdf.

12. Quoted in C. Druce and P. Lymbery, *Outlawed in Europe: How America Is Falling Behind Europe in Farm Animal Welfare* (New York: Archimedean Press, 2002), p. 20.

13. L. J. Rogers: *The Development of Brain and Behaviour in the Chicken* (Wallingford, UK: CAB International, 1996), p. 219.

14. See Juliet Gellatley, with Tony Wardle, *The Silent Ark: A Chilling Exposé of Meat—the Global Killer* (San Francisco: HarperCollins, 1996), pp. 12–40. The "Laying Hens Fact Sheet" on the Web site of the Humane Society of the United States (www.hsus.org) is a useful source of information, as is Karen Davis's *Prisoned Chickens, Poisoned Eggs: An Inside Look at the Modern Poultry Industry* (Summertown, TN: Book Publishing Co., 1996).

15. Ruth Harrison, who wrote the first book on factory farming, looked at the situation for birds in 1990 and wrote: "The 'barn' eggs can be from a dimly lit, windowless building, with no litter in which the hens could scratch or have dust baths, and with each bird allocated only 400 square centimeters [about 60 square inches]. The 'free-range' eggs could come from similar buildings, albeit with continuous daytime access to open-air runs. In practice, this often means a continuation of the practice of providing only one pop-hole for hundreds of hens, so that few ever go outside or *probably even realize that such access exists*" (emphasis added). The article can be found online at http://www.upc-online.org/battery_hens/102105harrison.html.

16. Her book was very favorably reviewed, with particular attention paid to Kingsolver's ability to kill. Here is one example, from *The Guardian Weekly,* July 20, 2007, by Kathryn Hughes: "Kingsolver describes a daily programme of exhausting tough love in which she is frequently called upon to snap the neck of a chicken that she has raised as tenderly as her own children."

17. Michael Pollan, *The Omnivore's Dilemma: A Natural History of Four Meals* (New York: Penguin, 2006), p. 232.

18. Martha Rosenberg, "Dick Cheney's Sadistic Passion for Shooting Tame Animals," *AlterNet,* posted November 14, 2007.

19. The USDA itself admits this is due to the hazards of the job: see http://www.ers.usda.gov/publications/aer785/aer785d.pdf.

20. J. Turner and P. J. Lymbery, "Brittle Bones: Osteoporosis and the Battery Cage," *Compassion In World Farming* (Petersfield, UK, 1999).

21. N. G. Gregory and L. J. Wilkins, "Broken bones in domestic fowl: Handling and processing damage in end-of-lay battery hens," *British Poultry Science*, 30 (1989), pp. 555–62.

22. For a good description of the behavior of feral chickens, see G. McBride, et al., "The Social Organization and Behaviour of the Feral Domestic Fowl," *Animal Behaviour Monographs,* vol. 2, no. 3 (1969), pp. 127–81. On chickens in general, I recommend Page Smith and Charles Daniel, *The Chicken Book: Being an Inquiry into the Rise and Fall, Use and Abuse, Triumph and Tragedy of Gallus Domesticus* (Boston: Little, Brown, 1975, 2000). For a revolutionary new view of chicken intelligence, see Lesley J. Rogers, *The Development of Brain and Behaviour in the Chicken* (Wallingford, UK: CAB International, 1996). The viewpoint I take here has been best described by Karen Davis, the president and founder of the chicken advocacy group United Poultry Concerns, in her *Prisoned Chickens, Poisoned Eggs: An Inside Look at the Modern Poultry Industry*. I also recommend a paper she presented at the International Conference on the Chicken at Yale University in May 2002, called "The Dignity, Beauty, and Abuse of Chickens: As Symbols and in Reality." It can be found on the Web at http://www.upc-online.org/thinking/dignity.html.

23. An excellent source of information about chicken eggs is the ten-page article in the two-volume *Cambridge World History of Food,* ed. Kenneth F. Kiple and Kriemhild Conee Ornelàs (Cambridge: Cambridge University Press, 2000), with its forty reference citations.

24. A. I. Romanoff and A. J. Romanoff, *The Avian Egg* (New York: John Wiley, 1949).

25. William Grimes, *My Fine Feathered Friend* (New York: North Point Press, 2002).

26. For information on cows in general, I recommend Peter Lovenheim, *Portrait of a Burger as a Young Calf: The Story of One Man, Two Cows, and the Feeding of a Nation* (New York: Harmony Books, 2002); Valerie Porter, *Caring for Cows* (London: Whittet Books, 1991); John Webster, *Understanding the Dairy Cow,* 2nd edn. (Oxford: Blackwell Science, 1993); also his *Animal Welfare: Limping Towards Eden* (Oxford: John Wiley/Blackwell, 2005); and Laurie Winn Carlson, *Cattle: An Informal History* (Chicago: Ivan R. Dee, 2001).

27. Joyce D'Silva, "Faster, Cheaper, Sicker," *New Scientist,* November 15, 2003. See too the excellent 33-page report by Toni Vermelli, *Viva!: The Dark Side of Dairy,* available as a PDF file at www.animalrightsafrica.org/Archive/dairy_report.pdf.

28. See J. N. Marchant-Forde, et al., "Responses of dairy cows and calves to each other's vocalisations after early separation," *Applied Animal Behaviour Science,* 78 (2002), pp. 19–28.

29. Oliver Sacks, *An Anthropologist on Mars: Seven Paradoxical Tales* (New York: Vintage Books, 1996).

30. See A. J. S. Heinrichs, et al., "A study on the use of milk replacers for dairy calves in the United States," *Journal of Dairy Science* 78 (1995), pp. 2831–37.

31. Natural weaning has seldom been observed, because cows have rarely been allowed to live the lives they were designed for. There are a few reports from feral cattle and wild-type cattle. V. and A. Reinhardt, "Natural sucking performance and age of weaning in zebu cattle," *Journal of Agricultural Science* (Cambridge, UK), 96 (1981), pp. 309–12, found that female calves were weaned by their mothers at a bit less than nine months and males at a bit more than eleven months. See also P. Jensen, ed., *The Ethology of Domestic Animals* (Cambridge, MA: CAB International, 2005); A. Fraser and D. M. Broom, *Farm Animal Behaviour and Welfare,* 3rd edn. (Oxford: CAB International, 1997); J. L. Albright and C. W. Arave, *The Behaviour of Cattle* (Wallingford, UK: CAB International, 1997); and John Webster's *Understanding the Dairy Cow.* I also recommend B. E. Rollins, *Farm Animal Welfare: Social, Bioethical, and Research Issues* (Ames: Iowa University Press, 1995).

32. Quoted in Peter Singer and Jim Mason, *The Way We Eat: Why Our*

Food Choices Matter, p. 58. I highly recommend this book in general, as well as for the description of the lives of cows (pp. 55–68). See too Michael Pollan, "Power Steer," *New York Times Sunday Magazine*, March 31, 2002, and Peter Lovenheim, *Portrait of a Burger as a Young Calf* (New York: Knopf, 1995). In the United Kingdom, over 1 million male calves have been slaughtered at less than twenty-one days old, under the so-called Herod scheme—see Geoff Tansey and Joyce D'Silva, eds., *The Meat Business: Devouring a Hungry Planet* (London: Earthscan Publications, 1995), p. 80.

33. Note that such housing and feeding have both been banned in the European Union as of 2007—calves raised for veal there must live in herds and must receive some roughage and iron in their diet.

34. See Webster, *Animal Welfare: Limping Towards Eden*, p. 147.

35. I know these facts are hard to believe. But see sources on the net that provide them, such as the reliable site of the Humane Society of the United States, http://www.hsus.org/farm/resources/animals/cattle/the_dairy_cow_factory_farm.html.

36. Webster, *Understanding the Dairy Cow*, pp. 250–58, has the most elaborate discussion of mastitis I have found.

37. According to John Webster, "lameness is indisputably the major welfare problem for the dairy cow." He continues: "Most surveys of lameness in dairy cattle in Europe and the USA report an annual incidence of about 50% and prevalence of over 20%. In simple words this means half the cows go lame in any one year and 20% are lame at any one time"—*Animal Welfare: Limping Towards Eden*, p. 141. In *Understanding the Dairy Cow*, Webster writes: "Inspection of the feet of cull cows at slaughter reveals that nearly every animal is suffering or has suffered some form of foot damage. In other words, the dairy industry is living with a painful crippling disease with a morbidity rate close to 100%!" (p. 227). When I went for a walk in the country with Professor Webster, we passed a herd of cows and could clearly see which ones were lame. I asked him how the cows experienced the pain, and he told me to imagine what it would feel like if my fingers were slammed in a door and then I was asked to walk on them. "Like that," he said. Cf. M. J. Clarkson, et al., "Incidence and prevalence of lameness in dairy cattle," *Veterinary Record*, 138 (1996), pp. 563–67. See also P. R. Greenough

and A. D. Weaver, *Lameness in Cattle,* 3rd edn. (Philadelphia: W. B. Saunders, 1997).

38. For the information in this entire paragraph, see in particular John Webster, *Understanding the Dairy Cow;* also A. J. F. Webster, *Calf Husbandry, Health and Welfare* (London: Collins, 1985).

39. *Food Democracy* in an article entitled "The reality of feed at animal factories" points out that "most animals are still allowed to eat meat from their own species . . . Even cattle can still be fed cow blood and some other cow parts." See http://fooddemocracy.wordpress.com/2007/10/15/the-reality-of-feed-at-animal-factories.

40. Webster, *Animal Welfare: Limping Towards Eden.*

41. The video can be viewed at http://www.hsus.org/farm/news/ournews/undercover_investigation.html. It has been extensively covered in the media, cited by more than 1,200 newspapers around the world.

42. Gail A. Eisnitz, *Slaughterhouse: The Shocking Story of Greed, Neglect, and Inhumane Treatment Inside the U.S. Meat Industry* (New York: Prometheus, 2006). Sue Coe, *Dead Meat* (New York: Four Walls Eight Windows, 1996). Eric Schlosser, *Fast Food Nation* (New York: Harper Perennial, 2005).

43. Rosamund Young, *The Secret Life of Cows* (London: Farming Books, 2005). I visited her and interviewed her in England in May 2000.

44. I visited Marphona Farms and interviewed Marcin Paloaka on February 12, 2008.

45. The Web site Eatwild that specializes in grass-fed foods lists less than two dozen such farms in the United States; they are few and far between. See also *Alternative Farming,* an annotated database from the Animal Welfare Institute, at http://www.awionline.org/farm/alt-farming.html.

46. There are a number of good books about pigs—their intelligence, their sensitivity, their cleanliness, their gentleness, their *joie de vivre,* their concern for the emotional state of others, and their ability to show affection and be companionable. One of the best and most recent is by Sy Montgomery, *The Good, Good Pig* (New York: Ballantine, 2007). After reading this book, one reader told her, "No pork on my fork!" I also highly recommend the chapter on his visit to a pig

farm in Matthew Scully's *Dominion: The Power of Man, the Suffering of Animals, and the Call to Mercy* (New York: St. Martin's Griffin, 2003). It is a beautifully written and searing account that cannot be read without a change of life or at least of diet.

47. See Heinz Meynhardt, *Schwarzwild-Report: Mein Leben unter Wildschweinen* (Leipzig: Neumann Verlag, 1986).

48. According to USDA for the year 2000. See http://www.upc-online .org/slaughter/2000slaughter_stats.html for all animal slaughter statistics. Worldwide, the figure for pigs was over 1 billion. Singer and Mason, in *The Way We Eat,* write: "More than 90 percent of pigs raised for meat today are raised indoors in crowded pens of concrete and steel. They never get to go outside or root around in pasture and don't even have straw to lie down in" (p. 45). They provide the exact statistics in a footnote.

49. An excellent source of information is the 190-page report of the Scientific Veterinary Committee, "The Welfare of Intensively Kept Pigs" (1997), available as a PDF download at www.ec.europa.eu/food/ani mal/welfare/farm/out17_en.pdf. See too the excellent information from the HSUS about gestation crates for pigs at http://www.hsus .org/farm/resources/research/practices/gestation_crates.html.

50. M. Gustafsson, P. Jensen, F. H. de Jonge, et al., "Maternal behaviour of domestic pigs and crosses between domestic pig and wild boar," *Applied Animal Behaviour Science,* 65 (1999), pp. 29–42. See also P. Jensen, *Maternal Behaviour of Free-Ranging Domestic Pigs. Vol. 1: Results of a Three-Year Study,* Swedish University of Agricultural Sciences, Department of Animal Hygiene, Report 22, Skara, 1988.

51. See A. Strolba and D. Wood-Gush, "The behavior of pigs in a semi-natural environment," *Animal Production,* 48 (1989).

52. A. B. Lawrence, et al., "The effect of environment on behaviour, plasma cortisol and prolactin in parturient sows," *Applied Animal Behaviour Science,* 39 (1994), pp. 313–30.

53. See Per Jensen, "Behaviour of Pigs," in P. Jensen, ed., *The Ethology of Domestic Animals* (Oxford: CAB International, 2002): "Castration is normally done without anaesthesia . . . this is a painful procedure . . . also in most countries, the tails are cut off the young piglets, again without anaesthesia . . . neuromas may develop in the cutting area of the tail, and such neuromas in humans are associated with

so-called phantom pain" (pp. 159–72). See also the many experiments done on animals to induce, prove, and alleviate phantom pain in humans, described in Richard A. Sherman, Marshall Devor, and Kim Heermann-Do, eds., *Phantom Pain* (New York: Springer, 1997).

54. See Janet L. Treasure and John B. Owen, "Intriguing links between animal behavior and anorexia nervosa," *International Journal of Eating Disorders,* vol. 21, no. 4 (1998), pp. 307–11. The equivalent in pigs is called "thin sow syndrome."

55. See D. G. M. Wood-Gush and K. Vestergaard, "Inquisitive exploration in pigs," *Animal Behaviour,* 45 (1993), pp. 185–87. Also H. B. Graves, "Behaviour and ecology of wild and feral swine (*Sus scrofa),*" *Journal of Animal Science,* 58 (1984), pp. 1785–91.

56. William M. Healy, "Behavior," in James G. Dickson, ed., *The Wild Turkey: Biology and Management* (Harrisburg, PA: Stackpole Books, 1992), pp. 44–65.

57. Joe Hutto, *Illumination in the Flatwoods: A Season with the Wild Turkey* (New York: Lyons & Burford, 1995). For the passages quoted and others like it, see pp. 149–55.

58. Quoted in Karen Davis, *More Than a Meal: The Turkey in History, Myth, Ritual, and Reality* (New York: Lantern Books, 2001), p. 150; also available at http://www.abirdshome.com/Audubon/VolV/00509.html.

59. Karen Davis, *More Than A Meal*, p. 150.

60. Quoted in ibid., p. 138.

Chapter Three
THE FISHY BUSINESS OF AQUACULTURE

1. Mark Paul Mattson, *Neurobiology of Aggression: Understanding and Preventing Violence* (New York: Humana, 2003), p. 39.

2. See *The New Genetics,* published by the U.S. Department of Health and Human Services, the National Institutes of Health, and the National Institute of General Medical Sciences, 2006; available for free download as a PDF file at http://publications.nigms.nih.gov/thenewgenetics/livinglab.html.

3. Quoted by Irwin Cotler, former minister of justice in Canada, in a

keynote address on January 29, 2007, at the Holocaust Commemoration, United Nations, Geneva, in *UN Watch,* No. 155 (2007).

4. Philip Zimbardo, *The Lucifer Effect: Understanding How Good People Turn Evil* (New York: Random House, 2008).

5. Freeman House, *Totem Salmon: Life Lessons from Another Species* (Boston: Beacon Press, 2000), p. 19.

6. Patrick Bateson, "Assessment of pain in animals," *Animal Behaviour,* 42 (1991), pp. 827–39. See also his article "Do animals feel pain?" *New Scientist* (April 1992), pp. 30–33, in which he writes: "Few people have much fellow feeling for fish even though many fish are long-lived, have complicated nervous systems and are capable of learning complicated tasks." And see T. J. Hara, "Role of Olfaction in Fish Behaviour," in T. J. Pitcher, ed., *The Behaviour of Teleost Fishes* (London: Croom Helm, 1986), pp. 152–76.

7. Dr. Lynne U. Sneddon, Dr. Victoria A. Braithwaite, and Dr. Michael J. Gentle, "Do Fish Have Nociceptors?: Evidence for the Evolution of a Vertebrate Sensory System," *Royal Society Scientific Academy,* June 7, 2003; available at http://www.pubs.royalsoc.ac.uk/proc_bio _content/news/sneddon.html.

8. See Alex Kirby, "Fish do feel pain: The first conclusive evidence of pain perception in fish is said to have been found by UK scientists," http://news.bbc.co.uk/2/hi/science/nature/2983045.stm. Another leading study is I. J. H. Duncan, et al., "Can fish suffer? Perspectives on sentience, pain, fear and stress," *Applied Animal Behaviour Science,* 86 (2004), pp. 225–50. The answer is a decisive yes.

9. Quoted at http://www.fishinghurts.com/FishFeelPain.asp.

10. " 'That Fish You Caught Was in Pain.' Research challenges the myth among anglers that fish can't feel pain from barbed hooks," *Los Angeles Times,* October 11, 2006.

11. See Gee's Web page http://www.geocities.com/culumbrown/, and his book with Kevin Laland and Jens Krause, *Fish Cognition and Behaviour* (London: Blackwell, 2006), for much information on such fascinating topics as eavesdropping in fish, the ability to avoid dangerous habitats, the audience or bystander effect, and individual recognition. See also R. M. Tarrant, "Rate of extinction of a conditioned response in juvenile sockeye salmon," *Transactions of the American Fish Society,* 93 (1964), pp. 399–401.

12. Personal e-mail from Phil Gee to the author, January 2008.

13. Culum Brown and K. N. Laland, "Social learning in fishes: A review," *Fish and Fisheries*, 4 (2003), pp. 280–88. See also Culum Brown, "Heritable and experiential effects on boldness in a tropical poeciliid," *Behavioral Ecology and Sociobiology*, 62 (December 2007), pp. 237–43.

14. These statistics come from the American Pet Products Manufacturers Association (APPMA) 2007–08 National Pet Owners Survey (www.appma.org).

15. M. DeShriver and Carol Riddick, "Effects of watching aquariums on elders' stress," *Anthrozoos*, 4 (1990), pp. 44–48.

16. http://news.uns.purdue.edu/html4ever/1999/990628.Edwards.fish.html.

17. Richard Ellis, *The Empty Ocean* (Washington, DC: Island Press, 2004). See also his book *No Turning Back: The Life and Death of Animal Species* (New York: HarperCollins, 2004).

18. There is an excellent 2002 report from the Sierra Club, written by Kim Todd, "What's Lost, What's Left: A Status Report of the Lewis & Clark Expedition," available as a PDF on the Sierra Club Web site.

19. B. Worm, et al., "Impacts of Biodiversity Loss on Ocean Ecosystem Services," *Science*, November 3, 2006, pp. 787–90.

20. Peter Steinhart, *Mother Jones* (July–August 1994); http://www.motherjones.com/news/special_reports/1994/07/steinhart.html.

21. See Manuel Barange of the Plymouth Marine Laboratory, "Ecosystem science and the sustainable management of marine resources: From Rio to Johannesburg," *Frontiers in Ecology and the Environment*, vol. 1, no. 4 (2003), pp. 190–96, available as a PDF file at web.pml.ac.uk/globec/structure/ipo/manuel/Frontiers-Barange.pdf.

22. Colin Woodard, *Ocean's End: Travels Through Endangered Seas* (New York: Basic Books, 2000), says that some fishing practices are so harmful they should be eliminated altogether, just as large-scale drift nets were banned around the world in 1989 when the public was outraged at the damage they were causing to marine life. He feels that factory-freezer trawlers should share the same fate because of the horrendous damage they do to ecosystems, and even smaller drift nets and bottom trawlers should be carefully regulated because of the widespread damage they can cause.

23. See the Natural Resources Defence Council comment in 2007: "If bottom trawling happened on land instead of at sea, someplace where we could see it and where cameras could film it, perhaps it would provoke the same sort of public outcry that strip-mining does. But unlike the raw, torn earth laid bare by strip-mining, the similar devastation of the ocean floor caused by bottom trawling is hidden beneath thousands of feet of water. In some cases, the damage could be irreparable"—http://www.nrdc.org/water/oceans/ftrawling.asp.

24. Fen Montaigne, "Everybody loves Atlantic salmon: Here's the catch," *National Geographic* (July 2003).

25. See http://www.citizen.org/cmep/foodsafety/shrimp/.

26. The site http://nis.gsmfc.org/nis_factsheet.php?toc_id=7 gives the details and many references from the scientific literature on White Spot Syndrome Baculovirus Complex.

27. See "Chemical Cocktail: The Health Impacts of Eating Farm-Raised Shrimp," special report by the Public Citizen's Food Program, available with complete list of scientific references at http://www.citizen.org/print_article.cfm?ID=12706#_edn9.

28. Philip Lymbery, *In Too Deep: The Welfare of Intensively Farmed Fish* (2002). A report for Compassion in World Farming (CIWF) by Lymbery, now its chief executive, is available at www.ciwf.org.uk. In 2007, the World Society for the Protection of Animals and CIWF produced a new report, *Closed Waters: The Welfare of Farmed Atlantic Salmon, Rainbow Trout, Atlantic Cod and Atlantic Halibut*. It is written by Peter Stevenson, chief policy advisor of CIWF, and is available online at http://www.ciwf.org.uk/publications/fish.html. Useful information on the different species of farmed fish can be found on the Web site of the Food and Agriculture Organization of the United Nations (FAO), in the Fisheries and Aquaculture Department, http://www.fao.org/fishery/culturedspecies.

29. See P. Southgate and T. Wall, "Welfare of farmed fish at slaughter," *Practice*, vol. 23, no. 5 (2001), pp. 277–84.

30. http://www.nytimes.com/2007/12/15/world/asia/15fish.html.

31. Since salmon seem to have more trouble finding their way on overcast days, some scientists think they use the North Star or the sun to navigate, but this has not been proven. But they definitely are known

to use olfaction to find their home river or stream. They also seem to be sensitive to the earth's magnetic poles.

31. I recommend in particular David R. Montgomery, *King of Fish: The Thousand-Year Run of Salmon* (Boulder, CO: Westview Press, 2003); Rik Scarce: *Fishy Business: Salmon, Biology, and the Social Construction of Nature* (Philadelphia: Temple University Press, 2000); and Peter Coates, *Salmon* (London: Reaktion Books, 2006). For a scholarly study, see Thomas P. Quinn, *The Behavior and Ecology of Pacific Salmon and Trout* (Seattle: University of Washington Press, 2005), and C. Groot and L. Margolis, *Pacific Salmon Life Histories* (Vancouver: University of British Columbia Press, 1991).

31. For an impartial view, see Peter A. Robson, *Salmon Farming: The Whole Story* (Victoria, BC: Heritage House, 2006). For the industry standard, see Selina M. Stead and Lindsay Laird, *The Handbook of Salmon Farming* (New York: Springer, 2002). I also recommend *World Watch* magazine, vol. 16, no. 5 (September–October 2003), "Feedlots of the sea."

32. See http://persianoad.wordpress.com/2007/11/26/organic-salmon-fish for more information on the small difference between organic farmed salmon and conventional farmed salmon. The issue of so-called organic farmed salmon has been widely written about in England. Iain Tolhurst, a highly respected organic grower and a key figure in the foundation of the modern British organic movement, points out that "However you try to dress it up, you are taking a free-ranging creature genetically programmed to swim the oceans and sticking it in a cage. Organic farming doesn't allow hens to be kept in cages even though they would actually walk only very short distances. So how can it be all right to keep a truly wild creature such as a salmon in one?" Peter Kindersley, another respected organic farmer who resigned as a trustee of the Soil Association over its certification of organic salmon, calculates that an organic salmon farm can produce a quantity of untreated sewage equivalent to the population of a small town. I agree, as does Joanna Blythman, in her article "Why Organic Salmon Is Causing a Nasty Smell," *The Observer Food Monthly*, October 22, 2006. When I approached the largest New Zealand organic salmon farm, they refused to allow me to visit the facility and gave me no explanation. I take this as a bad sign.

35. A picture of a typical salmon fish farm can be seen at http://www
    .foe.org/camps/reg/nw/salmon/farms.html.
36. I have used several sources for this paragraph. See especially Peter Ste-
    venson, *Closed Waters: Farmed Salmon,* published in 2007 by CIWF
    and the *World Society for the Protection of Animals,* and available at
    www.ciwf.org/publications/reports/closed_waters. Stevenson includes
    a full set of scientific references. Of the killing methods, he says: "A
    range of slaughter methods are used in fish farming some of which
    cause stress and aversion and involve the fish taking a long time
    to lose consciousness. In its 2004 Opinion, the Scientific Panel on
    Animal Health and Welfare of the European Food Safety Authority
    concluded: 'Many commercial killing methods expose fish to sub-
    stantial suffering over a prolonged period of time.' " Other relevant
    sources include: T. T. Poppe, A. Barnes, and P. J. Midtlyng, "Welfare
    and ethics in fish farming," *Bulletin of the European Association of
    Fish Pathologists,* vol. 22, no. 2 (2000), pp. 148–51; L. S. Chervova,
    "Pain sensitivity and behaviour of fishes," *Journal of Ichthyology,*
    37 (1997), pp. 621–37; D. H. F. Robb, et al., "Commercial slaughter
    methods used on Atlantic salmon: Determination of the onset of
    brain failure by electroencephalography," *Veterinary Record,* 147
    (2000), pp. 298–303; T. Tobiassen and N. K. Sørensen, "Influence of
    killing methods on time of death of Atlantic salmon and rainbow
    trout," *Aquaculture Europe,* Trondhein, Norway (1999); and Ken-
    neth D. Black, ed., *Environmental Impacts of Aquaculture* (Lon-
    don: Blackwells, 2001). See also E. Stokstad, "Salmon survey stokes
    debate about farmed fish," *Science,* 303 (2004), pp. 154–55.
37. Quoted on the BBC News, April 12, 2000. See http://news.bbc
    .co.uk/1/hi/scotland/710476.stm.
38. *Vital Choices,* vol. 3, no. 58 (2006), "Farmed salmon's diet yields
    unhealthful cardiovascular effects: Fish doctors find plant oils in
    standard feed regimen may slash heart benefits of farmed salmon."
39. I e-mailed Dr. Pimentel, just to make certain, and he wrote back:
    "Yes, pig dung is fed to fish (carp) in China. Sewage and other sources
    of nutrients are also fed to fish." In Asia, it is not unusual for a human
    toilet to be situated directly over a fishpond. A scholarly article clari-
    fying (and justifying) the use of human and fish sewage and waste on
    fish farms in China and Indonesia can be found at http://www.unu

.edu/unupress/unupbooks/80434e/80434E0g.htm. John E. Bardach and Michael T. Santerre, from the East-West Resource Systems Institute, EastWest Center, Honolulu, conclude: "Socio-cultural objections to the use of sewage for fish culture seem to be decreasing in several societies as ecological information becomes disseminated and as fertilizer costs increase." But see R. L. Naylor, et al., "Effect of aquaculture on world fish supplies," *Nature,* 4005 (2000), pp. 1017–24. Most farmed fish are still fed with other fish: since on average it takes 2–5 pounds of wild caught ocean fish to produce 1 pound of farmed fish, it seems inescapable that aquaculture is contributing to the destruction of ocean fisheries. This is the conclusion of many scientists—see, e.g., S. Grende, et al., "Pacific salmon in aquatic and terrestrial ecosystems," *Bioscience,* vol. 52, no. 10 (2002), pp. 917–28. That there is contaminant loading in these farmed fish seems irrefutable—M. D. L. Easton, et al., "Preliminary examination of contaminant loadings in farmed salmon, wild salmon and commercial salmon feed," *Chemosphere,* 46 (2002), pp. 1053–74.

40. David Pimentel, Laura Westra, and Reed F. Noss, eds., *Ecological Integrity: Integrating Environment, Conservation, and Health* (Washington, DC: Island Press, 2000), p. 131.

41. For up-to-date information, see http://www.davidsuzuki.org/Oceans/Aquaculture/.

42. See the useful Internet site http://www.salmonfarmmonitor.org/problems.shtml.

43. To be fair, there does seem to be evidence that the dyes used, even though artificial, are not unduly dangerous: a careful discussion on the pigments in salmon aquaculture can be found at http://www.seafood monitor.com/sample/salmon.html. The conclusion here is: "There are plenty of grounds on which to question salmon farming—and they will be dealt with in other installments of The Salmon Files—but the use of pigmented feed is not a very compelling one." A different take is found in Bruce Babbitt's "Aquaculture's troubled harvest," *Mother Jones* (November–December 2001), and also in articles from the National Audubon Society, Environmental Defense, the Sierra Club, the David Suzuki Foundation, and the Living Oceans Society. What many critics dislike is the fact that Hoffmann–La Roche (a major supplier of the pigment used in salmon farming)

uses SalmoFan, a set of color swatches used by farmers and buyers to judge and specify the color of farmed salmon. It all seems very artificial, far removed from the real lives of these wild animals, even if the dyes present no health problem for humans, which is at least still debatable.

44. See the useful site http://www.imakenews.com/vitalchoiceseafood/e_article000161842.cfm.

45. The European Commission Health and Consumer Protection Directorate-General issued an "Opinion of the Scientific Committee on Animal Nutrition on the use of canthaxanthin in feedingstuffs for salmon and trout, laying hens, and other poultry Adopted on 17 April 2002." It is a long document, which gives all the scientific evidence, background, and conclusions leading to the decision taken. It can be downloaded as a PDF file at http://ec.europa.eu/food/fs/sc/scan/out81_en.pdf. For further discussion, see *Focus on Pigments,* vol. 2003, no. 6 (June 2003), p. 7. While the U.S. government does not seem unduly concerned, some scientists feel there is some danger to the human eye, especially at high levels of consumption (but how much we would have to consume to face danger remains unclear). See R. T. M. Baker, "Canthaxanthin in aquafeed applications: Is there any risk?" *Trends in Food Science and Technology,* 12 (2002), pp. 240–43.

46. All this information and more can be found in "Silent Spring of the Sea" in an excellent book that deserves to be widely read, *A Stain Upon the Sea: West Coast Salmon Farming* (Madeira Park, BC: Harbour Publishing, 2004). Also useful is Otto E. Langer, director of Marine Conservation at the David Suzuki Foundation, "Is There a Bottom Line in the Wild Salmon—Farmed Salmon Debate?—A Technical Opinion." See too their Web site: www.davidsuzuki.org.

47. See R. Goldburg, et al., "Marine Aquaculture in the United States: Environmental Impacts and Policy Options" Pew Ocean Commission (2001), pp. 16–17, available at http://www.pewoceans.org/oceanfacts/2002/01/11/fact_22988.asp. The conclusion is that the use of antibiotics is a health risk for people and farmed fish, since it promotes the spread of antibiotic resistance in both human and fish pathogens. At least a few types of bacteria associated with fish, such

as *Streptococcus,* can be pathogenic to humans. If strains of these bacteria develop higher levels of resistance to antibiotics, infections may be difficult to treat. More generally, resistance can potentially spread to other types of bacteria, including human pathogens. A U.S. Centers for Disease Control and Prevention review indicates that certain antibiotic resistance genes in *Salmonella*—bacteria that can cause severe food poisoning in people—might have emerged following antibiotic use in Asian aquaculture. See Madeline Drexler, *Secret Agents: The Menace of Emerging Infections* (Washington, DC: Joseph Henry Press, 2002), where she explains the origins of DT 104 (a frightening and enigmatic drug-resistant strain of *Salmonella tymphimurium*) in the use of antibiotics in Asian aquaculture that probably came to the United States via ground-up fishmeal fed to chickens.

48. On the dangers of PCBS (polychlorinated biphenyls), see the American Chemical Society study, "Investigation of Selected Persistent Organic Pollutants in Farmed Atlantic Salmon (Salmo salar), Salmon Aquaculture Feed, and Fish Oil Components of the Feed," in *Environmental Science and Technology,* vol. 36, no. 13 (2002), pp. 2797–805, by Miriam N. Jacobs (from the School of Biomedical and Life Sciences, University of Surrey), Adrian Covaci, and Paul Schepens. They are cautious scientists, but nonetheless report that their study "confirms previous reports of relatively high concentrations of PCBs." Less cautious, but a fine article, by EarthSave, is "What's the Catch? If the earth's oceans were a human being, they'd be rushed to the hospital, admitted to the intensive care unit and listed in grave condition," at http://earthsave.org/news/fish what.htm. In 2007 and 2008, according to David Anderson, president of the World Fisheries Trust, and former minister of fisheries in the Canadian government, far less antibiotics and hormones are being fed to farmed salmon. On the other hand, Food and Water Watch's Web site states that feed derived from wild fish contributes to the decline of wild fish populations and can contain high levels of contaminants such as PCBs. Their conclusion: "The 2007 National Offshore Aquaculture Act does not include safeguards to mitigate the human health and environmental risks created by chemical use

and contamination in offshore aquaculture. Members of Congress must oppose this and any aquaculture bill that does not protect consumers from unsafe levels of chemicals, hormones, antibiotics, and heavy metals that could accumulate in the flesh of farmed fish, and any dangerous substances used in or around fish farming operations that could contaminate wild seafood." See www.foodandwaterwatch.org, which provides a complete list of all the contaminants and chemicals involved—copper, mercury, pesticides, antibiotics, fertility drugs, etc.

49. M. D. Easton and D. Luszniak, "Preliminary examination of contaminant loadings in farmed salmon, wild salmon and commercial salmon feed," *Chemosphere,* vol. 46, no. 7 (February 2002), pp. 1053–74. See also Food Safety Authority of Ireland (FSAI), 2002a, Summary of investigation of dioxins, furans, and PCBs in farmed salmon, wild salmon, farmed trout, and fish oil capsules (March 2002), accessed online, July 21, 2003, at http://www.fsai.ie/industry/Dioxins3.htm. See also the National Academy of Sciences, *Dioxins and Dioxin-like Compounds in the Food Supply: Strategies to Decrease Exposure* (Washington, DC: National Academies Press, 2003). However, a study by Dariush Mozaffarian of the Harvard School of Public Health in the *Journal of the American Medical Association,* 296 (October 2006), pp. 1885–99, shows that the benefits of eating fish—even farmed salmon, and despite the mercury, PCBs, and dioxins, greatly outweigh the risks. There are many physicians who would disagree, including my wife, Leila.

50. See W. K. Stevens, "As a Species Vanishes, No One Can Say Why," *New York Times,* September 14, 1999; and also "The Hidden Cost of Farmed Salmon" at http://www.sectionz.info/issue_1/facts_footnotes.html, which speaks of both Atlantic and Pacific salmon.

51. Many scientific articles on this topic can easily be found on the Internet. One I read was published at the end of 2005, and reports research on pancreas disease in farmed salmon. It can be found at www.marine.ie/NR/rdonlyres/0BAFCCB0-8CEC-49A6-914E-AC22D5AE974B/0/Mehs22.pdf.

52. See http://www.sciencemag.org/cgi/content/abstract/318/5857/1772. This site points to an article by some of the most respected scientists in the field—*Science,* December 14, 2007, pp. 1772–75. They found

that wild pink salmon populations north of Vancouver Island suffered recurrent louse infestations and population declines because of salmon farms. They also analyze the impacts of salmon farms around the globe and report that farms dramatically reduce survival rates of wild salmonids that migrate past aquaculture operations as juveniles on their way to the ocean. One of the authors, Ransom Myers, whose recent death claimed a powerful voice for marine conservation, developed the first mathematical models to show that industrial fisheries caused the cod collapse, and later revealed a catastrophic decline of the ocean's large predatory fish.

53. This is reported by Don Staniford in a paper presented at the European Parliament's Committee on Fisheries public hearing on "Aquaculture in the European Union: Present Situation and Future Prospects," October 1, 2002. See also R. Cusack and G. Johnson, "A Study of Dichlorvos (Nuvan; 2,2 dichloroethenyl phosphate), a Therapeutic Agent for Sea Lice (Lepeophtheirus salmonis)," ERDA Report No. 14, 1988, Department of Microbiology and Pathology, University of Prince Edward Island, Charlottetown.

54. According to the David Suzuki Foundation article "Drugs used in the salmon farming industry" (http://www.davidsuzuki.org/oceans/ aquaculture/salmon/drugs.asp), all of the drugs mentioned below, and many others, are still in common use. On cypermethrin, see L. E. Burridge, et al., "The lethality of the cypermethrin formulation Excis (R) to larval and post-larval stages of the American lobster (*Homarus americanus*)," *Aquaculture,* vol. 182, no. 1 (February 2000), pp. 37–47. For the Scottish Environment Protection Agency (SEPA) position, see http://govdocs.aquake.org/cgi/content/abstract/ 2003/1025/10250030.

55. Teflubenzuron is highly toxic to all aquatic crustacean invertebrates. See http://www.fluoridealert.org/pesticides/epage.tefluben zuron.htm. A 1999 report by SEPA found teflubenzuron to be "potentially highly toxic to any species which undergo moulting within their life cycle." See http://www.sundayherald.com/news/heraldnews/display .var.1758638.0.toxic_pesticide_again_in_use_on_salmon_farms.php.

56. L. M. Collier and E. H. Penn, "An assessment of the acute impact of the sea lice treatment ivermectin on a benthic community," *Journal of Experimental Marine Biology and Ecology,* 230 (1998),

pp. 131–47. See also I. M. Davies, "A review of the use of ivermectin as a treatment for sea lice [Lepeophtheirus salmonis (Kroyer) and Caligus elongatus Nordmann] infestation in farmed Atlantic salmon (Salmo salar L.)," *Aquaculture Research,* 31 (2000), pp. 869–83.

57. The safety information Web site of Oxford University's Physical and Theoretical Chemistry Laboratory lists the compound as "very toxic," having a half-life in the environment of up to fifteen months and killing 50 percent of rainbow trout after 96 hours at exposure levels of 174 parts per billion. It is hard for non-scientists (like me and most of my readers) to interpret the data on many of these pesticides, but surely it is common sense to avoid them if possible.

58. "Friends of the Earth" Scotland has noted that the cocktail of toxic chemicals used on Scottish salmon farms may be having a "large-scale effect" on the environment, according to leaked government research. The research, part of an ongoing $8 million study into the impacts of the industry, has uncovered an "almost complete absence" of certain key species of crustaceans. According to the scientists, this "suggests the possibility of a large-scale effect that may be related to the use of chemicals on fish farms." *New Scientist* for April 2002 also reports on this document, a 180-page report led by a consortium of government agencies, which was the result of a three-year project begun in late 1999, specifically designed to assess the environmental impact of sea lice treatments used in farmed salmon. See http://www.fluoridealert .org/pesticides/teflubenzuron.foe.uk.2002.htm.

59. See William T. Fairgrieve and Michael B. Rust, "Interactions of Atlantic salmon in the Pacific northwest v. human health and safety," *Fisheries Research,* 62 (2003), pp. 329–38.

60. David Barboza, "In China, Farming Fish in Toxic Waters," *New York Times,* December 15, 2007.

61. A report published in *Nature* finds that commercial fish farms have a "disastrous impact on both the environment and stocks of wild fish"—see http://home.alltel.net/bsundquist1/fi10.html. See also M. MacGarvin, "Scotland's Secret—Aquaculture, Nutrient Pollution Eutrophication and Toxic Blooms" (Aberfeldy: World Wildlife Fund Scotland, 2000).

62. See Richard Ellis, *The Empty Ocean: Plundering the World's Marine Life* (Washington, DC: Island Press, 2003), pp. 82ff. More recent release figures can be found at a Friends of the Earth site: http://www.foe.org/camps/reg/nw/salmon/farms.html.

63. See this excellent site: http://www.mtholyoke.edu/~lyfarrel/new.html.

64. T. Ellis, et al., "The relationship between stocking density and welfare in farmed rainbow trout," *Journal of Fish Biology,* 61 (2002), pp. 493–531.

65. There is a valuable book with this title by Laurence Hutchinson— see www.permaculture.co.uk.

66. For the problems associated with organic salmon fish farms, see http://www.salmonfarmmonitor.org/problems.shtml.

67. *In Too Deep: The Welfare of Intensively Farmed Fish,* Compassion in World Farming (2002), p. 45.

68. See Jim Lichatowich, *Salmon Without Rivers: A History of the Pacific Salmon Crisis* (Washington, DC: Island Press, 2001), p. 214.

69. The Blue Ocean Institute, founded by Carl Safina, has a "Guide to Ocean Friendly Seafood" that can be downloaded at http://www.blueocean.org/seafood/.

70. John Hersey, *Blues* (New York: Vintage, 1988).

71. *The Guardian Weekly,* June 23–29, 2006, p. 4.

Chapter Four DENIAL

1. Bill Buford, *Heat: An Amateur's Adventures as Kitchen Slave, Line Cook, Pasta-Maker, and Apprentice to a Dante-Quoting Butcher in Tuscany* (New York: Alfred A. Knopf, 2006), p. 256.

2. Julia Moskin, "Chefs' New Goal: Looking Dinner in the Eye," *New York Times,* January 16, 2008.

3. Hugh Fearnley-Whittingstall, *The River Cottage Meat Book* (London: Hodder & Stoughton, 2004), p. 16.

4. Quoted in Jim Mason, *An Unnatural Order: Uncovering the Roots of Our Domination of Nature and Each Other* (New York: Simon & Schuster, 1993), p. 78.

5. Roger Scruton, "A Carnivore's Credo," in *The Best American Essays 2007,* ed. David Foster Wallace (Boston: Houghton Mifflin, 2007).

6. Peter Singer and Jim Mason, *The Way We Eat: Why Our Food Choices Matter* (New York: Rodale Press, 2006), quoted in Tamar Haspel, "Meat Eaters Without Guilt," *Washington Post*, August 14, 2006, p. A13.

7. R. M. Hare, "Why I am Only a Demi-Vegetarian," in Dale Jamieson, ed., *Singer and His Critics (Philosophers and Their Critics)* (New York: Wiley-Blackwell, 1999).

8. James Lovelock, *The Revenge of Gaia: Earth's Climate Crisis & The Fate of Humanity* (New York: Basic Books, 2007).

9. *The Guardian Weekly,* Dr. Jeph Mathias, Letters to the Editor, March 17–23, 2006.

10. Bruce Chatwin, *In Patagonia* (New York: Penguin Classics, 2003).

11. Henry L. Feingold, *Bearing Witness: How America and Its Jews Responded to the Holocaust* (Syracuse, NY: Syracuse University Press, 1995).

12. The British government did little to save Jews. There was a very small quota on Jewish refugee immigration, as well as a consistent refusal to help Jewish resistance in Europe. See Bernard Wasserstein, *Britain and the Jews of Europe, 1939–45,* 2nd rev. edn. (Leicester, UK: Leicester University Press, 1999).

13. Feingold, *Bearing Witness.*

14. Bob Woodward, "Greenspan Is Critical of Bush in Memoir," *Washington Post,* September 15, 2007, p. A01.

15. Michel Foucault, *The History of Sexuality,* 3 vols. (New York: Vintage Books, 1990), p. 293.

16. S. Freud, "Some Additional Notes on Dream-Interpretation as a Whole," *The Standard Edition of the Complete Psychological Works of Sigmund Freud,* vol. 19 (London: Hogarth Press, 1961), pp. 131–34.

17. Quoted by Luce Irigaray, *Speculum of the Other Woman* (Ithaca, NY: Cornell University Press, 1985), p 59. See also the historical comments on the concept of "disavowal" in Freud: James Strachey, *The Standard Edition of the Complete Psychological Works of Sigmund Freud,* vol. 19 (London: Hogarth Press, 1961), p. 143.

18. Anna Freud, *The Writings of Anna Freud,* vol. 1, *Introduction of Psychoanalysis: Lectures for Child Analysts and Teachers, 1922–1935* (New York: International Universities Press, 1974), p. 83

(emphasis added). The paper dates from 1930, so Anna Freud cannot be faulted for the false information about animals.

19. Upton Sinclair, *The Jungle: The Uncensored Original Edition,* foreword by Earl Lee, introduction by Kathleen DeGrave (Tucson, AZ: See Sharp Press, 2003), p. 2. The text can be viewed online at http://www.pagebypagebooks.com/Upton_Sinclair/The_Jungle/Chapter_3_p4.html

20. C. David Coats, *Old MacDonald's Factory Farm: The Myth of the Traditional Farm and the Shocking Truth About Animal Suffering in Today's Agribusiness* (New York: Continuum, 1989), p. 13.

21. I have rarely seen this more vividly expressed than in the film *The Emotional World of Farm Animals,* where a young girl describes an animal she raised from birth only to see it taken for slaughter. The look of pain and sorrow on her face affects just about everyone who watched this remarkable segment. (Full disclosure: the film is about the writing of one of my books, *The Pig Who Sang to the Moon.*)

Chapter Five A DAY IN THE LIFE OF A VEGAN

1. For a critique of the Atkins Diet, see Michael Gregor: *Carbophobia: The Scary Truth About America's Low-carb* Craze (New York: Lantern Books, 2005).

2. Marion Nestle has written extensively on these issues in her book *Food Politics: How the Food Industry Influences Nutrition, and Health,* rev. and expanded edn., California Studies in Food and Culture (Berkeley: University of California Press, 2007). She was director of Nutrition Policy at the U.S. Department of Health and Human Services, a longtime chair of the Department of Nutrition at New York University, and the editor of the 1988 Surgeon General's Report. See also Michele Simon, *Appetite for Profit: How the Food Industry Undermines Our Health and How to Fight Back* (New York: Nation Books, 2006). The quote from Nestle is found in the article by Laura Shapiro, "Feeding Frenzy," in *Newsweek,* March 12, 2008; http://www.newsweek.com/id/122237/output/print.

3. "Position of the American Dietetic Association and Dietitians of

Canada: Vegetarian diets," *Journal of the American Dietetic Association,* vol. 103, no. 6 (June 2003), p. 748.

4. See Bruce Fife and Jon J. Kabara: *The Coconut Oil Miracle* (New York: Avery, 2004), "Coconuts and coconut oils are major food sources in Malaysia, Polynesia, and parts of the Philippines and India. Interestingly the people who use these products have a much lower incidence of heart disease, hypertension, atherosclerosis, stroke, diabetes, and cancer than those who eat modern foods in which vegetable oils, meat, and dairy are the predominant dietary sources for fat" (p. 33). Not sure how rigorously researched this small book is, but I like the sentiment! Thanks to Marti Kheel for the reference.

5. The Center for Science in the Public Interest ran an excellent article in the October 1996 issue of their *Nutrition Action Healthletter* on the health and environmental benefits of plant-based diets. The Nestle quote comes from there.

6. Those doctors are: Dean Ornish, head of the Preventive Medicine Research Institute in Sausalito, California (www.ornish.com), whom President Bill Clinton credits with saving his life; Dr. Caldwell B. Esselstyn, former renowned surgeon at the famed Cleveland Clinic (www.heartattackproof.com); Dr. John A. McDougall (www.drmcdougall.com), possibly the first to put the theory to the test with a large number of patients; Dr. Joel Fuhrman (www.drfuhrman.com), who has a thriving vegan-centered private practice for preventing heart disease and cancer; Jeffrey Novick, a PhD researcher, director of nutrition at the Pritikin Longevity Center (www.pritikin.com); the Coronary Health Improvement Project, founded by Dr. Hans Diehl (www.chipusa.org), which has enrolled countless people in these helpful diets; and the ever popular Dr. Michael Greger (www.drgreger.org), now at the Humane Society of the United States.

Many of them highly recommend T. Colin Campbell's *The China Study: Startling Implications for Diet, Weight Loss and Long-Term Health* (Dallas: Benbella Books, 2005). The original study, which costs over $300, is J. Chen, T. C. Campbell, et al., *Diet, Life-Style and Mortality in China. A Study of the Characteristics of 65 Chinese Counties* (Oxford; Ithaca, NY; and Beijing: Oxford University Press; Cornell University Press; People's Medical Publishing House, 1990).

I would add the many popular books by Dr. Neal Barnard of the Physicians Committee for Responsible Medicine: *Dr. Neal Barnard's Program for Reversing Diabetes* (New York: Rodale Press, 2007); *Eat Right; Live Longer: Using the Natural Power of Foods to Age-Proof Your Body* (New York: Harmony Books, 1995); *Food for Life: How the New Four Food Groups Can Save Your Life* (New York: Three Rivers Press, 1994); *Foods That Fight Pain* (New York: Three Rivers Press, 1998); and *Breaking the Food Seduction: The Hidden Reasons Behind Food Cravings* (New York: St. Martin's, 2003). Perhaps most popular of all are the excellent books by John Robbins, the man who was disowned for turning his back on the Baskin Robbins fortune, only to save his father years later from a heart attack by turning him vegan! His *Diet for a New America,* first published in 1987, is responsible for encouraging many Americans to become vegetarian and is still a wonderful read twenty years later. See too *The Food Revolution: How Your Diet Can Help Save Your Life and Our World* (Newburyport, MA: Conari Press, 2001); *Reclaiming Our Health: Exploding the Medical Myth and Embracing the Source of True Healing* (Tiburon, CA: H. J. Kramer, 1996); and most recently, *Healthy at 100: The Scientifically Proven Secrets of the World's Healthiest and Longest-Lived Peoples* (New York: Random House, 2007).

For the science of veganism, I have been guided primarily by three books: Gary E. Fraser's *Diet, Life Expectancy, and Chronic Disease: Studies of Seventh-day Adventists and Other Vegetarians* (New York: Oxford University Press, 2003); Mark and Virginia Messina's *The Dietitian's Guide to Vegetarian Diets: Issues and Applications* (Gaithersburg, MD: Aspen Publishers, 1996); and Stephen Walsh, *Plant Based Nutrition and Health* (London: The Vegan Society, 2003).

7. E-mail from Neal Barnard to the author, May 12, 2008.

8. Joanne Slavin, et al., "The role of whole grains in disease prevention," *Journal of the American Dietetic Association,* 101 (2001), pp. 780–85. See also D. R. Jacobs, et al., "Whole-grain intake and cancer: An expanded review and meta-analysis," *Nutrition and Cancer,* 30 (1998), pp. 85–96.

9. For coronary heart disease, see C. B. Esselstyn, et al., "A strategy to arrest and reverse coronary artery disease: A 5-year longitudinal

study of a single physician's practice," *Journal of Family Practice,* 41 (1995), pp. 560–68. See too Esselstyn's recent book, *Prevent and Reverse Heart Disease* (New York: Avery Penguin, 2008). Also D. Ornish, S. E. Brown, L. W. Scherwitz, et al., "Can lifestyle changes reverse coronary heart disease?" *Lancet,* 336 (1990), pp. 129–33. For diabetes, see N. D. Barnard, et al., "The effects of a low-fat, plant-based dietary intervention on body weight, metabolism, and insulin sensitivity," *American Journal of Medicine,* 118 (2005), pp. 991–97. See too his recent book, *Dr. Neal Barnard's Program for Reversing Diabetes.* On MS and other autoimmune diseases, see *The China Study,* mentioned above, as well as the Web site of Dr. John McDougall (www.drmcdougall.com).

10. For kidneys, see Neil J. Breslau, et al., "Relationship of animal protein-rich diet to kidney stone formation and calcium metabolism," *Journal of Clinical Endocrinology and Metabolism,* 66 (1988), pp. 140–46. On bone: Linda K. Massey, "Dietary animal and plant protein and human bone health: a whole foods approach," *Journal of Nutrition,* 133 (2003), pp. 862S–65S. Also Marian T. Hannan, et al., "Effect of dietary protein on bone loss in elderly men and women: The Framingham osteoporosis study," *Journal of Bone and Mineral Research,* 15 (2000), pp. 2504–12. Susan A. New, et al., "Dietary influence on bone mass and bone metabolism: Further evidence of a positive link between fruit and vegetable consumption and bone health?" *American Journal of Clinical Nutrition,* 71 (2000), pp. 142–51.

For the eyes, see J. M. Robertson, et al., "A possible role for vitamins C and E in cataract prevention," *American Journal of Clinical Nutrition,* 53 (1991), pp. 346S–551S. Also P. F. Jacques, et al., "Epidemiologic evidence of a role for the antioxidant vitamins and carotenoids in cataract prevention," *American Journal of Clinical Nutrition,* 53 (1991), pp. 352S–55S. On the brain, see Marianne J. Engelhardt, et al., "Dietary intake of antioxidants and risk of Alzheimer disease," *Journal of the American Medical Association,* 287 (2002), pp. 3223–29. Also Martha Clare Morris, et al., "Dietary intake of antioxidant nutrients and the risk of incident Alzheimer disease in a biracial community study," *Journal of the American Medical Association,* 287 (2002), pp. 3230–37.

11. The chart is widely available. I use the one in Stephen Walsh's *Plant-Based Nutrition and Health*.

12. See James A. Joseph, Daniel A. Nadeau, and Anne Underwood, *The Color Code: A Revolutionary Eating Plan for Optimum Health* (New York: Hyperion, 2002).

13. In 2002, the USDA put out a National Organic Program and guidelines, easily downloadable from the net, on labeling and standards. On their Web site (updated 2008), they state that agricultural products labeled "100 percent organic" and "organic" cannot be produced using what they call "excluded methods, sewage sludge, or ionizing radiation." The produce must be certified, unless it comes from a small farm where the sale of organic products amounts to less than $5,000 yearly.

14. Organic food tastes better, helps the soil retain its fertility, and keeps those who eat it healthier. But I am well aware of the economic and class issues here, that most people cannot afford fresh healthy food, and that fast food outlets take advantage of this problem to sell them cheap, poor-quality food. This book does not seem like the right place to address this problem, however. In general, organic produce can cost up to 50 percent more than the conventionally grown. Of course, the first rule of thumb is to buy what is in season. But it is also true, I understand from organic farmers, that some products retain pesticides more readily than others. These include apples, grapes, peaches, nectarines, cherries, raspberries, strawberries, spinach, carrots, oranges, and potatoes. Organic makes less of a difference for other foods, such as avocados, bananas, papaya, mango, blueberries, asparagus, broccoli, pineapple, kiwi, corn, and, at the very bottom of the list, onions, which carry the smallest pesticide load.

15. In an e-mail to me, May 12, 2008, David Pimentel writes: "Sweden during the past 10 years has reduced pesticide use about 68% without any reduction in crop losses to pests. At the same time the number of pesticide human poisonings have declined 77%."

16. See the Web site EXTOXNET: The Extension Toxicology Network at http://pmep.cce.cornell.edu/profiles/extoxnet/24d_captan124d-ext .html.

17. The Sierra Club of Canada offers a site called The Truth About

Pesticides: http://www.sierraclub.ca/national/programs/health-envi ronment/pesticides/pesticide-truth.html.

18. Gary Paul Nabhan, *Coming Home to Eat: The Pleasures and Politics of Local Foods* (New York: W. W. Norton, 2002). See also Michael Pollan's popular *In Defense of Food: An Eater's Manifesto* (New York: Penguin, 2008), with its wonderful logo: "Eat food, not too much, mostly plants."

19. So many people ask why one is vegetarian, or vegan, it occurred to me that the reverse question would be interesting: why do you eat meat? I have maintained that often the reason comes down to a lack of information. But feminists such as Marti Kheel and Carol Adams argue forcefully that eating meat is deeply connected to masculine identity: *real men* eat meat—a symbol of power and dominance! According to this view, vegetarian foods require the addition of the superior flesh foods to become a complete meal.

20. http://www.vegsource.com/articles2/novick_full.htm. USDA also has a good Web site called "How to understand and use the nutrition facts label," along with a video—http://www.cfsan.fda.gov/~dms/ foodlab.html.

21. I received an e-mail from Dr. Esselstyn after he read this chapter. He sent me a link to an article by Jeff Novick against olive oil: http:// www.pritikin.com/eperspective/0611/oliveOil.shtml. Esselstyn says: "Olive oil (all oils) is very destructive to endothelium. Drs. McDougall, Campbell, Ornish, Furhman, Barnard and I all agree with Novick on the down side of olive oil and all other oils. Example: 'Olive, soybean, and palm oil intake have a similarly acute detrimental effect over the endothelial function in healthy young subjects,' by Christian F. Rueda-Clausen, Frederico A. Silva, et al, in *Nutrition, Metabolism, and Cardiovascular Diseases* (2007), 17, 50–57." I am sure their medical knowledge is correct, but most people, including me, find it very difficult to give up all oils. However, if one is ill, then their recommendation is essential.

22. I like the response of David Katz, a professor at the Yale University School of Medicine, and director of their CDC-funded Prevention Research Center: "It's basically a slow form of poison. I applaud New York City, and frankly, I think there should be a nationwide ban."

23. http://www.foodrevolution.org/what_about_soy.htm. The FDA Web

site has a news item: "FDA approves new health claim for soy protein and coronary heart disease"—see http://www.fda.gov/bbs/topics/ANSWERS/ANS00980.htm. The Nutrition Committee of the American Heart Association made the recommendation about soy "because Soy protein contains all of the essential amino acids in sufficient quantities to support human life—in other words, it is a complete protein." See John W. Erdman, Jr., "Soy protein and cardiovascular disease: A statement for healthcare professionals from the Nutrition Committee of the AHA," *Circulation*, 102, November 14, 2000, pp. 2555–59.

24. One of the great medical detective stories, well told in Kenneth J. Carpenter's *Beriberi, White Rice, and Vitamin B: A Disease, A Cause, and a Cure* (Berkeley: University of California Press, 2000).

25. There is an excellent article by Jeanne Yacoubou, "Is your sugar vegan? An update on sugar processing practices," *Vegetarian Journal*, 4 (2007), pp. 15–19 (available on the Web as a PDF file). Treat yourself, too, to *Sugar Blues*, a remarkable book by William Dufty about how he transformed his health by going off sugar (Radnor, PA: Chilton, 1975).

26. Only about 40,000 people are currently diagnosed with celiac disease in the United States. But researchers at the Center for Celiac Research at the University of Maryland School of Medicine found that when primary care physicians offer to test all patients with celiac symptoms, the diagnostic rate increases 32- to 43-fold.

27. S. Boyd Eaton, Marjorie Shostak, and Melvin Konner, *The Paleolithic Prescription: A Program of Diet and Exercise and a Design for Living* (New York: HarperCollins, 1988). For a similar perspective, see Randolph Nesse, *Why We Get Sick: The New Science of Darwinian Medicine* (New York: Vintage Books, 1996), the classic work on the evolutionary basis of disease.

28. See Artemis P. Simopoulos and Jo Robinson, *The Omega Plan* (New York: HarperCollins, 1998). Dr. Simopoulos was the nutritional adviser to the Office of Consumer Affairs at the White House, and was chair of the Nutrition Coordinating Committee of the NIH for nine years.

29. The Paleolithic diet has good advice about avoiding processed foods, in particular carbohydrates, but they also recommend meat and dairy products.

30. http://www.wcrf.org.

31. G. E. Fraser, et al., "A possible protective effect of nut consumption on risk of coronary heart disease," *Archives of Internal Medicine*, 252 (1992), pp. 1416–24.

32. Frank A. Oski, *Don't Drink Your Milk: New Frightening Medical Facts About the World's Most Overrated Nutrient*, 9th edn. (Brushton, NY: Teach Services, 1992). Oski, the author of the most widely used textbook on pediatrics, was the head of the Department of Pediatrics at the Johns Hopkins University School of Medicine until his premature death in 1996 at the age of sixty-four. His article "Is bovine milk a health hazard?" *Pediatrics*, 75 (1985), showed that drinking whole milk after the first year of life plays a potential role in atherosclerosis, recurrent abdominal pain of childhood, cataracts, and milk-borne infections. His short book concludes that "Cow milk has no valid claim as the perfect food. As nutrition, it produces allergies in infants, diarrhea and cramps in the older child and adult, and may be a factor in the development of heart attacks and strokes. Perhaps when the public is educated as to the hazards of milk only calves will be left to drink the real thing. Only calves should drink the real thing"(p. 86).

38. Spock went vegan himself, after a series of illnesses, in 1991. He said it gave him a new lease on life and improved his health greatly (he died in 1998). Many pediatricians, however, thought his advice was wrong and said so; his old friend T. Berry Brazelton said it was "absolutely insane." See Jane Brody, "Final Advice from Dr. Spock: Eat Only All Your Vegetables," *New York Times*, June 20, 1998. But some recent research does seem to show that high dairy intake in childhood can lead to later colorectal cancer, as reported by Dr. Jolieke C. van der Pols in the *American Journal of Nutrition* (December 2007).

39. Joy Pierson, et al., *The Candle Café Cookbook* (New York: Clarkson Potter, 2003). You can go to such sites as *Compassion Over Killing* (www.goveg.com), *Physicians Committee for Responsible Medicine* (http://pcrm.org/health/recipes/index.html), or *Mercy for Animals* (http://chooseveg.com/). In addition, I use vegweb.com, http://www .vrg.org/recipes, and for international recipes, http://www.ivu.org/ recipes/, as well as http://allrecipes.com/Recipes/Everyday-Cooking/

Vegetarian/Vegan/Main.aspx. I think my two all-time favorites are (1) my friends Jeff and Sabrina Nelson's Vegsource (http://www .vegsource.com/talk/recipes/index.html) and (2) Colleen Patrick-Goudreau's Compassionate Cooks (http://www.compassionatecooks .com/blog/index.html). Don't forget one of America's best small magazines, *VegNews*, which has many excellent recipes and interesting news about the vegan lifestyle, available at a newsstand near you.

RECOMMENDED READING

All of the following books were helpful in forming my ideas, even if I don't necessarily agree with the authors' views. The books are arranged chronologically under categories, with the most recent titles cited first.

MEAT

Nibert, D. "The Promotion of 'Meat' and Its Consequences," in L. Kalof, ed., *The Animals Reader: The Essential Classic and Contemporary Writings*. Oxford: Berg, 2007.

Marcus, Erik. *Meat Market: Animals, Ethics, and Money*. Boston: Brio Press, 2005.

Gellatley, Juliet, with Tony Wardle. *The Silent Ark: A Chilling Exposé of Meat—The Global Killer*. London: HarperCollins, 1996.

Fiddes, Nicke. *Meat: A Natural Symbol*. New York: Routledge, 1991.

Adams, Carol. *The Sexual Politics of Meat: A Feminist Vegetarian Critical Theory*. New York: Continuum, 1990.

Sinclair, Upton. *The Jungle: The Uncensored Original Edition*. Tucson, AZ: Sharp Press, 2003 (orig. pub. 1906).

VEGANISM

Popick, Jeff. *The Real Forbidden Fruit: How Meat Destroys Paradise and How Veganism Can Get It Back*. Marco Island, FL: VeganWorld Publishing, 2007.

Singer, Peter, and Jim Mason. *The Way We Eat: Why Our Food Choices Matter*. New York: Rodale Press, 2006.

Torres, Bob, and Jenna Torres. *Vegan Freak: Being Vegan in a Non-Vegan World*. Colton, NY: Tofu Hound Press, 2006.

Lyman, Howard F. *No More Bull! The Mad Cowboy Targets America's Worst Enemy: Our Diet*. New York: Scribner, 2005.

Freedman, Rory, and Kim Barnouin. *Skinny Bitch*. Philadelphia: Running Press, 2005.

Tuttle, Will. *The World Peace Diet: Eating for Spiritual Health and Social Harmony*. New York: Lantern Books, 2005.

Saunders, Kerrie K. *The Vegan Diet as Chronic Disease Prevention*. New York: Lantern Books, 2003.

Walsh, Stephen. *Plant Based Nutrition and Health*. London: The Vegan Society, 2003.

Davis, Brenda, and Vesanto Melina. *Becoming Vegan: The Complete Guide to Adopting a Healthy Plant-Based Diet*. Summertown, TN: Book Publishing Co., 2000.

Stepaniak, Joanne. *Being Vegan: Living with Conscience, Conviction and Compassion*. Los Angeles: Lowell House, 2000.

Marcus, Erik. *Vegan: The New Ethics of Eating.* Ithaca, NY: McBooks, 1998.

Clements, Kath. *Why Vegan: The Ethics of Eating and the Need for Change.* London: Heretic Books, 1995.

Lanley, Gill. *Vegan Nutrition: A Survey of Research.* Oxford: The Vegan Society, 1988.

Sussman, Victor. *The Vegetarian Alternative: A Guide to a Healthful and Humane Diet.* Emmaus, PA: Rodale Press, 1978.

VEGETARIANISM

Stuart, Tristram. *The Bloodless Revolution: A Cultural History of Vegetarianism from 1600 to Modern Times.* New York: W. W. Norton, 2006.

Rice, Pamela. *101 Reasons Why I'm a Vegetarian.* New York: Lantern Books, 2005.

Sapontzis, Steve F., ed. *Food for Thought: The Debate Over Eating Meat.* Amherst, NY: Prometheus Books, 2004.

Iacobbo, Karen, and Michael Iacobbo. *Vegetarian America: A History.* Westport, CT: Praeger, 2004.

Rangdrol, Shabkar Tsogdruk. *Food of Bodhisattvas: Buddhist Teachings on Abstaining from Meat,* trans. by the Padmakara Translation Group. Boston: Shambala, 2004.

Williams, Howard, ed. *The Ethics of Diet: A Catena of Authorities Deprecatory of the Practice of Flesh-Eating.* Chicago: University of Illinois Press, 2003.

Adams, Carol J. *Living Among Meat Eaters: The Vegetarian's Survival Handbook.* New York: Continuum, 2003.

Lanou, Amy Joy, and the Physicians Committee for Responsible Medicine Expert Nutrition Panel: *Healthy Eating for Life for Children*. New York: John Wiley & Sons, 2002.

Maurer, Donna. *Vegetarianism: Movement or Moment?* Philadelphia: Temple University Press, 2002.

Walters, Kerry S., and Lisa Portmess, eds. *Ethical Vegetarianism: From Pythagoras to Peter Singer*. Albany: State University of New York Press, 1999.

Fox, Michael A. *Deep Vegetarianism*. Philadelphia: Temple University Press, 1999.

Havala, Suzanne. *The Complete Idiot's Guide to Being Vegetarian*. New York: Macmillan, 1999.

Moll, Lucy. *The Vegetarian Child: A Complete Guide for Parents*. New York: Berkley Publishing Group, 1997.

Messina, Virginia, and Mark Messina. *Total Health for You and Your Family the Vegetarian Way*. New York: Crown, 1996.

Harris, William. *The Scientific Basis of Vegetarianism*. Honolulu: Health Publishers, 1996.

Hill, John Lawrence. *The Case for Vegetarianism: Philosophy for a Small Planet*. London: Rowman & Littlefield, 1996.

Spencer, Colin. *The Heretic's Feast: A History of Vegetarianism*. Hanover, NH: University Press of New England, 1995.

Cox, P. *The New Why You Don't Need Meat*. London: Bloomsbury, 1994.

Amato, Paul R., and Sonia A. Partridge. *The New Vegetarians: Promoting Health and Protecting Life*. New York: Plenum Press, 1989.

Tracy, Lisa. *The Gradual Vegetarian*. New York: M. Evans & Co., 1985.

Dombrowski, Daniel A. *The Philosophy of Vegetarianism*. Amherst: University of Massachusetts Press, 1984.

Braunstein, Martha Mathew. *Radical Vegetarianism*. Los Angeles: Panjandrum Books, 1981.

Giehl, Dudley. *Vegetarianism, a Way of Life* (Foreword by Isaac Bashevis Singer). New York: Harper & Row, 1979.

Barkas, Janet. *The Vegetable Passion: A History of the Vegetarian State of Mind*. New York: Scribner, 1975.

ANIMAL RIGHTS

Kheel, Marti. *Nature Ethics: An Ecofeminist Perspective*. Lanham, MD: Rowman & Littlefield, 2008.

Dawn, Karen. *Thanking the Monkey: Rethinking the Way We Treat Animals*. New York: Harper Paperbacks, 2008.

Donovan, J., and Carol J. Adams, eds. *The Feminist Care Tradition in Animal Ethics*. New York: Columbia University Press, 2007.

Jensen, Derrick, and Karen Tweedy-Holmes. *Thought to Exist in the Wild: Awakening from the Nightmare of Zoos*. Santa Cruz, CA: No Voice Unheard, 2007.

Singer, Peter, ed. *In Defense of Animals: The Second Wave*. Malden, MA: Blackwell, 2006.

Hall, Lee. *Capers in the Churchyard: Animal Rights Advocacy in the Age of Terror*. Darien, CT: Nectar Bat Press, 2006.

Beers, Diane L. *For the Prevention of Cruelty: The History and Legacy of Animal Rights Activism in the United States*. Athens, OH: Swallow Press / Ohio University Press, 2006.

Sunstein, Cass R., and Martha C. Nussbaum, eds. *Animal Rights: Current Debates and New Directions*. New York: Oxford University Press, 2005.

Bulliet, Richard W. *Hunters, Herders, and Hamburgers: The Past and Future of Human-Animal Relationships*. New York: Columbia University Press, 2005.

Regan, Tom. *Empty Cages: Facing the Challenge of Animal Rights*. New York: Rowman & Littlefield, 2004.

Scully, Matthew. *Dominion: the Power of Man, the Suffering of Animals, and the Call to Mercy*. New York: St. Martin's Press, 2002.

Patterson, Charles. *Eternal Treblinka: Our Treatment of Animals and the Holocaust*. New York: Lantern Books, 2002.

Rowlands, Mark. *Animals Like Us*. New York: Verso, 2002.

Stallwood, Kim W., ed. *A Primer on Animal Rights: Leading Experts Write About Animal Cruelty and Exploitation*. New York: Lantern Books, 2002.

Preece, Rod, ed. *Awe of the Tiger, Love of the Lamb: A Chronology of Sensibility to Animals*. New York: Routledge, 2002.

Coetzee, J. M. *The Lives of Animals*. Princeton, NJ: Princeton University Press, Tanner Lectures, 1997, 2001.

Dunayer, Joan. *Animal Equality: Language and Liberation*. Derwood, MD: Ryce, 2001.

Francione, Gary. *Introduction to Animal Rights: Your Child or the Dog?* Philadelphia: Temple University Press, 2000.

de Grazia, David. *Taking Animals Seriously: Mental Life and Moral Status*. New York: Cambridge University Press, 1996.

Serpell, J. *In the Company of Animals: A Study of Human-Animal Relationships*. Cambridge: Cambridge University Press, 1996.

Pluhar, Evelyn B. *Beyond Prejudice: The Moral Significance of Human and Nonhuman Animals*. Durham, NC: Duke University Press, 1995.

Mason, Jim. *An Unnatural Order: Uncovering the Roots of Our Domination of Nature and Each Other*. New York: Simon & Schuster, 1993.

Sorabji, Richard. *Animal Minds and Human Morals: The Origins of the Western Debate*. Ithaca, NY: Cornell University Press, 1993.

Turner, E. S. *All Heaven in a Rage*. London: Open Gate Press, 1992.

Rollin, Bernard. *The Unheeded Cry: Animal Consciousness, Animal Pain and Science*. New York: Oxford University Press, 1989.

Wynne-Tyson, Jon. *The Extended Circle: A Dictionary of Humane Thought*. Fontwell, UK: Centaur Press, 1985.

Lackner, Stephan. *Peaceable Nature: An Optimistic View of Life on Earth*. San Francisco: Harper & Row, 1984.

Regan, Tom. *The Case for Animal Rights*. Berkeley: University of California Press, 1983.

Midgley, Mary. *Beast and Man: The Roots of Human Nature*. Ithaca, NY: Cornell University Press, 1978.

Regan, Tom, and Peter Singer, eds. *Animal Rights and Human Obligations*. Englewood Cliffs, NJ: Prentice Hall, 1976.

Singer, Peter. *Animal Liberation*, 2nd edn. New York: New York Review of Books, 1990 (orig. pub. 1975).

Godlovitch, Stanley, Roslind Godlovitch, and John Harris. *Animals,*

Men and Morals: An Inquiry into the Maltreatment of Non-Humans.
New York: Grove Press, 1971.

ANIMAL EMOTIONS

Bekoff, Marc. *The Emotional Lives of Animals: A Leading Scientist Explores Animal Joy, Sorrow, and Empathy—and Why They Matter.*
New York: New World Library, 2007.

Balcombe, Jonathan. *Pleasurable Kingdom: Animals and the Nature of Feeling Good.* New York: Macmillan, 2007.

Ryder, Richard. *Painism: A Modern Morality.* London: Open Gate Press, 2002.

Bekoff, Marc. *Smile of a Dolphin: Remarkable Accounts of Animal Emotions* (Foreword by Stephen Jay Gould). New York: Discovery Books, 2000.

Panksepp, Jaak. *Affective Neuroscience: The Foundations of Human and Animal Emotions.* New York: Oxford University Press, 1998.

Moussaieff Masson, Jeffrey. *When Elephants Weep: The Emotional Lives of Animals.* New York: Delacorte, 1995.

INDIVIDUAL ANIMALS

Chickens

Grimes, William. *My Fine Feathered Friend.* New York: North Point Press, 2002.

Davis, Karen. *Prisoned Chickens, Poisoned Eggs: An Inside Look at the Modern Poultry Industry.* Summertown, TN: Book Publishing Co., 1996.

Smith, Page, and Charles Daniel. *The Chicken Book.* San Francisco: North Point Press, 1982.

Kruijt, J. P. *Ontogeny of Social Behaviour in Burmese Red Junglefowl* (*Gallus gallus spadiecues*). Leiden, Holland: E. J. Brill, 1964.

Cows

Velten, Hannah. *Cow*. London: Reaktion Books, 2007.

Carlson, Laurie Winn. *Cattle: An Informal Social History*. Chicago: Ivan R. Dee, 2001.

Webster, John. *Understanding the Dairy Cow*. Oxford: Blackwell Science, 1993.

Rifkin, Jeremy. *Beyond Beef: The Rise and Fall of the Cattle Culture*. New York: Dutton, 1992.

Pigs

Watson, Lyall. *The Whole Hog: Exploring the Extraordinary Potential of Pigs*. Washington, DC: Smithsonian Books, 2004.

Fabre-Vassas, Claudine. *The Singular Beast: Jews, Christians, and the Pig*. New York: Columbia University Press, 1997.

Schwenke, Karl. *In a Pig's Eye*. Chelsea, VT: Chelsea Green Publishing, 1985.

Hedpeth, William. *The Hog Book*. New York: Doubleday, 1978.

Sillar, F. C., and R. M. Meyler. *The Symbolic Pig: An Anthology of Pigs in Literature and Art*. Edinburgh: Oliver & Boyd, 1961.

Turkeys

Davis, Karen. *More Than a Meal: The Turkey in History, Myth, Ritual, and Reality*. New York: Lantern Books, 2001.

Hutto, Joe. *Illuminations in the Flatwoods: A Season with the Wild Turkeys*. New York: Lyons & Burford, 1995.

Schorger, A. W. *The Wild Turkey: Its History and Domestication*. Norman: University of Oklahoma Press, 1966.

THE ENVIRONMENT

Vanderheiden, Steve. *Atmospheric Justice: A Political Theory of Climate Change*. New York: Oxford University Press, 2008.

Simontacchi, Carol. *The Crazy Makers: How the Food Industry Is Destroying Our Brains and Harming Our Children*. Los Angeles: Jeremy Tarcher, 2007.

Pawlick, Thomas. *The End of Food*. New York: Barricade Books, 2006.

Brown, Lester R. *Plan B 2.0: Rescuing a Planet Under Stress and a Civilization in Trouble,* updated and expanded edn. New York: W. W. Norton, 2006.

Fitzgerald, Randall. *The Hundred-Year Lie: How Food and Medicine Are Destroying Your Health*. New York: E. P. Dutton, 2006.

Reisner, Marc. *Cadillac Desert: The American West and Its Disappearing Water,* rev. edn. New York: Penguin, 1993.

Carson, Rachel. *Silent Spring*. New York: Mariner Books, 2002 (104th edn., with an Introduction by Al Gore; orig. pub. 1962).

FACTORY FARMS

Mason, Jim, and Peter Singer. *Animal Factories,* rev. edn. New York: Harmony Books, 1990.

Coats, C. David. *Old MacDonald's Factory Farm: The Myth of the Traditional Farm and the Shocking Truth About Animal Suffering in Today's Agribusiness.* New York: Continuum, 1989.

Harrison, Ruth. *Animal Machines: The New Factory Farming Industry.* London: Vincent Stuart, 1964.

DIET AND HEALTH

Esselstyn, Caldwell B. *Prevent and Reverse Heart Disease: The Revolutionary, Scientifically Proven, Nutrition-Based Cure.* New York: Avery, 2008.

Campbell, T. Colin. *The China Study: The Most Comprehensive Study of Nutrition Ever Conducted and the Startling Implications for Diet, Weight Loss and Long-Term Health.* Dallas: Benbella Books, 2005.

Messina, Virginia, Reed Mangles, and Mark Messina. *The Dietitian's Guide to Vegetarian Diets: Issues and Applications,* 2nd edn. Boston: Jones & Bartless, 2004.

Fraser, Gary. *Diet, Life Expectancy, and Chronic Disease: Studies of Seventh-Day Adventists and Other Vegetarians.* New York: Oxford University Press, 2003.

Fuhrman, Joel. *Eat to Live.* Boston: Little, Brown, 2003.

Bowlby, Rex. *Plant Roots: 101 Reasons Why the Human Diet Is Rooted Exclusively in Plants.* Burbank, CA: Outside the Box, 2003.

Barnard, Neal D. *Eat Right, Live Longer: Using the Natural Power of Foods to Age-Proof Your Body.* New York: Harmony Books, 1995.

Messina, Mark, and Virginia Messina, with Ken Setchell. *The Simple Soybean and Your Health.* New York: Avery, 1994.

Barnard, Neal D. *Food for Life: How the New Four Food Groups Can Save Your Life*. New York: Three Rivers Press, 1993.

McDougall, John A. *The McDougall Program*. New York: Penguin, 1991.

Ornish, Dean. *Dr. Dean Ornish's Program for Reversing Heart Disease*. New York: Ballantine, 1990.

Oski, Frank. *Don't Drink Your Milk: New Frightening Medical Facts About the Word's Most Overrated Nutrient*. Brushton, NY: Teach Services, 1992 (orig. pub. 1983).

PERMACULTURE

Fukuoka, Masanobu. *The One-Straw Revolution: An Introduction to Natural Farming*. Emmaus, PA: Rodale Press, 1978.

Howard, Sir Albert. *An Agricultural Testament*. New York: Oxford University Press, 1940.

FOOD ISSUES

Friend, Catherine. *The Compassionate Carnivore*. New York: Perseus, 2008.

Pollan, Michael. *In Defense of Food: An Eater's Manifesto*. New York: Penguin, 2008.

Fullteron-Smith, Jill. *The Truth About Food: What You Eat Can Change Your Life*. New York: Bloomsbury, 2007.

Imhoff, Daniel. *The Citizen's Guide to a Food and Farm Bill* (Foreword by Michael Pollan). Berkeley: University of California Press, 2007.

McNamee, Gregory. *Moveable Feasts: The History, Science, and Lore of Food*. Westport, CT: Praeger, 2007.

Menzel, Peter, and Faith D'Aluisio. *Hungry Planet: What the World Eats* (Foreword by Marion Nestle). Berkeley: Ten Speed Press, 2007.

Pollan, Michael. *The Omnivore's Dilemma: A Natural History of Four Meals.* New York: Penguin, 2006.

Belasco, Warren. *Meals to Come: A History of the Future of Food.* Berkeley: University of California Press, 2006.

Nestle, Marion. *What to Eat.* New York: North Point Press, 2006.

Davidson, Alan. *The Oxford Companion to Food*, 2nd edn. New York: Oxford University Press, 2006.

Goodall, Jane, Gary McAvoy, and Gail Hudson. *Harvest for Hope: A Guide to Mindful Eating.* New York: Grand Central Publishing, 2005.

Anderson, E. N. *Everyone Eats: Understanding Food and Culture.* New York: New York University Press, 2005.

Watson, James I., and Melissa I. Caldwell, eds. *The Cultural Politics of Food and Eating: A Reader.* Oxford: Blackwell, 2005.

Cook, Christopher D. *Diet for a Dead Planet: How the Food Industry Is Killing Us.* New York: The New Press, 2004.

Kelleher, Colm. A. *Brain Trust: The Hidden Connections Between Mad Cow and Misdiagnosed Alzheimer's Disease.* New York: Pocket Books, 2004.

Brownell, Kelly D., and Katherine Battle Horgen. *Food Fight: The Inside Story of the Food Industry, America's Obesity Crisis, and What We Can Do About It.* New York: Contemporary Books, 2004.

Waldman, Murray, and Marjorie Lamb. *Dying for a Hamburger: The Alarming Link Between the Meat Industry and Alzheimer's Disease.* New York: Thomas Dunne, 2004.

Halweil, Brian. *Eat Here: Reclaiming Homegrown Pleasures in a Global Supermarket*. New York: W. W. Norton, 2004.

Critser, Greg. *Fat Land: How Americans Became the Fattest People in the World*. Boston: Houghton Mifflin, 2003.

Severson, Kim, and Cindy Burke. *The Trans Fat Solution: Cooking and Shopping to Eliminate the Deadliest Fat from Your Diet*. Berkeley: Ten Speed Press, 2003.

Nestle, Marion. *Food Politics: How the Food Industry Influences Nutrition and Health*. Berkeley: University of California Press, 2002.

Pretty, Jules. *Agri-Culture: Reconnecting People, Land and Nature*. Sterling, VA: Earthscan, 2002.

Jacobson, Michael F., and Jayne Hurley. *Restaurant Confidential: The Shocking Truth About What You're Really Eating When You're Eating Out*. New York: Workman Publishing, 2002.

Nabhan, Gary Paul. *Coming Home to Eat: The Pleasures and Politics of Local Foods*. New York: W. W. Norton, 2002.

Kimbrell, Andrew, ed. *The Fatal Harvest Reader: The Tragedy of Industrial Agriculture*. Washington, DC: Island Press, 2002.

Fernandez-Armesto, Felipe. *Near a Thousand Tables: A History of Food*. New York: Free Press, 2002.

Pollan, Michael. *The Botany of Desire: A Plant's-Eye View of the World*. New York: Random House, 2001.

Rebora, Giovanni. *Culture of the Fork: A Brief History of Food in Europe*. New York: Columbia University Press, 2001.

Robbins, John. *The Food Revolution: How Your Diet Can Help Save Your Life and Our World*. New York: Conari Press, 2001.

Petrini, Carlo, ed. *Slow Food: Collected Thoughts on Taste, Tradition, and the Honest Pleasures of Food*. White River Junction, VT: Chelsea Green Publishing, 2001.

Schlosser, Eric. *Fast Food Nation: The Dark Side of the All-American Meal*. Boston: Houghton Mifflin, 2001.

Allport, Susan. *The Primal Feast: Food, Sex, Foraging and Love*. New York: Harmony Books, 2000.

Simontacchi, Carol. *The Crazy Makers: How the Food Industry Is Destroying Our Brains and Harming Our Children*. New York: Jeremy T. Tarcher/Putnam, 2000.

Kiple, Kenneth F., and Kriemhild Coneè Ornelas, et al., eds. *The Cambridge World History of Food*. 2 vols. Cambridge: Cambridge University Press, 2000.

Manning, Richard. *Food's Future: The Next Green Revolution*. New York: North Point Press, 2000.

Barer-Stein, Thelma. *You Eat What You Are: People, Culture and Food Traditions*. Willowdale, Ont.: Firefly Books, 1999.

Kass, Leon R. *The Hungry Soul: Eating and the Perfecting of Our Nature*, 2nd edn. Chicago: University of Chicago Press, 1999.

Macbeth, Helen, ed. *Food Preferences and Taste: Continuity and Change*. Providence, RI: Berghahn Books, 1997.

Mintz, Sidney W. *Tasting Food, Tasting Freedom: Excursions into Eating, Culture, and the Past*. Boston: Beacon Press, 1996.

Maurer, D. "Meat as a Social Problem: Rhetorical Struggles in the Contemporary Vegetarian Literature," in D. Maurer and J. Sobal, eds., *Eating Agendas: Food and Nutrition as Social Problems*. New York: Aldine de Gruyter, 1995.

Simoons, Frederick J. *Eat Not This Flesh: Food Avoidances from Prehistory to the Present,* 2nd edn. Madison: University of Wisconsin Press, 1994.

Toussaint-Samat, Maguelonne. *History of Food,* trans. by Anthea Bell. Cambridge, MA: Blackwell, 1994.

Levenstein, Harvey. *Paradox of Plenty: A Social History of Eating in Modern America.* New York: Oxford University Press, 1993.

Pitchford, Paul. *Healing with Whole Foods: Oriental Traditions and Modern Nutrition.* Berkeley: North Atlantic Books, 1993.

Mennell, Stephen, et al. *The Sociology of Food: Eating, Diet and Culture.* New York: Sage Publications/International Sociological Association, 1992.

Simoons, Frederick J. *Food in China: A Cultural and Historical Inquiry.* Boca Raton, FL: CRC Press, 1991.

Visser, Margaret. *The Rituals of Dinner: The Origins, Evolution, Eccentricities, and Meaning of Table Manners.* New York: Grove Weidenfeld, 1991.

Logue, A. W. *The Psychology of Eating and Drinking: An Introduction.* New York: W. H. Freeman, 1989.

Belasco, Warren J. *Appetite for Change: How the Counterculture Took on the Food Industry, 1966–1988.* New York: Pantheon, 1989.

Robbins, John. *Diet for a New America.* Walpole, NH: Stillpoint Publishing, 1987.

Bryant, Carol A., et al. *The Cultural Feast: An Introduction to Food and Society.* New York: West Publishing, 1985.

Jerome, Norge W., Randy F. Kandel, and Gretel H. Pelto, eds. *Nutritional Anthropology: Contemporary Approaches to Diet and Culture.* Pleasantville, NY: Redgrave Publishing, 1980.

Farb, Peter, and George Armelagos. *Consuming Passions: The Anthropology of Eating.* Boston: Houghton Mifflin, 1980.

Tannahill, Reay. *Food in History.* New York: Three Rivers Press, 1988 (orig. pub. 1973).

Lappé, Francis Moore. *Diet for a Small Planet,* rev. edn. New York: Ballantine, 1975 (orig. pub. 1971).

GREAT BOOKS ABOUT ANIMALS

Kalof, Linda, and Amy Fitzgerald. *The Animals Reader: The Essential Classic and Contemporary Writings.* New York: Berg, 2007.

Ellis, Hattie. *Sweetness and Light: The Mysterious History of the Honeybee.* New York: Harmony Books, 2004.

Cassie, B., J. Sandved, and R. M. Pyle. *A World of Butterflies.* New York: Bulfinch Press, 2004.

Spotila, James R. *Sea Turtles: A Complete Guide to Their Biology, Behavior, and Conservation.* Baltimore: Johns Hopkins University Press, 2004.

Beckmann, Paul. *Living Jewels: The Natural Design of Beetles.* New York: Prestel, 2004.

McCarthy, Susan. *Becoming a Tiger: How Baby Animals Learn to Live in the Wild.* New York: HarperCollins, 2004.

Byers, John. *Built for Speed: A Year in the Life of Pronghorn.* Cambridge, MA: Harvard University Press, 2003.

Davis, Susan E., and Margo Demello. *Stories Rabbits Tell: A Natural and Cultural History of a Misunderstood Creature.* New York: Lantern Books, 2003.

Mech, L. David, and Luigi Boitani. *Wolves: Behavior, Ecology, and Conservation*. Chicago: University of Chicago Press, 2003.

Sunquist, Mel, and Fiona Sunquist. *Wild Cats of the World*. Chicago: University of Chicago Press, 2002.

Skutch, Alexander F. *The Minds of Birds*. College Station: Texas A&M University Press, 1996.

Cartmill, Matt. *A View to a Death in the Morning: Hunting and Nature Through History*. Cambridge, MA: Harvard University Press, 1993.

Thomas, Elizabeth Marshall. *The Hidden Life of Dogs*. Boston: Houghton Mifflin, 1993.

Ryden, Hope. *Lily Pond: Four Years with a Family of Beavers*. New York: William Morrow, 1989.

Midgley, Mary. *Animals and Why They Matter*. Athens: University of Georgia Press, 1983.

Griffin, Donald. *The Question of Animal Awareness: Evolutionary Continuity of Mental Experience*, 2nd edn. New York: Rockefeller University Press, 1981.

van Gulik, R. H. *The Gibbon in China: An Essay in Chinese Animal Lore*. Leiden, Holland: E. J. Brill, 1967.

Prévoste, Jean. *Ecologie du Manchot Empereur*. Paris: Hermann, 1961.

Schorger, A. W. *The Passenger Pigeon: Its Natural History and Extinction*. Norman: University of Oklahoma Press, 1955.

RECOMMENDED WEB SITES

Note: These are sites that I like and have found useful. I do not necessarily agree with all of the opinions expressed in them, but intellectual debate is always invigorating and valuable.

ANIMAL ISSUES

Abolitionist: A Voice for Animal Rights (Australia)
http://www.abolitionist-online.com/

Alley Cat Allies
http://www.alleycat.org/

American Anti-Vivisection Society
http://www.aavs.org/

Animal Liberation Victoria (Patty Mark, Australia)
http://www.alv.org.au/

The Animal Rights Library
http://www.animal-rights-library.com/

Animals & Society
http://www.animalsandsociety.com/

Animals Australia
http://www.animalsaustralia.org/

Arkangel for Animal Liberation
http://www.arkangelweb.org/

The Captive Animals' Protection Society
http://www.captiveanimals.org/

Cetacean Freedom Network
http://www.captivitystinks.org/

Compassion in World Farming (UK)
http://www.ciwf.org/

Compassion Over Killing
http://www2.cok.net/

Freedom for Animals
http://www.freedomforanimals.org/

Friends of Animals
http://www.friendsofanimals.org/

Great Ape Standing and Personhood (GRASP)
http://www.personhood.org/

Human Society of the United States
http://www.hsus.org/

In Defense of Animals
http://www.idausa.org/

Jane Goodall
http://www.janegoodall.org/

Last Chance for Animals (Chris DeRose)
http://www.lcanimal.org/

Lobster Liberation
http://www.lobsterlib.com/

The Meatrix
http://www.themeatrix.com/

New England Anti-Vivisection Society
http://www.neavs.org/

People for the Ethical Treatment of Animals
http://www.peta-online.org/

Save Animals from Exploitation (New Zealand)
http://www.safe.org.nz/

Tribe of Heart: The Art of Peaceful Transformation
http://www.tribeofheart.org/

United Poultry Concerns (Karen Davis)
http://www.upc-online.org/

Viva! (UK)
http://www.viva.org.uk/

Voiceless: The Fund for Animals (Australia)
http://www.voiceless.org.au/

Zoocheck Canada
http://www.zoocheck.com/

ENVIRONMENTAL ISSUES

Earth Island Institute
http://www.earthisland.org/

Ecofeminism
http://www.ecofem.org/

Rainforest Action Network
http://www.ran.org/

Sea Shepherd Conservation Society (Paul Watson)
http://www.seashepherd.org/

Wetlands Activism Collective
http://wetlands-preserve.org/

HEALTH

Dr. Colin Campbell
http://www.thechinastudy.com/

Dr. Caldwell B. Esselstyn, Jr.
http://www.heartattackproof.com/

Dr. Joel Fuhrman
http://drfuhrman.com/

Dr. Michael Greger
http://www.veganmd.com/

Dr. Michael Klaper
http://www.vegsource.com/klaper/

Dr. John A. McDougall
http://www.drmcdougall.com/

Milk Sucks
http://www.milksucks.com/

Physicians Committee for Responsible Medicine
http://www.pcrm.org/

John Robbins
http://www.earthsave.org/

Veg Cooking
http://www.vegcooking.com/

World Cancer Research Fund (UK)
http://www.wcrf-uk.org/

ONLINE JOURNALS

Satya
http://www.satyamag.com/

Vegnews
http://www.vegnews.com/

PROGRESSIVE POLITICS

AlterNet
http://www.alternet.org/

Centre for Research on Globalization
http://www.globalresearch.ca/

Common Dreams Newscenter
http://www.commondreams.org/

The Huffington Post
http://www.huffingtonpost.com/

Independent Media Center
http://www.indymedia.org/

TruthOut
http://www.truthout.org/

SANCTUARIES

Animal Place
http://www.animalplace.org/

Farm Sanctuary
http://www.farmsanctuary.org/

Peaceful Choices
http://www.peacefulchoices.com/

Peaceful Prairie
http://www.peacefulprairie.org/

VEGETARIAN AND VEGAN SITES

Compassionate Cooks (Colleen Patrick-Goudreau)
http://www.compassionatecooks.com/

Gary L. Francione
http://www.animal-law.org/

Go Veg
http://www.goveg.com/

Howard Lyman
http://www.madcowboy.com/

Meet Your Meat
http://www.meat.org/

Matthew Scully
http://www.matthewscully.com/

Supervegan
http://www.supervegan.com/

Vegan (Erik Marcus)
http://www.vegan.com/

Vegan Action
http://www.vegan.org/

Vegan Freak: Being Vegan in a Non-vegan World
http://www.veganfreak.com/

Vegan Outreach
http://www.veganoutreach.org/

Vegan Society (UK)
http://www.vegansociety.com/html/

Vegetarian Resource Group
http://www.vrg.org/

Veg for Life
http://www.vegforlife.org/

Vegsource
http://www.vegsource.com/

INDEX